IP Routing

Ravi Malhotra

O'REILLY®

Beijing · Cambridge · Farnham · Köln · Paris · Sebastopol · Taipei · Tokyo

IP Routing
by Ravi Malhotra

Copyright © 2002 O'Reilly & Associates, Inc. All rights reserved.
Printed in the United States of America.

Published by O'Reilly & Associates, Inc., 1005 Gravenstein Highway North,
Sebastopol, CA 95472.

O'Reilly & Associates books may be purchased for educational, business, or sales promotional
use. Online editions are also available for most titles (*safari.oreilly.com*). For more information
contact our corporate/institutional sales department: (800) 998-9938 or *corporate@oreilly.com*.

Editor:	Jim Sumser
Production Editor:	Rachel Wheeler
Cover Designer:	Ellie Volckhausen
Interior Designer:	Melanie Wang

Printing History:

January 2002:	First Edition.

ISBN: 0-596-00275-0
[C]

*This book is dedicated to my grandfather, the late
P.D. Gandhi, who taught me the love of learning.*

Table of Contents

Preface

Ants, single-celled creatures such as the cellular slime mold, plants and animals in ecosystems, and (even) human beings can congregate and display miraculously complex behaviors.* Say a colony of ants in a tree needs to move to another tree, perhaps in search of food. Some ants build a bridge by joining their bodies in a chain stretching from one limb in one tree to another limb in another tree. Other ants cross over this ant structure, walking over their peers. Once all the ants have crossed over, the ants in the bridge begin to gracefully undo the structure, crossing one by one. Each ant only repeats simple actions, over and over again; the net result of thousands of ants working together is the miracle of the bridge, which allows the ant colony to migrate.

In our own human society we hope to emulate this level of cooperation. Each one of us is useful to others in some way: we write, lay bricks, act in the theater, farm, drive buses, repair helicopters, tend to the sick, make coffee... As individuals, we repeat the same acts again and again, whether it be making coffee cup after coffee cup or seeing patient after patient. The net result of all these acts is our complex, wonderful society.

So, what does all this have to do with IP routing? Each router in a network repeats simple processes over and over again, as described in the specification of the routing protocol it is executing. The net result of all the routers in a network repeating these simple processes is IP routing, or the movement of IP packets in a network.

---

* *The New York Times* has reported some intriguing examples of such behavior, quoting research work from the Santa Fe Institute in New Mexico ("Mindless Creatures Acting Mindfully," *The New York Times*, March 23, 1999, Science Times).

My advice to you, the student of IP routing, is this: study the simple behaviors of each ant, and make sure you understand them in detail. There is no other way to understand how IP networks behave as ordered organisms.

Audience

This text assumes that the reader has knowledge of basic networking concepts—the ISO/OSI model, bridging versus routing, IP addressing, TCP/IP, etc.

This text is not meant to replace Cisco manuals. Use this text to build concepts. IP routing commands are described as they are used to illustrate concepts; however, this text does not contain an exhaustive list of all IP routing commands. Use Cisco documentation for details on commands, to find out which IOS release supports new features, and for the (inevitable) bug lists.

Most of the time I have used addresses from the private address pool. However, sometimes I have had to dip into the registered address pool, especially when talking about BGP. If you use the examples in this book, be careful that you do not choose addresses that conflict with existing addresses in your environment.

Organization

This book is comprised of eight chapters:

Chapter 1, *Starting Simple*
> This chapter introduces the basic concepts of IP routing. It will show you the simplest method of creating entries in a routing table—by defining static routes.

Chapter 2, *Routing Information Protocol (RIP)*
> RIP is the earliest dynamic routing protocol. This chapter describes RIP in detail, including a discussion of the Distance Vector (DV) algorithms that are the foundation of RIP and other routing protocols. Since RIP is the simplest dynamic routing protocol, it is a great tool from which to learn. It may be a good idea to study this chapter even if you do not intend to use RIP.

Chapter 3, *Interior Gateway Routing Protocol (IGRP)*
> IGRP is Cisco's proprietary routing protocol, which directly descended from RIP. IGRP contains some features that make it much more useful than RIP. This chapter focuses on these new features (study Chapter 2 to learn about the foundations of IGRP—the DV protocols).

Chapter 4, *Enhanced Interior Gateway Routing Protocol (EIGRP)*
> The DV algorithms employed by RIP and IGRP have inherent limitations. EIGRP is Cisco's proprietary routing protocol, which interworks seamlessly with IGRP but attempts to overcome these limitations. EIGRP supports classless networks and Variable Length Subnet Masks (VLSM).

Chapter 5, *Routing Information Protocol Version 2 (RIP-2)*

RIP-2 is an attempt to bring RIP back into vogue. RIP-2 is really RIP with support for classless networks and VLSM. RIP-2 still has all the limitations of DV protocols, such as long convergence times.

Chapter 6, *Open Shortest Path First (OSPF)*

OSPF is an open routing protocol. It is most commonly used to build large IP networks. The standards bodies are focusing their work on OSPF, and it is constantly evolving. OSPF is not a DV protocol: OSPF is based on the Dijkstra algorithm. This chapter explains Dijkstra in detail and lays the foundation of how to build hierarchical networks using OSPF.

Chapter 7, *Border Gateway Protocol 4 (BGP-4)*

BGP is the glue that binds the thousands of networks that comprise the Internet. Routing in the Internet is quite different from routing in intranets. There are several new concepts in this chapter.

Chapter 8, *Administrative Controls*

This chapter describes the administrative tools available to all the routing protocols. These tools are used to block the advertisement of routing updates, set up preferences for one routing protocol over another, and more.

Conventions Used in This Book

Italic

Used for emphasis and the first use of technical terms, as well as for the names of networks and routers used in the examples.

Constant Width

Used for IP addresses.

Constant width italic

Used for replaceable parameter names in command syntax.

Code blocks are used throughout the text to make concepts concrete. Line numbers in the lefthand margins are used to refer to specific pieces of the code block. To avoid confusion, within each chapter the line numbers used in the code blocks start at 1 and continue consecutively through the end of the chapter. Code lines that are in bold but are not numbered are also of particular relevance to the surrounding text.

```
  NewYork#sh ip ospf interface
  ...
  Ethernet0 is up, line protocol is up
1   Internet Address 172.16.1.1/24, Area 0
2   Process ID 10, Router ID 172.16.251.1, Network Type BROADCAST, Cost: 10
    ...
  Serial0 is up, line protocol is up
    Internet Address 172.16.250.1/24, Area 0
    Process ID 10, Router ID 172.16.251.1, Network Type POINT_TO_POINT, Cost: 64
```

The use of "..." in the code block indicates that some lines (which were not useful in the discussion) have been omitted.

Indicates a tip, suggestion, or general note.

Indicates a warning or caution.

How to Contact Us

Please address comments and questions concerning this book to the publisher:

O'Reilly & Associates, Inc.
1005 Gravenstein Highway North
Sebastopol, CA 95472
(800) 998-9938 (in the United States or Canada)
(707) 829-0515 (international/local)
(707) 829-0104 (fax)

There is a web page for this book, which lists errata, examples, or any additional information. You can access this page at:

http://www.oreilly.com/catalog/iprouting/

To comment or ask technical questions about this book, send email to:

bookquestions@oreilly.com

For more information about books, conferences, Resource Centers, and the O'Reilly Network, see the O'Reilly web site at:

http://www.oreilly.com

Acknowledgments

I would like to thank Andrew Sun for suggesting this book. Andrew's work on PPP was not only an inspiration but also a model for my endeavors on this text. Mark H. Degner, Edgar Danielyan, and especially Elsa Lankford made some key suggestions on improving the technical content.

Rachel Wheeler served as a very gracious Production Editor, coordinating the details that were essential to producing the book on time. Thanks also to Jessamyn Read, the O'Reilly Illustrator who transformed my rough sketches into the figures you'll find in this book.

As the first editor, Mike Loukides helped define the organization and content of the book. Jim Sumser took over from Mike partway through the project. Jim helped me see the work in perspective and led me through the mire of the detailed work. I want to thank Jim for the patience with which he worked with me. Everything that could prevent me from getting to the book seemed to happen: even I did not believe it would get done, but somehow Jim believed in it. I must have worked through two summers with him, for I remember him talking about two very sweet crops from his cherry tree.

Writing this book was a long, winding road that led me away from my loved ones on many an evening. I have missed Char, my wife, all those evenings when I was locked away somewhere, rewriting a chapter. I am not sure how much Char missed me, but she certainly missed having me around to look after Lucas and Theo, who are quite young and absolutely adorable to be around.

This last piece of this book is being written in the weeks after September 11, 2001. Much of this book was written around the World Trade Center: in it, under it, in its shadow, looking up at it, in a bus traveling to it, in a subway moving away from it, under the influence of coffee bought there, while waiting to meet my family in a nearby park. The Towers symbolize a time of freedom and innocence. We live in a different era now, and I have come to think of this book as belonging to that era of freedom and happiness and innocence.

Starting Simple

What Is IP Routing?

A young woman boards a commuter train in a small town in Quebec, changes trains a couple of times, and, a day later, arrives in New York City. She walks up the stairs from the platform into Grand Central Terminal, looks up above her head, and, for the first time, sees the constellations, hundreds of feet above on the ceiling.

A high school student in New Zealand downloads maps of Sri Lanka from a local (Sri Lankan) web site. The maps show the natural features, the political boundaries, the flora and fauna, rainfall, ancient kingdoms, languages, and religions. The download takes thousands of IP packets that find their way from Sri Lanka to the student's PC in New Zealand.

Just as our Canadian friend changed trains at several stations along the way, the IP packets from the Sri Lankan web site may have bounced through dozens of routers before arriving at the student's machine.

The routing of IP packets in an IP network is the set of tasks required to move an IP packet from router to router to its destination, as specified in the IP header field. This book is about the set of tasks that accomplish IP routing.

There are similarities in routing concepts between IP networks, transportation systems, and mail delivery operations. Throughout this text, we will often illustrate IP routing concepts by comparison with these other systems.

Directly Connected Networks

When our Canadian visitor finally picks up her bags and is ready to head out of Grand Central Terminal, she looks around for the exit signs. On one end, below a row of immense windows, is a sign saying "Vanderbilt Avenue." Below the opposite row of tall windows is a sign saying "Lexington Avenue." Under the large stone arches is a sign reading "42nd Street" (Figure 1-1).

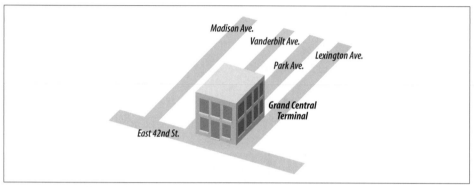

Figure 1-1. Grand Central Terminal and the adjoining streets

Just as the streets around Grand Central Terminal are immediately accessible to any traveler, a router has directly attached networks that are immediately accessible (in other words, that do not require any specific routing mechanism to discover). Consider router *R*, in the following example. Networks 1.0.0.0, 10.1.1.0, and 10.1.2.0 are directly connected to the router:

```
hostname R
!
interface Ethernet0
ip address 1.1.1.1 255.0.0.0
!
interface Ethernet1
ip address 10.1.1.4 255.255.255.0
!
interface Ethernet2
ip address 10.1.2.4 255.255.255.0
...
```

In fact, the moment these networks are connected to the router they are visible in *R*'s routing table. Note in the following output that the command to display the routing table is *show ip route* (in EXEC mode). Also note the "C" that is prepended to the entries in the routing table, indicating that the routes were discovered as directly connected to the router:

```
R#show ip route
Codes: C - connected, S - static, I - IGRP, R - RIP, M - mobile, B - BGP
```

```
        D - EIGRP, EX - EIGRP external, O - OSPF, IA - OSPF inter area
        N1 - OSPF NSSA external type 1, N2 - OSPF NSSA external type 2
        E1 - OSPF external type 1, E2 - OSPF external type 2, E - EGP
        i - IS-IS, L1 - IS-IS level-1, L2 - IS-IS level-2, * - candidate default

Gateway of last resort is 0.0.0.0 to network 0.0.0.0

C    1.0.0.0/8 is directly connected, Ethernet0
     10.0.0.0/8 is subnetted, 2 subnets
C       10.1.1.0/24 is directly connected, Ethernet1
C       10.1.2.0/24 is directly connected, Ethernet2
```

Directly connected networks are automatically installed in the routing table if the interface to the network is up. Figure 1-2 shows router R with its directly connected networks. (The EXEC command *show interface* will show the state of the interfaces). In the previous example, it is assumed that all three interfaces to the directly connected networks are up. If an interface to a directly connected network goes down, the corresponding route is removed from the routing table.

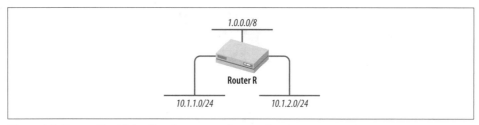

Figure 1-2. Router R with its directly connected networks

If multiple IP addresses are attached to an interface (using secondary addresses), all the associated networks are installed in the routing table.

Static Routing

Our Canadian friend has always wanted to see the New York Public Library. She gets directions at the information booth: "Make a right on 42nd Street; walk three blocks; look for the lions in front of the library." The information-booth attendant may have no idea that the library is closed that day, or that the sidewalk on 42nd Street is blocked just then because of fire trucks and 41st Street may be the preferable route. The information booth has given the same directions to the library for the last hundred years and hopefully will for hundreds more—the route from Grand Central Station to the library, in other words, is static.

In a similar vein, a network administrator can create a static route. So, to reach network 146.1.0.0, we may add the command:

```
ip route 146.1.0.0 255.255.0.0 1.1.1.2
```

which says to get to network 146.1.0.0/16, go to the next hop of 1.1.1.2. This specifies a fixed path to 146.1.0.0/16, as shown here, where the contents of the routing table are displayed using the EXEC command *show ip route*:

```
R#sh ip route
...
1  S    146.1.0.0/16 [1/0] via 1.1.1.2
```

Even if 1.1.1.2 goes down, an alternate path—shown via *R2* in Figure 1-3—cannot be used until a second static route is specified:

```
ip route 146.1.0.0 255.255.0.0 1.1.1.3
```

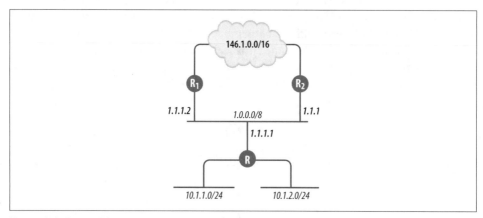

Figure 1-3. Router R's connectivity to 146.1.0.0

The syntax of the static route command is:

```
ip route network [mask] {address | interface} [distance]
```

where *network* and *mask* specify the IP address and mask of the destination. The next hop may be specified by its IP address or by the interface on which to send the packet. To point a static route to an interface (*Ethernet0* in this case), use:

```
ip route 146.1.0.0 255.255.0.0 interface Ethernet0
```

Static routes are smart to the extent that if the next hop (interface or IP address) specified goes down, the router will remove the static route entry from the routing table.

In line 1, the static route in the routing table is accompanied by "[1/0]". This specifies the administrative distance and the metric associated with the route. We'll discuss distance and metrics in the next section.

As should be obvious, static routing does not scale well. As the network grows, the task of maintaining static routes becomes more and more horrendous.

Dynamic Routing

After the public library, our Canadian visitor jumps into a taxi to go crash at a friend's place in Brooklyn. "Go over the Brooklyn Bridge," she tells the driver. They head downtown. Suddenly, the driver slams on his brakes and makes an abrupt turn. Cars all around jam on their brakes, and pedestrians run hither and thither. "The radio said it is an hour to go over the bridge! We will take the tunnel!" the driver shouts to the back seat. This is an example of dynamic routing in a transportation system. What is dynamic routing in IP networks? Dynamic routing protocols allow each router to automatically discover one or more paths to each destination in the network. When the network topology changes, such as when new paths are added or when paths go out of service, dynamic routing protocols automatically adjust the contents of the routing table to reflect the new network topology.

Dynamic routing relies on (frequent!) updates to discover changes in network topology. In the example in Figure 1-3, when the path *R3 → R4* is added to the network it can be automatically discovered by a routing protocol, such as RIP, EIGRP, or OSPF.

The routing protocols in use today are based on one of two algorithms: *Distance Vector* or *Link State*. Distance Vector (DV) algorithms broadcast routing information to all neighboring routers. In other words, each router tells all of its neighbors the routes it knows. When a router receives a route (from a neighbor) that is not in its routing table, it adds the route to its table; if the router receives a route that is already in its routing table, it keeps the *shorter* route in its table. DV algorithms are sometimes also described as routing by rumor: bad routing information propagates just as quickly as good information. Link State algorithms operate on a different paradigm. First, each router constructs its own topological map of the entire network, based on updates from neighbors. Next, each router uses Dijkstra's algorithm to compute the *shortest* path to each destination in this graph. Both DV and Link State algorithms are described in further detail in the chapters that follow.

In the previous paragraph, we spoke of the "shorter" or "shortest" path in the context of both DV and Link State algorithms. Since a router may know of multiple paths to a destination, each routing protocol must provide a mechanism to discover the "shorter" or "shortest" path based on one or more of the following criteria: number of hops, delay, throughput, traffic, reliability, etc. A *metric* is usually attached to this combination; lower metric values indicate "shorter" paths. For each routing protocol discussed in the chapters that follow, we will describe how the route metric is computed.

A network under a single administrative authority is described as an *autonomous system* (AS) in routing parlance. *Interior gateway protocols* (IGPs) are designed to support the task of routing internal to an AS. IGPs have no concept of political boundaries between ASs or the metrics that may be used to select paths between ASs. RIP, IGRP, EIGRP, and OSPF are IGPs. *Exterior gateway protocols* (EGPs) are designed to support routing between ASs. EGPs deploy metrics to select one inter-AS path over another. BGP is the most commonly used EGP.

Routing architectures may be broadly classified as *flat* or *hierarchical*. Flat routing implies that all routes are known to all peers—all routers in the network are equal, possessing the same routing information. Hierarchical routing implies that some routers possess only local routes, whereas others possess a little bit more information, and still others possess even more.

Let's draw an analogy to the postal system. When I write a letter to a friend in India, the postman in the U.S. may have no idea where India is. He forwards all foreign mail to a designated post office in his state. That designated post office must know every postal system in the world. Such a system, in which some post offices are regional and some handle foreign mail, could be described as hierarchical.

In large IP networks, only a few routers need to know every route in the network. These routers are sometimes described as *core* routers. Around the core routers is a layer of *distribution* routers that need not possess the complete routing table. When a distribution router receives a packet whose destination IP address does not appear in its local routing table, the distribution router simply forwards the packet to a core router.

In the earlier example of the high school student in New Zealand accessing a web site in Sri Lanka, the small router in the high school in New Zealand probably has only a tiny routing table, with no routing entries for Sri Lanka. The high school router will forward all traffic for unknown destinations to another router, which in turn may forward the traffic to another one. Large IP networks exhibit several layers of hierarchy.

As we will see in the chapters that follow, some routing protocols have features that make it easier to build hierarchies. These features include route aggregation, classlessness, the use of default routes, and the flexibility with which routes can be exchanged with other routing protocols.

RIP is an example of an almost completely flat routing protocol. OSPF exhibits several features that permit the design of hierarchical networks.

As with any other algorithm, routing algorithms may also be categorized based on their complexity, flexibility, overhead, memory and CPU utilization, robustness, and stability. These properties of routing algorithms are of interest to the routing engineer, since he provides the (router) infrastructure to execute these algorithms.

The Routing Table

At Grand Central Terminal, a big wall lists all the destinations and their corresponding track numbers (see Figure 1-4). Passengers find their destination on this wall and then proceed to the indicated platforms. Similarly, a routing table must contain at least two pieces of information: the destination network and the next hop toward that destination. This reflects a fundamental paradigm of IP routing: hop-by-hop routing. In other words, a router does not know the full path to a destination, but only the next hop to reach the destination.

Departures

Time	Destination	Track number
9:18	New Haven	17
9:21	Cos Cob	22
9:24	Valhalla	11
9:31	Dover Plains	19
9:42	Bronxville	12

Figure 1-4. Destinations and track numbers at Grand Central Terminal

Routes are installed in the routing table as they are learned through the mechanisms we have been discussing: directly connected networks, static routes, and dynamic routing protocols. A typical routing table in a Cisco router looks like this:

```
Router>show ip route
Codes: C - connected, S - static, I - IGRP, R - RIP, M - mobile, B - BGP
       D - EIGRP, EX - EIGRP external, O - OSPF, IA - OSPF inter area
       N1 - OSPF NSSA external type 1, N2 - OSPF NSSA external type 2
       E1 - OSPF external type 1, E2 - OSPF external type 2, E - EGP
       i - IS-IS, L1 - IS-IS level-1, L2 - IS-IS level-2, * - candidate default

Gateway of last resort is 0.0.0.0 to network 0.0.0.0
```

```
2        177.130.0.0/30 is subnetted, 2 subnets
   C        177.130.17.152 is directly connected, Serial1
   C        177.130.17.148 is directly connected, Serial0
3        10.0.0.0/8 is variably subnetted, 2 subnets, 2 masks
4  S        10.0.0.0/8 [1/0] via 160.4.115.74
5  S        10.254.101.0/24 [1/0] via 160.4.101.4
6        162.162.0.0/24 is subnetted, 2 subnets
   O IA     162.162.101.0 [110/3137] via 11.175.238.4, 02:16:02, Ethernet0
                          [110/3137] via 11.175.238.3, 02:16:02, Ethernet0
   O IA     162.162.253.0 [110/3127] via 11.175.238.4, 02:25:43, Ethernet0
                          [110/3127] via 11.175.238.3, 02:25:43, Ethernet0
7  O E2 192.188.106.0/24 [110/20] via 11.175.238.33, 20:49:59, Ethernet0
   ...
```

Note that the first few lines of the output attach a code to the source of the routing information: "C" and "S" denote "connected" and "static", respectively, as we saw earlier, "I" denotes IGRP, etc. This code is prepended to each routing entry in the routing table, signifying the source of that route.

The body of the routing table essentially contains two pieces of information: the destination and the next hop. So, 177.130.0.0 (line 2) has two subnets, each with a 30-bit mask. The two subnets are listed in the following two lines.

Line 3 shows an interesting case. 10.0.0.0 has two subnets: 10.0.0.0/8 and 10.254.101.0/24. Not only are the subnet masks different, but the subnets are overlapping. A destination address of 10.254.101.1 would match both route entries! So, should a packet for 10.254.101.1 be routed to 160.4.115.74 or 160.4.101.4? Routing table lookups follow the rule of *longest prefix match*. 10.254.101.1 matches 8 bits on line 4 and 24 bits on line 5—the longer prefix wins, and the packet is forwarded to 160.4.101.4. 162.162.0.0 (line 6) has two subnets, each of which is known via two paths. 192.188.106.0 (line 7) is not subnetted.

What if a route is learnt via multiple sources—say, via OSPF and as a static entry? Each source of routing information has an attached measure of its trustworthiness, called *administrative distance* in Cisco parlance. The lower the administrative distance, the more trustworthy the source.

Table 1-1 shows the default administrative distances.

Table 1-1. Default administrative distances

Route source	Default distance
Connected interface	0
Static route	1
External BGP	20
IGRP	100
OSPF	110
IS-IS	115
RIP	120
EGP	140
Internal BGP	200
Unknown	255

Thus, if a route is known both via OSPF and as a static entry, the static entry, not the entry known via OSPF, will be installed in the routing table.

Note that distance information and the route metric appear in the output of *show ip route* inside square brackets with the distance information first, followed by a "/" and the route metric: [distance/metric].

Administrative distance is only considered internally within a router; distance information is not exchanged in routing updates.

Underlying Processes

Behind the scenes, there are three key sets of processes running on each router that make up IP routing. I have already discussed examples from each of these three sets in the preceding sections. These processes may be organized into three categories:

1. Processes associated with the discovery of paths to various destinations in the network. These processes include dynamic routing protocols, such as RIP and IGRP, as well as static route entries. This text describes these processes in detail.

2. Processes that maintain the IP routing table. These processes receive updates from all dynamic routing protocols running on the router as well as from static route entries. By attaching administrative distance values to each routing information source, these processes break ties when multiple sources (e.g., OSPF and static route entries) report paths to the same destination. I discussed the use of administrative distance values in the previous section. Other examples from this group of processes will be discussed in Chapter 8.

3. Processes involved with the forwarding of IP packets. These processes are invoked when a router receives a packet to forward. The result of the match between the destination IP address in the packet and the contents of the IP routing table may be a match with one entry in the routing table, a match with more than one entry in the routing table, a match with a default route, etc. One general rule here is the rule of longest prefix match—if there is more than one match, the match with the longest subnet mask (or prefix) wins. Further, the outcome of these processes depends on whether the router is configured for classful or classless route lookups.

Several concepts that have not yet been discussed were thrown into the preceding discussion. For instance, we have not yet talked about classful versus classless route lookups or about default routes. These concepts will be addressed in later chapters. However, this early lesson in the division of processes should help you to understand and classify concepts more quickly.

Summing Up

Dynamic routing protocols are the mainstay of IP routing. Thus, without ado, I will begin with RIP and then, moving on in order of complexity, will discuss IGRP, EIGRP, OSPF, and BGP-4.

CHAPTER 2
Routing Information Protocol (RIP)

RIP is the first in a family of dynamic routing protocols that we will look at closely. Dynamic routing protocols *automatically* compute routing tables, freeing the network administrator from the task of specifying routes to every network using static routes. Indeed, given the complexity of and number of routes in most networks, static routing usually is not even an option.

In addition to computing the "shortest" paths to all destination networks, dynamic routing protocols discover alternative (second-best) paths when a primary path fails and balance traffic over multiple paths (load balancing).

Most dynamic routing protocols are based on one of two distributed algorithms: Distance Vector or Link State. RIP, upon which Cisco's IGRP was based, is a classic example of a DV protocol. Link State protocols include OSPF, which we will look at in a later chapter. The following section gets us started with configuring RIP.

Getting RIP Running

Throughout this book, we'll be using a fictional network called TraderMary to illustrate the concepts with which we're working. TraderMary is a distributed network with nodes in New York, Chicago, and Ames, Iowa, as shown in Figure 2-1.

As a distributed process, RIP needs to be configured on every router in the network:

```
hostname NewYork
...
interface Ethernet0
```

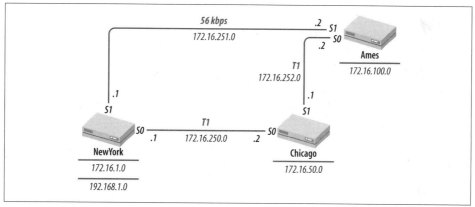

Figure 2-1. TraderMary's network

```
ip address 172.16.1.1 255.255.255.0
!
interface Ethernet1
ip address 192.168.1.1 255.255.255.0
!
interface Serial0
ip address 172.16.250.1 255.255.255.0
!
interface Serial1
ip address 172.16.251.1 255.255.255.0
...
router rip
network 172.16.0.0


hostname Chicago
...
interface Ethernet0
ip address 172.16.50.1 255.255.255.0
!
interface Serial0
ip address 172.16.250.2 255.255.255.0
!
interface Serial1
ip address 172.16.252.1 255.255.255.0
...

router rip
network 172.16.0.0


hostname Ames
...
interface Ethernet0
ip address 172.16.100.1 255.255.255.0
```

```
!
interface Serial0
ip address 172.16.252.2 255.255.255.0
!
interface Serial1
ip address 172.16.251.2 255.255.255.0
...

router rip
network 172.16.0.0
```

Notice that all that is required of a network administrator to start RIP on a router is to issue the following command:

```
router rip
```

in global configuration mode and to list the networks that will be participating in the RIP process:

```
network 172.16.0.0
```

What does it mean to list the network numbers participating in RIP?

1. Router *NewYork* will include directly connected 172.16.0.0 subnets in its updates to neighboring routers. For example, 172.16.1.0 will now be included in updates to the routers *Chicago* and *Ames*.

2. *NewYork* will receive and process RIP updates on its 172.16.0.0 interfaces from other routers running RIP. For example, *NewYork* will receive RIP updates from *Chicago* and *Ames*.

3. By exclusion, network 192.168.1.0, connected to *NewYork*, will not be advertised to *Chicago* or *Ames*, and *NewYork* will not process any RIP updates received on *Ethernet0* (if there is another router on that segment).

Next, let's verify that all the routers are seeing all the 172.16.0.0 subnets:

```
NewYork>sh ip route
Codes: C - connected, S - static, I - IGRP, R - RIP, M - mobile, B - BGP
       D - EIGRP, EX - EIGRP external, O - OSPF, IA - OSPF inter area
       N1 - OSPF NSSA external type 1, N2 - OSPF NSSA external type 2
       E1 - OSPF external type 1, E2 - OSPF external type 2, E - EGP
       i - IS-IS, L1 - IS-IS level-1, L2 - IS-IS level-2, * - candidate default

Gateway of last resort is not set

C        192.168.1.0 is directly connected, Ethernet1
         172.16.0.0/16 is subnetted, 6 subnets
C        172.16.1.0 is directly connected, Ethernet0
C        172.16.250.0 is directly connected, Serial0
C        172.16.251.0 is directly connected, Serial1
R        172.16.50.0 [120/1] via 172.16.250.2, 0:00:11, Serial0
R        172.16.100.0 [120/1] via 172.16.251.2, 0:00:19, Serial1
R        172.16.252.0 [120/1] via 172.16.250.2, 0:00:11, Serial0
                      [120/1] via 172.16.251.2, 0:00:19, Serial1
```

```
Chicago>sh ip route
Codes: C - connected, S - static, I - IGRP, R - RIP, M - mobile, B - BGP
       D - EIGRP, EX - EIGRP external, O - OSPF, IA - OSPF inter area
       N1 - OSPF NSSA external type 1, N2 - OSPF NSSA external type 2
       E1 - OSPF external type 1, E2 - OSPF external type 2, E - EGP
       i - IS-IS, L1 - IS-IS level-1, L2 - IS-IS level-2, * - candidate default

Gateway of last resort is not set

     172.16.0.0/16 is subnetted, 6 subnets
C        172.16.50.0 is directly connected, Ethernet0
C        172.16.250.0 is directly connected, Serial0
C        172.16.252.0 is directly connected, Serial1
R        172.16.1.0 [120/1] via 172.16.250.1, 0:00:01, Serial0
R        172.16.100.0 [120/1] via 172.16.252.2, 0:00:10, Serial1
R        172.16.251.0 [120/1] via 172.16.250.1, 0:00:01, Serial0
                      [120/1] via 172.16.252.2, 0:00:10, Serial1


Ames>sh ip route
Codes: C - connected, S - static, I - IGRP, R - RIP, M - mobile, B - BGP
       D - EIGRP, EX - EIGRP external, O - OSPF, IA - OSPF inter area
       N1 - OSPF NSSA external type 1, N2 - OSPF NSSA external type 2
       E1 - OSPF external type 1, E2 - OSPF external type 2, E - EGP
       i - IS-IS, L1 - IS-IS level-1, L2 - IS-IS level-2, * - candidate default

Gateway of last resort is not set

1     172.16.0.0/16 is subnetted, 6 subnets
C        172.16.100.0 is directly connected, Ethernet0
C        172.16.252.0 is directly connected, Serial0
C        172.16.251.0 is directly connected, Serial1
R        172.16.50.0 [120/1] via 172.16.252.1, 0:00:21, Serial0
R        172.16.1.0 [120/1] via 172.16.251.1, 0:00:09, Serial1
R        172.16.250.0 [120/1] via 172.16.252.1, 0:00:21, Serial0
                      [120/1] via 172.16.251.1, 0:00:09, Serial1
```

The left margin in the output of the routing tables shows how the route was derived. "C" indicates a directly connected network; "R" indicates RIP. Further note that there is some indentation in the output. The subnets of 172.16.0.0 are indented under line 1, which gives us the number of subnets (6) in 172.16.0.0 and the subnet mask that is associated with this network (/16). The routing table provides this information for every major network number it knows, indenting the subnets below the major network number.

Configuring RIP is fairly straightforward. We'll examine how RIP works in more detail in the next section.

How RIP Finds Shortest Paths

All DV protocols essentially operate the same way: routers exchange routing updates with neighboring (directly connected) routers; the routing updates contain a list of network numbers along with the distance (metric, in routing terminology) to the networks. Each router chooses the shortest path to a destination network by comparing the distance (or metric) information it receives from its various neighbors. Let's look at this in more detail in the context of RIP.

Let's imagine that the network is cold-started—i.e., all three routers are powered up at the same time. The first thing that happens after IOS has finished loading is that the router checks for its connected interfaces and determines which ones are up. Next, these directly connected networks are installed in each router's routing table. So, right after IOS has been loaded and before any routing updates have been exchanged, the routing table would look like this:

```
NewYork>sh ip route
Codes: C - connected, S - static, I - IGRP, R - RIP, M - mobile, B - BGP
       D - EIGRP, EX - EIGRP external, O - OSPF, IA - OSPF inter area
       N1 - OSPF NSSA external type 1, N2 - OSPF NSSA external type 2
       E1 - OSPF external type 1, E2 - OSPF external type 2, E - EGP
       i - IS-IS, L1 - IS-IS level-1, L2 - IS-IS level-2, * - candidate default

Gateway of last resort is not set

C       171.16.1.0 is directly connected, Ethernet0
C       171.16.250.0 is directly connected, Serial0
C       171.16.251.0 is directly connected, Serial1


Chicago>sh ip route
Codes: C - connected, S - static, I - IGRP, R - RIP, M - mobile, B - BGP
       D - EIGRP, EX - EIGRP external, O - OSPF, IA - OSPF inter area
       N1 - OSPF NSSA external type 1, N2 - OSPF NSSA external type 2
       E1 - OSPF external type 1, E2 - OSPF external type 2, E - EGP
       i - IS-IS, L1 - IS-IS level-1, L2 - IS-IS level-2, * - candidate default

Gateway of last resort is not set

C       171.16.50.0 is directly connected, Ethernet0
C       171.16.250.0 is directly connected, Serial0
C       171.16.252.0 is directly connected, Serial1


Ames>sh ip route
Codes: C - connected, S - static, I - IGRP, R - RIP, M - mobile, B - BGP
       D - EIGRP, EX - EIGRP external, O - OSPF, IA - OSPF inter area
       N1 - OSPF NSSA external type 1, N2 - OSPF NSSA external type 2
       E1 - OSPF external type 1, E2 - OSPF external type 2, E - EGP
       i - IS-IS, L1 - IS-IS level-1, L2 - IS-IS level-2, * - candidate default

Gateway of last resort is not set

C       171.16.100.0 is directly connected, Ethernet0
C       171.16.250.0 is directly connected, Serial0
C       171.16.252.0 is directly connected, Serial1
```

The routers are now ready to update their neighbors with these routes.

RIP Update

RIP updates are encapsulated in UDP. The well-known port number for RIP updates is 520. The format of a RIP packet is shown in Figure 2-2.

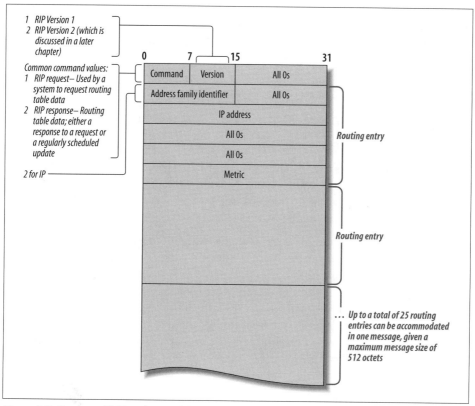

Figure 2-2. Format of RIP update packet

Note that RIP allows a station to request routes, so a machine that has just booted up can request the routing table from its neighbors instead of waiting until the next cycle of updates.

The destination IP address in RIP updates is 255.255.255.255. The source IP address is the IP address of the interface from which the update is issued.

If you look closely at the update you will see that a key piece of information is missing: the subnet mask. Let's say that an update was received with the network number 172.31.0.0. Should this be interpreted as 172.31.0.0/16 or 172.31.0.0/24 or 172.31.0.0/26 or ...? This question is addressed later, in the "Subnet Masks" section.

RIP Metric

The RIP metric is simply a measure of the number of hops to a destination network. 172.16.100.0, which is directly connected to *Ames*, is zero hops from *Ames* but one hop from *NewYork* and *Chicago*. You can see RIP metrics in the routing table:

```
NewYork>sh ip route
...
Gateway of last resort is not set

C       192.168.1.0 is directly connected, Ethernet1
        172.16.0.0/16 is subnetted, 6 subnets
C       172.16.1.0 is directly connected, Ethernet0
C       172.16.250.0 is directly connected, Serial0
C       172.16.251.0 is directly connected, Serial1
R       172.16.50.0 [120/1] via 172.16.250.2, 0:00:11, Serial0
R       172.16.100.0 [120/1] via 172.16.251.2, 0:00:19, Serial1
R       172.16.252.0 [120/1] via 172.16.250.2, 0:00:11, Serial0
                     [120/1] via 172.16.251.2, 0:00:19, Serial1
```

This routing table shows the [distance/metric] tuple in bold. Every hop between two routers adds 1 to the RIP metric. Thus, *NewYork* sees the *Ames* segment (172.16. 100.0) as one hop via the direct 56-kbps link and two hops via the T-1 to *Chicago*. *NewYork* will prefer the direct one-hop path to *Ames*.

The simplicity of the RIP metric is an asset in small, homogenous networks but a liability in networks with heterogeneous media. Consider the following comparison: the transmission delay for a 1,000-octet packet is 143 ms over a 56-kbps link and 5 ms over a T-1 link. Neglecting buffering and processing delays, two T-1 hops will cost 10 ms in comparison to 143 ms via the 56-kbps link. Thus, the two-hop T-1 path between *NewYork* and *Ames* is quicker; indeed, the designers of TraderMary's network may have put in the 56-kbps link only for backup purposes. However, RIP does not account for line speed, delay, or reliability. For this, we will look to the next DV protocol—IGRP.

Let's look at one more example of RIP metrics for TraderMary's network. Let's say that the T-1 link between *NewYork* and *Chicago* fails. As soon as *NewYork* (or *Chicago*) detects a failure in the link, all routes associated with that link are purged from the routing table, and, upon receipt of the next update, *NewYork* (*Chicago*) will learn the routes to *Chicago* (*NewYork*) via *Ames*. *NewYork*'s routing table would look like this:

```
NewYork>sh ip route
...
Gateway of last resort is not set

C       192.168.1.0 is directly connected, Ethernet1
        172.16.0.0/16 is subnetted, 6 subnets
C       172.16.1.0 is directly connected, Ethernet0
C       172.16.251.0 is directly connected, Serial1
```

```
R       172.16.50.0 [120/2] via 172.16.251.2, 0:00:23, Serial1
R       172.16.100.0 [120/1] via 172.16.251.2, 0:00:23, Serial1
R       172.16.252.0 [120/1] via 172.16.251.2, 0:00:23, Serial1
```

As we discussed in the previous chapter, the distance value associated with RIP is 120. Note that directly connected routes do not show a distance or metric value. Directly connected routes have a distance value of 0 and thus show the most preferred route to a destination, no matter how low the metric value of a route to the same network may be through another routing source (such as RIP).

The RIP metrics we saw in the previous examples were 1 or 2. It turns out that a RIP metric of 16 signals infinity (or unreachability). Why is it necessary to choose a maximum value for the RIP metric? Without a maximum hop count, a route can propagate indefinitely during certain failure scenarios, resulting in indefinitely long convergence times. This is discussed further in the "Convergence" section under "Counting to infinity."

Processing RIP Updates

The following rules summarize the steps a router takes when it receives a RIP update:

1. If the destination network number is unknown to the router, install the route using the source IP address of the update (provided the hop count is less than 16).

2. If the destination network number is known to the router but the update contains a smaller metric, modify the routing table entry with the new next hop and metric.

3. If the destination network number is known to the router but the update contains a larger metric, ignore the update.

4. If the destination network number is known to the router and the update contains a higher metric that is from the same next hop as in the table, update the metric.

5. If the destination network number is known to the router and the update contains the same metric from a different next hop, RFC 1058 calls for this update to be ignored, in general. However, Cisco differs from the standard here and installs up to four parallel paths to the same destination. These parallel paths are then used for load balancing.

Thus, when the first update from *Ames* reaches *NewYork* with the network 172.16. 100.0, *NewYork* installs the route with a hop count of 1 using rule 1. *NewYork* will also receive 172.16.100.0 in a subsequent update from *Chicago* (after *Chicago* itself has learned the route from *Ames*), but *NewYork* will discard this route because of rule 3.

Steady State

It is important for you as the network administrator to be familiar with the state of the network during normal conditions. Deviations from this state will be your clue to troubleshooting the network during times of network outage.

The following output will show you the values of the RIP timers. Note that RIP updates are sent every 30 seconds and the next update is due in 24 seconds, which means that an update was issued about 6 seconds ago. We will discuss the invalid, hold-down, and flush timers later, in the "Convergence" section.

```
NewYork>sh ip protocol

Routing Protocol is "rip"
Sending updates every 30 seconds, next due in 24 seconds
Invalid after 90 seconds, hold down 90, flushed after 180
```

One key area to look at in the routing table is the timer values. The format Cisco uses for timers is *hh:mm:ss* (hours:minutes:seconds). You would expect the time against each route to be between 0 and 30 seconds. If a route was received more than 30 seconds ago, that indicates a problem in the network. You should begin by checking to see if the next hop for the route is reachable. As an example, in line 1, 172.16. 50.0 was learned 11 seconds ago from 172.16.250.2 (on *Serial0*).

```
NewYork>sh ip route
...
Gateway of last resort is not set

     C       192.168.1.0 is directly connected, Ethernet1
             172.16.0.0/16 is subnetted, 6 subnets
     C       172.16.1.9 is directly connected, Ethernet0
     C       172.16.250.0 is directly connected, Serial0
     C       172.16.251.0 is directly connected, Serial1
  2  R       172.16.50.0 [120/1] via 172.16.250.2, 0:00:11, Serial0
     R       172.16.100.0 [120/1] via 172.16.251.2, 0:00:19, Serial1
     R       172.16.252.0 [120/1] via 172.16.250.2, 0:00:11, Serial0
                         [120/1] via 172.16.251.2, 0:00:19, Serial1
```

Parallel Paths

There are two equal-cost paths to network 172.16.252.0 from *NewYork*—one advertised by *Ames* and the other by *Chicago. NewYork* will install both routes in its routing table:

```
NewYork>sh ip route
...
Gateway of last resort is not set

     C       192.168.1.0 is directly connected, Ethernet1
             172.16.0.0/16 is subnetted, 6 subnets
     C       172.16.1.9 is directly connected, Ethernet0
     C       172.16.250.0 is directly connected, Serial0
     C       172.16.251.0 is directly connected, Serial1
     R       172.16.50.0 [120/1] via 172.16.250.2, 0:00:11, Serial0
     R       172.16.100.0 [120/1] via 172.16.251.2, 0:00:19, Serial1
     R       172.16.252.0 [120/1] via 172.16.250.2, 0:00:11, Serial0
                         [120/1] via 172.16.251.2, 0:00:19, Serial1
```

Both paths are utilized to forward packets. How is traffic split over the two links? The answer depends on the switching mode configured on the Cisco router. Two common switching modes are process switching and fast switching.

Process Switching

Process switching results in packet-by-packet load balancing—one packet travels out on *serial0* and the next packet travels out on *serial1*. Packet-by-packet load balancing is possible while process switching because in this switching mode the router examines its routing table for every packet it receives.

Process switching is configured as follows:

```
NewYork#-config#interface serial0
NewYork#-config-if#no ip route-cache
```

Packet switching is very CPU-intensive, as every packet causes a routing table lookup.

Fast Switching

In this mode, only the first packet for a given destination is looked up in the routing table, and, as this packet is forwarded, its next hop (say, *serial0*) is placed in a cache. Subsequent packets for the same destination are looked up in the cache, not in the routing table. This implies that all packets for this destination will follow the same path (*serial0*).

Now, if another packet arrives that matches the routing entry 204.148.185.192, it will be cached with a next hop of *serial1*. Henceforth, all packets to this second destination will follow *serial1*.

Fast switching thus load-balances destination-by-destination (or session-by-session). Fast switching is configured as follows:

```
NewYork#-config#interface serial0
NewYork#-config-if#ip route-cache
```

In fast switching, the first packet for a new destination causes a routing table lookup and the generation of a new entry in the route cache. Subsequent packets consult the route cache but not the routing table.

Convergence

Changes—planned and unplanned—are normal in any network:

- A serial link breaks
- A new serial link is added to a network
- A router or hub loses power or malfunctions
- A new LAN segment is added to a network

All routers in the routing domain will not reflect these changes right away. This is because RIP routers rely on their direct neighbors for routing updates, which in turn rely on another set of neighbors. The routing process that is set into motion from the time of a network change (such as the failure of a link) until all routers correctly reflect the change is referred to as convergence. During convergence, routing connectivity between some parts of the network may be lost and, hence, an important question that is frequently asked is "How long will the network take to converge after such-and-such failure in the network?" The answer depends on a number of factors, including the network topology and the timers that have been defined for the routing protocol.

The following list defines the four timers that are key to the operation of any DV protocol, including RIP:

Update timer (default value: 30 seconds)
> After sending a routing update, RIP sets the update timer to 0. When the timer expires, RIP issues another routing update. Thus, RIP updates are sent every 30 seconds.

Invalid timer (default value: 180 seconds)
> Every time a router receives an update for a route, it sets the invalid timer to 0. The expiration of the invalid timer indicates that six consecutive updates were missed—at this time, the source of the routing information is considered suspect. Even though the route is declared invalid, packets are still forwarded to the next hop specified in the routing table. Note that prior to the expiration of the invalid timer RIP would process any updates received by updating the route's timers.

Hold-down timer (default value: 180 seconds)
> When the invalid timer expires, the route automatically enters the hold-down phase. During hold-down, all updates regarding the route are disregarded—it is assumed that the network may not have converged and that there may be bad routing information circulating in the network. The hold-down timer is started when the invalid timer expires. Thus, a route goes into hold-down state when the invalid timer expires. A route may also go into hold-down state when an update is received indicating that the route has become unreachable—this is discussed further later in this section.

Flush timer (default value: 240 seconds)
> The flush timer is set to 0 when an update is received. When the flush timer expires, the route is removed from the routing table and the router is ready to receive an update with this route. Note that the flush timer overrides the hold-down timer.

Let's consider Figure 2-3. Here is a snapshot of *A*'s routing table (when all entities are up):

```
A>sh ip route
...

C       192.168.1.0 is directly connected, Ethernet1
        172.17.0.0/16 is subnetted, 6 subnets
```

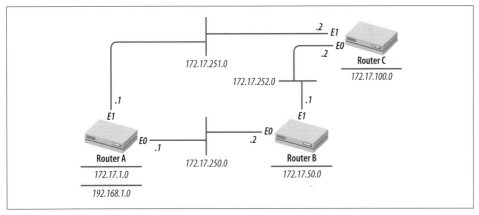

Figure 2-3. Three routers connected using Ethernet segments

```
C       172.17.1.9 is directly connected, Ethernet0
C       172.17.250.0 is directly connected, Ethernet1
C       172.17.251.0 is directly connected, Ethernet2
R       172.17.50.0 [120/1] via 172.17.250.2, 0:00:11, Ethernet1
R       172.17.100.0 [120/1] via 172.17.251.2, 0:00:19, Ethernet2
R       172.17.252.0 [120/1] via 172.17.250.2, 0:00:11, Ethernet1
                     [120/1] via 172.17.251.2, 0:00:19, Ethernet2
```

This table shows that 11 seconds ago *A* received an update for 172.17.50.0 from 172.17.250.2 (*B*). The update and invalid timers for a route are reset (set to 0) every time a valid update is received for the route. At the moment this routing-table snapshot was taken, *A*'s invalid timer for 172.16.50.0 and *B*'s update timer for 172.16.50.0 would both be 11 seconds.

Let's say that at this very time, *B* was disconnected from its LAN attachment to *A*. *A* would now stop receiving updates from *B*. 30 seconds after the cut, the routing table would look like this:

```
A>sh ip route
...

C       192.168.1.0 is directly connected, Ethernet1
        172.17.0.0/16 is subnetted, 6 subnets
C       172.17.1.9 is directly connected, Ethernet0
C       172.17.250.0 is directly connected, Serial0
C       172.17.251.0 is directly connected, Serial1
R       172.17.50.0 [120/1] via 172.17.250.2, 0:00:41, Serial0
R       172.17.100.0 [120/1] via 172.17.251.2, 0:00:19, Serial1
R       172.17.252.0 [120/1] via 172.17.250.2, 0:00:41, Serial0
                     [120/1] via 172.17.251.2, 0:00:19, Serial1
```

The invalid timer for 172.16.50.0 is now at 41 seconds. *A* would still continue to forward traffic for 172.17.50.0 via *Ethernet0*. The assumption RIP makes is that an update was lost or damaged in transit from *B* to *A*, even though the route is still good. This assumption holds good until the invalid timer expires (180 seconds or 6 update intervals from the last update). Before the invalid timer expires, *A* will receive and process any updates received regarding 172.16.50.0. Once the invalid timer expires, the route is placed in hold-down and subsequent updates about 172.16.0.0 are suppressed under the assumption that the route has gone bad and that bad routing information may be circulating in the network. The route will go into hold-down 180 seconds from the last update, or 169 seconds after the cut. At this time, the routing table would look like this:

```
A>sh ip route
...

C       192.168.1.0 is directly connected, Ethernet1
        172.17.0.0/16 is subnetted, 6 subnets
C       172.17.1.9 is directly connected, Ethernet0
C       172.17.250.0 is directly connected, Serial0
C       172.17.251.0 is directly connected, Serial1
R       172.17.50.0 is possibly down,
          routing via 172.17.250.2, Serial0
R       172.17.100.0 [120/1] via 172.17.251.2, 0:00:19, Serial1
R       172.17.252.0 [120/1] is possibly down,
          routing via 172.16.250.2, Ethernet1
                    [120/1] via 172.17.251.2, 0:00:19, Serial1
```

The route remains in hold-down until the hold-down timer expires or until the route is flushed, whichever happens first. Using default timers, the flush timer would go off first, 229 seconds after the cut. Router *A* would then learn the route to 172.17.50.0 when the next update arrived from *C*, which could be between 0 and 30 seconds after the route has been flushed, or 229 to 259 seconds from the cut.

The events just described are illustrated in Figure 2-4.

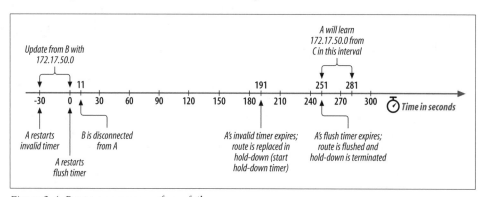

Figure 2-4. Route convergence after a failure

Speeding Up Convergence

When a router detects that an interface is down, it immediately flushes all routes it knows via that interface. This speeds up convergence, avoiding the invalid, hold-down, and flush timers.

Can you now guess the reason why the case study used earlier (routers *A*, *B*, and *C* connected via Ethernet segments) differs slightly from TraderMary's network in New York, Chicago, and Ames?

We couldn't illustrate the details of the invalid, hold-down, and flush timers in TraderMary's network because if a serial link is detected in the down state, all routes that point through that interface are immediately flushed from the routing table. In our case study, we were able to pull *B* off its Ethernet connection to *A* while keeping *A* up on all its interfaces.

Split horizon

Consider a simple network with two routers connected to each other (Figure 2-5).

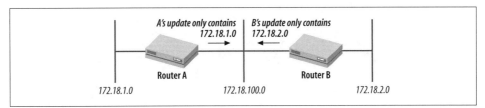

Figure 2-5. Split horizon

Let's say that router *A* lost its connection to 172.18.1.0, but before it could update *B* about this change, *B* sent *A* its full routing table, including 172.18.1.0 at one hop. Router *A* now assumes that *B* has a connection to 172.18.1.0 at one hop, so *A* installs a route to 172.18.1.0 at two hops via *B*. *A*'s next update to *B* announces 172.18.1.0 at two hops, so *B* adjusts its route 172.18.1.0 to three hops via *A*! This cycle continues until the route metric reaches 16, at which stage the route update is discarded.

Split horizon solves this problem by proposing a simple solution: when a router sends an update through an interface, it does not include in its update any routes that it learned via that interface. Using this rule, the only network that *A* would send to *B* in its update would be 172.18.1.0, and the only network that *B* would send to *A* would be 172.18.2.0. *B* would never send 172.18.1.0 to *A*, so the previously described loop would be impossible.

Counting to infinity

Split horizon works well for two routers directly connected to each other. However, consider the following network (shown in Figure 2-6).

Let's say that router *A* stopped advertising network *X* to its neighbors *B* and *E*. Routers *B*, *D*, and *E* will finally purge the route to *X*, but router *C* may still advertise *X* to *D* (without violating split horizon). *D*, in turn, will advertise *X* to *E*, and *E* will advertise *X* to *A*. Thus, the router (*C*) that did not purge *X* from its table can propagate a bad route.

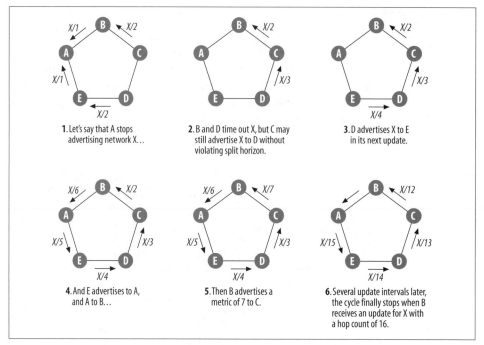

Figure 2-6. Counting to infinity

This problem is solved by equating a hop count of 16 to infinity and hence disregarding any advertisement for a route with this metric.

In Figure 2-6, when *B* finally receives an advertisement for *X* with a metric of 16, it will consider *X* to be unreachable and will disregard the advertisement. The choice of 16 as infinity limits RIP networks to a maximum diameter of 15 hops between nodes. Note that the choice of 16 as infinity is a compromise between convergence time and network diameter—if a higher number were chosen, the network would take longer to converge after a failure; if a lower number were chosen, the network would converge faster but the maximum possible diameter of a RIP network would be smaller.

Triggered updates

When a router detects a change in the metric for a route and sends an update to its neighbors right away (without waiting for its next update cycle), the update is referred to as a *triggered update*. The triggered update speeds convergence between two neighbors by as much as 30 seconds. A triggered update does not include the entire routing table, but only the route that has changed.

Poison reverse

When a router detects that a link is down, its next update for that route will contain a metric of 16. This is called *poisoning* the route. Downstream routers that receive this update will immediately place the route in hold-down (without going through the invalid period).

Poison reverse and triggered updates can be combined. When a router detects that a link has been lost or the metric for a route has changed to 16, it will immediately issue a poison reverse with triggered update to all its neighbors.

Neighbors that receive unreachability information about a route via a poison reverse with triggered update will place the route in hold-down if their next hop is via the router issuing the poison reverse. The hold-down state ensures that bad information about the route (say from a neighbor that may have lost its copy of the triggered update or may have issued a regular update just before it received the triggered update) does not propagate in the network.

Triggered updates and hold-downs can handle the loss of a route, preventing bad routing information. Why, then, do we need the count-to-infinity limits? Triggered updates may be dropped, lost, or corrupted. Some routers may not ever receive the unreachability information and may inject a path for a route into the network even when that path has been lost. Count to infinity would take care of these situations.

Setting timers

The value of RIP timers on a Cisco router can be seen in the following example:

```
Chicago>sh ip protocol

Routing Protocol is "rip"
Sending updates every 30 seconds, next due in 24 seconds
Invalid after 90 seconds, hold down 90, flushed after 180
```

These timers could be modified to allow faster convergence. The following command:

```
timers basic 10 25 30 40
```

would send RIP updates every 10 seconds instead of every 30 seconds. The other three timers specify the invalid, hold-down, and flush timers, respectively. These timers can be configured as follows:

```
NewYork#config
NewYork-config#router rip
NewYork-config#timers basic 10 25 30 40
```

However, RIP timers should not be modified without a detailed understanding of how RIP works. Potential problems with decreasing the timer values are that updates will be issued more frequently and can cause congestion on low-bandwidth networks, and that congestion in the network is more likely to cause routes to go into hold-down; this, in turn, can cause route flapping.

 Do not modify RIP timers unless absolutely necessary. If you modify RIP timers, make sure that all routers have the same timers.

If an interface on a router goes down, the router sends a RIP request out to the other, up interfaces. This speeds up convergence if any of the other neighbors can reach the destinations that were missed in the first request.

Subnet Masks

Looking closely at Figure 2-2, we see that there is no field for subnet masks in RIP. Let's say that router *SantaFe* received an update with the following routes in the IP address field:

```
192.100.1.48
192.100.1.64
192.100.2.0
10.0.0.0
```

And let's say that *SantaFe* has the following configuration:

```
hostname SantaFe
!
interface Ethernet 0
ip address 192.100.1.17 255.255.255.240
!
interface Ethernet 1
ip address 192.100.1.33 255.255.255.240
!
router rip
network 192.100.1.0
network 192.100.2.0
```

How would the router associate subnet masks with these routes?

- If the router has an interface on a network number received in an update, it would associate the same mask with the update as it does with its own interface. Consequently, RIP does not permit Variable Length Subnet Masks (VLSM).

- If the router does not have an interface on the network number received in an update, it would assume a natural mask for the network number.

SantaFe's routing table would look like this:

```
SantaFe>sh ip route
...
Gateway of last resort is not set

R       10.0.0.0 [120/1] via 192.100.1.18, 0:00:11, Ethernet0
R       192.100.2.0 [120/1] via 192.100.1.18, 0:00:11, Ethernet0
        192.100.1.0/16 is subnetted, 4 subnets
C       192.100.1.16 is directly connected, Ethernet0
C       192.100.1.32 is directly connected, Ethernet1
R       192.100.1.48 [120/1] via 192.100.1.18, 0:00:11, Ethernet0
R       192.100.1.64 [120/1] via 192.100.1.18, 0:00:11, Ethernet0
```

SantaFe represents 192.100.1.48 and 192.100.1.64 with a 28-bit mask even though the subnet mask was not conveyed in the RIP update. *SantaFe* was able to deduce the

28-bit mask because it has direct interfaces on 192.100.1.0 networks. This assumption is key to why RIP does not support VLSM.

SantaFe represents 192.100.2.0 and 10.0.0.0 with their natural 24-bit and 8-bit masks, respectively, because it has no interfaces on those networks. Chapter 5 covers RIP-2, an extension of RIP that supports VLSM.

Route Summarization

Consider the router *Phoenix*, which connects to *SantaFe* and sends the RIP updates shown earlier:

```
192.100.1.48
192.100.1.64
192.100.2.0
10.0.0.0
```

Phoenix may have been configured as follows (see Figure 2-8, later in this chapter):

```
hostname Phoenix
ip subnet-zero
!
interface Ethernet 0
ip address 192.100.1.18 255.255.255.240
!
interface Ethernet 1
ip address 192.100.1.49 255.255.255.240
!
interface Ethernet 2
ip address 192.100.1.65 255.255.255.240
!
interface Ethernet 3
ip address 192.100.2.1 255.255.255.240
!
interface Ethernet 4
ip address 192.100.2.17 255.255.255.240
!
interface Ethernet 5
ip address 10.1.0.1 255.255.0.0
!
interface Ethernet 6
ip address 10.2.0.1 255.255.0.0
!
router rip
network 192.100.1.0
network 192.100.2.0
network 10.0.0.0
```

Phoenix did not send detailed routes for 192.100.2.0 or 10.0.0.0 when advertising to *SantaFe* because *Phoenix* summarized those routes. As I stated earlier, since *Phoenix* did not have interfaces on those networks, it couldn't have made sense of those routes anyway.

Default Route

A routing table need not contain all routes in the network to reach all destinations. This simplification is arrived at through the use of a *default route*. When a router does not have an explicit route to a destination IP address, it looks to see if it has a default route in its routing table and, if so, forwards packets for this destination via the default route.

In RIP, the default route is represented as the IP address 0.0.0.0. This is convenient because 0.0.0.0 cannot be confused with any Class A, B, or C IP address.

One situation in which default routes can be employed in an intranet is in a core network that has branch offices hanging off it (Figure 2-7).

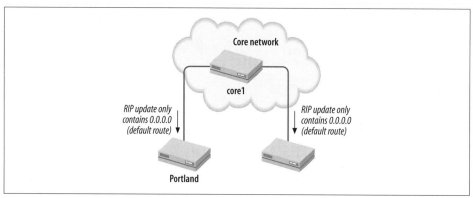

Figure 2-7. Branch offices only need a default route

Consider the topology of this figure. Since the branch offices have only one connection (to the core), all routes to the core network and to other branches can be replaced with a single default route pointing toward the core network. This implies that the size of the routing table in the branch offices is just the number of directly connected networks plus the default route.

So, router *Portland* may be configured as follows:

```
hostname Portland
...
interface Ethernet 0
ip address 192.100.1.17 255.255.255.240
!
interface Serial 0
ip address 192.100.1.33 255.255.255.240
!
router rip
network 192.100.1.0
```

An examination of *Portland*'s routing table would show the following:

```
Portland>sh ip route
...
Gateway of last resort is not set

     192.100.1.0/28 is subnetted, 2 subnets
C       192.100.1.16 is directly connected, Ethernet0
C       192.100.1.32 is directly connected, Serial0
R    0.0.0.0 [120/1] via 192.199.1.34, 0:00:21, Serial0
```

The default route may be sourced from router *core1* as follows:

```
hostname core1
...
interface Serial 0
ip address 192.100.1.34 255.255.255.240
!
router rip
network 192.100.1.0
!
ip route 0.0.0.0 0.0.0.0 null0
```

Note that the default route 0.0.0.0 is automatically carried by RIP—it is not listed in a network number statement under *router rip*.

The advantage of using a default in place of hundreds or thousands of more specific routes is obvious—network bandwidth and router CPU are not tied up in routing updates. The disadvantage of using a default is that packets for destinations that are down or not even defined in the network are still forwarded to the core network.

Default routes are tremendously useful in Internet connectivity—where all (thousands and thousands of) Internet routes may be represented by a single default route.

Yet another use of default routes is in maintaining reachability between a routing domain running RIP and another routing domain with VLSM. Since VLSM cannot be imported into RIP, a default route pointing to the second domain may be defined in the RIP network.

Routes to hosts

Some host machines listen to RIP updates in "quiet" or "silent" mode (Figure 2-8). These hosts do not respond to requests for RIP routes or issue regular RIP updates. Listening to RIP provides redundancy to the hosts in a scenario in which multiple routers are connected to a segment. If the routers have similar routing tables, it may make sense to send only the default route (0.0.0.0) to hosts.

Fine-Tuning RIP

We saw in the section on RIP metrics that the preferred path between *New York* and *Ames* would be the two-hop path via *Chicago* rather than the one-hop 56-kbps path

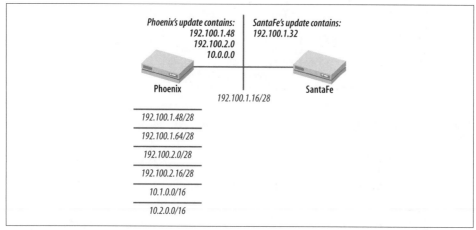

Figure 2-8. RIP routes to hosts

that RIP selects. The RIP metrics can be manipulated to disfavor the one-hop path through the use of offset lists:

```
hostname NewYork
...
router rip
network 172.16.0.0
offset-list 10 in 2 serial1
...
access-list 10 permit 172.16.100.0 0.0.0.0

hostname Chicago
...
router rip
network 172.16.0.0

Ames#config terminal
router rip
network 172.16.0.0
offset-list 20 in 2 serial1
...
access-list 20 permit 172.16.1.0 0.0.0.0
```

NewYork adds 2 to the metric for the routes specified in access list 10 when learned via *serial1*, and *Ames* adds 2 to the metric for the routes specified in access list 20 when learned via *serial1*. The direct route over the 56-kbps link thus has a metric of 3, and the route via *Chicago* has a metric of 2. The new routing tables look like this:

```
NewYork>sh ip route
...
Gateway of last resort is not set

C       192.168.1.0 is directly connected, Ethernet1
        172.16.0.0/16 is subnetted, 6 subnets
C       172.16.1.0 is directly connected, Ethernet0
```

```
C       172.16.250.0 is directly connected, Serial0
C       172.16.251.0 is directly connected, Serial1
R       172.16.50.0 [120/1] via 172.16.250.2, 0:00:11, Serial0
R       172.16.100.0 [120/2] via 172.16.250.2, 0:00:19, Serial0
R       172.16.252.0 [120/1] via 172.16.250.2, 0:00:11, Serial0
                     [120/1] via 172.16.251.2, 0:00:19, Serial1

Ames>sh ip route
...
Gateway of last resort is not set

        172.16.0.0/16 is subnetted, 6 subnets
C       172.16.100.0 is directly connected, Ethernet0
C       172.16.252.0 is directly connected, Serial0
C       172.16.251.0 is directly connected, Serial1
R       172.16.50.0 [120/1] via 172.16.252.1, 0:00:21, Serial0
R       172.16.1.0 [120/2] via 172.16.251.1, 0:00:09, Serial1
R       172.16.250.0 [120/1] via 172.16.252.1, 0:00:21, Serial0
                     [120/1] via 172.16.251.1, 0:00:09, Serial1
```

The syntax for offset lists is as follows:

```
offset-list {access-list} {in | out} offset [type number]
```

The offset list specifies the offset to add to the RIP metric on routes of interface *type* (Ethernet, serial, etc.) and *number* (interface number) that are being learned (*in*) or advertised (*out*).

An offset list can also be applied to default routes. Thus, in Figure 2-7, let's consider the scenario where *Portland* is given a second connection to a backup router *core2*. *core2* may originate a default with a higher metric:

```
hostname core2
...
interface Serial 0
ip address 192.100.2.34 255.255.255.240
!
router rip
network 192.100.2.0
offset-list 30 out 3 serial0
!
ip route 0.0.0.0 0.0.0.0 null0
!
access-list 30 permit 0.0.0.0 0.0.0.0
```

Portland would prefer the default via *core1* because the metric from *core1* would be lower by 3. *Portland* would use the default from *core2* if *core1* or the link to *core1* went down.

Summing Up

RIP is a relatively simple protocol, easy to configure and very reliable. The robustness of RIP is evident from the fact that various implementations of RIP differ in details and yet work well together. A standard for RIP wasn't put forth until 1988 (by Charles Hedrick, in RFC 1058). Small, homogeneous networks are a good match for RIP. However, as networks grow, other routing protocols may look more attractive for several reasons:

- The RIP metric does not account for link bandwidth or delay.
- The exchange of full routing updates every 30 seconds does not scale for large networks—the overhead of generating and processing all routes can be high.
- RIP convergence times can be too long.
- Subnet mask information is not exchanged in RIP updates, so Variable Length Subnet Masks are not supported.
- The RIP metric restricts the network diameter to 15 hops.

CHAPTER 3

Interior Gateway Routing Protocol (IGRP)

The second Distance Vector protocol that we will examine is the Interior Gateway Routing Protocol, or IGRP. IGRP and RIP are close cousins: both are based on the Bellman-Ford Distance Vector (DV) algorithms. DV algorithms propagate routing information from neighbor to neighbor; if a router receives the same route from multiple neighbors, it chooses the route with the lowest metric. All DV protocols need robust strategies to cope with *bad* routing information. Bad routes can linger in a network when information about the loss of a route does not reach some router (for instance, because of the loss of a route update packet), which then inserts the bad route back into the network. IGRP uses the same convergence strategies as RIP: triggered updates, route hold-downs, split horizon, and poison reverse.

IGRP has been widely deployed in small to mid-sized networks because it can be configured with the same ease as RIP, but its metric represents bandwidth and delay, in addition to hop count. The ability to discriminate between paths based on bandwidth and delay is a major improvement over RIP.

IGRP is a Cisco proprietary protocol; other router vendors do not support IGRP. Keep this in mind if you are planning a multivendor router environment.

The following section gets us started with configuring IGRP.

Getting IGRP Running

TraderMary's network, shown in Figure 3-1, can be configured to run IGRP as follows.

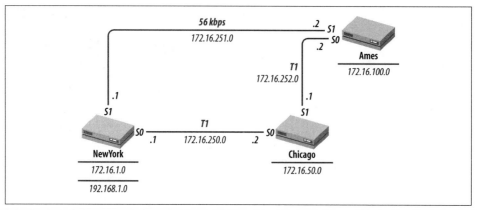

Figure 3-1. TraderMary's network

Like RIP, IGRP is a distributed protocol that needs to be configured on every router in the network:

```
hostname NewYork
...
interface Ethernet0
ip address 172.16.1.1 255.255.255.0
!
interface Ethernet1
ip address 192.168.1.1 255.255.255.0
!
interface Serial0
description New York to Chicago link
ip address 172.16.250.1 255.255.255.0
!
interface Serial1
description New York to Ames link
ip address 172.16.251.1 255.255.255.0
...
router igrp 10
network 172.16.0.0


hostname Chicago
...
interface Ethernet0
ip address 172.16.50.1 255.255.255.0
!
interface Serial0
ip address 172.16.250.2 255.255.255.0
!
interface Serial1
ip address 172.16.252.1 255.255.255.0
...
```

```
router igrp 10
network 172.16.0.0
```

```
hostname Ames
...
interface Ethernet0
ip address 172.16.100.1 255.255.255.0
!
interface Serial0
ip address 172.16.252.2 255.255.255.0
!
interface Serial1
ip address 172.16.251.2 255.255.255.0
...
```

```
router igrp 10
network 172.16.0.0
```

The syntax of the IGRP command is:

```
router igrp {process-id | autonomous-system-number}
```

in global configuration mode. The networks that will be participating in the IGRP process are then listed:

```
network 172.16.0.0
```

What does it mean to list the network numbers participating in IGRP?

1. *NewYork* will include directly connected `172.16.0.0` subnets in its updates to neighboring routers. For example, `172.16.1.0` will now be included in updates to the routers *Chicago* and *Ames*.

2. *NewYork* will receive and process IGRP updates on its `172.16.0.0` interfaces from other routers running IGRP 10. For example, *NewYork* will receive IGRP updates from *Chicago* and *Ames*.

3. By exclusion, network `192.168.1.0`, connected to *NewYork*, will not be advertised to *Chicago* or *Ames*, and *NewYork* will not process any IGRP updates received on *Ethernet0* (if there is another router on that segment).

Next, let's verify that all the routers are seeing all the `172.16.0.0` subnets. Here is *NewYork*'s routing table:

```
NewYork#show ip route
Codes: C - connected, S - static, I - IGRP, R - RIP, M - mobile, B - BGP
       D - EIGRP, EX - EIGRP external, O - OSPF, IA - OSPF inter area
       N1 - OSPF NSSA external type 1, N2 - OSPF NSSA external type 2
       E1 - OSPF external type 1, E2 - OSPF external type 2, E - EGP
       i - IS-IS, L1 - IS-IS level-1, L2 - IS-IS level-2, * - candidate default

Gateway of last resort is not set
```

```
       172.16.0.0/24 is subnetted, 6 subnets
I        172.16.252.0 [100/10476] via 172.16.251.2, 00:00:26, Serial1
                      [100/10476] via 172.16.250.2, 00:00:37, Serial0
C        172.16.250.0 is directly connected, Serial0
C        172.16.251.0 is directly connected, Serial1
I        172.16.50.0 [100/8576] via 172.16.250.2, 00:00:37, Serial0
C        172.16.1.0 is directly connected, Ethernet0
I        172.16.100.0 [100/8576] via 172.16.251.2, 00:00:26, Serial1
C     192.168.1.0/24 is directly connected, Ethernet1
```

Here is *Chicago*'s table:

```
Chicago#sh ip route
...
Gateway of last resort is not set

       172.16.0.0/24 is subnetted, 6 subnets
C        172.16.252.0 is directly connected, Serial1
C        172.16.250.0 is directly connected, Serial0
I        172.16.251.0 [100/10476] via 172.16.250.1, 00:01:22, Serial0
                      [100/10476] via 172.16.252.2, 00:00:17, Serial1
C        172.16.50.0 is directly connected, Ethernet0
I        172.16.1.0 [100/8576] via 172.16.250.1, 00:01:22, Serial0
I        172.16.100.0 [100/8576] via 172.16.252.2, 00:00:17, Serial1
```

And here is *Ames*'s table:

```
Ames#sh ip route
...
Gateway of last resort is not set

       172.16.0.0/24 is subnetted, 6 subnets
C        172.16.252.0 is directly connected, Serial0
I        172.16.250.0 [100/10476] via 172.16.251.1, 00:01:11, Serial1
                      [100/10476] via 172.16.252.1, 00:00:21, Serial0
C        172.16.251.0 is directly connected, Serial1
I        172.16.50.0 [100/8576] via 172.16.252.1, 00:00:21, Serial0
I        172.16.1.0 [100/8576] via 172.16.251.1, 00:01:11, Serial1
C        172.16.100.0 is directly connected, Ethernet0
```

The IGRP-derived routes in these tables are labeled with an "I" in the left margin. The first line in each router's table contains summary information:

```
172.16.0.0/24 is subnetted, 6 subnets
```

Note that all three routers show the same summary information—*NewYork*, *Chicago*, and *Ames* show all six subnets.

Note also that network 192.168.1.0, defined on *NewYork* interface *Ethernet1*, did not appear in the routing tables of *Chicago* and *Ames*. To be propagated, 192.168.1.0 would have to be defined in a network statement under the IGRP configuration on *NewYork*:

```
hostname NewYork
...
```

```
router igrp 10
network 172.16.0.0
network 192.168.1.0
```

Getting IGRP started is fairly straightforward. However, if you compare the routing tables in this section to those in the previous chapter on RIP, there is no difference in the next-hop information. More importantly, the route from *NewYork* to network `172.16.100.0` is still over the direct 56-kbps path rather than the two-hop T-1 path. The two-hop T-1 path is better than the one-hop 56-kbps link. As an example, take a 512-byte packet; it would take 73 ms to copy this packet over a 56-kbits/s link versus 5 ms over two T-1 links. Our expectation is that IGRP should install this two-hop T-1 path, since IGRP has been touted for its metric that includes link bandwidth and delay. The later section "IGRP Metric" explains why IGRP installs the slower path. The "Modifying IGRP metrics" section leads us through the configuration changes required to make IGRP install the faster path.

A key difference in this configuration is that, unlike in RIP, each IGRP process is identified by an autonomous system (AS) number. AS numbers are described in detail in the next section.

How IGRP Works

Since IGRP is such a close cousin of RIP, we will not repeat the details of how DV algorithms work, how updates are sent, and how route convergence is achieved. However, because IGRP employs a much more comprehensive metric, I'll discuss the IGRP metric in detail. I'll begin this discussion with AS numbers.

IGRP Autonomous System Number

Each IGRP process requires an autonomous system number:

```
router igrp autonomous-system-number
```

The AS number allows the network administrator to define routing domains; routers within a domain exchange IGRP routing updates with each other but not with routers in different domains. Note that in the context of IGRP the terms "autonomous system number" and "process ID" are often used interchangeably. Since the IGRP autonomous system number is not advertised to other domains, network engineers often cook up arbitrary process IDs for their IGRP domains.

Let's say that TraderMary created a subsidiary in Africa and that the new topology is as shown in Figure 3-2.

Note that IGRP is running in the U.S. and Africa with AS numbers of 10 and 20, respectively. The U.S. routers now exchange IGRP routes with each other, as before, and the routers *Nairobi* and *Casablanca* exchange IGRP updates with each other. IGRP updates are processed only between routers running the same AS number, so

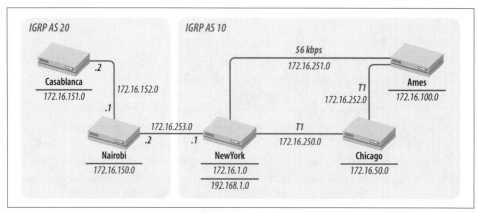

Figure 3-2. TraderMary's U.S. and African networks

NewYork and *Nairobi* do not exchange IGRP updates with each other. We will see this in more detail later, when we look at the format of an IGRP update.

The advantage of creating small domains with unique AS numbers is that a routing problem in one domain is not likely to ripple into another domain running a different AS number. So, for example, let's say that a network engineer in Africa configured network 172.16.50.0 on *Casablanca* (172.16.50.0 already exists on *Chicago*). The U.S. network would not be disrupted because of this duplicate address. In another situation, an IGRP bug in IOS on *Chicago* could disrupt routing in the U.S., but *Nairobi* and *Casablanca* would not be affected by this problem in the AS 10.

The problem with creating too many small domains running different IGRP AS numbers is that sooner or later the domains will need to exchange routes with each other. The office in New York would need to send files to Nairobi. This could be accomplished by adding static routes on *NewYork* (to 172.16.150.0) and *Nairobi* (to 172.16.1.0). However, static routes can be cumbersome to install and administer and do not offer the redundancy of dynamic routing protocols. Dynamic distribution of routes between routing domains is discussed in Chapter 8.

In the meantime, all I will say is to use good judgment when breaking networks into autonomous systems. Making a routing domain too small will require extensive redistributions or the creation of static entries. Making a routing domain too big exposes the network to failures of the type just described.

The boundary between domains is often geographic or organizational.

IGRP Metric

The RIP metric was designed for small, homogenous networks. Paths were selected based on the number of hops to a destination; the lowest hop-count path was installed in the routing table. IGRP is designed for more complex networks. Cisco's implementation of IGRP allows the network engineer to customize the metric based on bandwidth, delay, reliability, load, and MTU. In order to compare metrics between paths and select the least-cost path, IGRP converts bandwidth, delay, reliability, delay, and MTU into a scalar quantity—a *composite* metric that expresses the desirability of a path. Just as in the case of RIP, a path with a lower composite metric is preferred to a path with a higher composite metric.

The computation of the IGRP composite metric is user-configurable; i.e., the network administrator can specify parameters in the *formula* used to convert bandwidth, delay, reliability, load, and MTU into a scalar quantity.

The following sections define bandwidth, delay, reliability, load, and MTU. We will then see how these variables can be used to compute the composite metric for a path.

Interface bandwidth, delay, reliability, load, and MTU

The IGRP metric for a path is derived from the bandwidth, delay, reliability, load, and MTU values of every media in the path to the destination network.

The bandwidth, delay, reliability, load, and MTU values at any interface to a media can be seen as output of the *show interface* command:

```
router1#sh interface ethernet 0
Ethernet0 is up, line protocol is up
  Hardware is AmdP2, address is 0010.7bcf.e340 (bia 0010.7bcf.e340)
  Description: Lab Test
  Internet address is 1.13.96.1/16
  MTU 1500 bytes, BW 10000 Kbit, DLY 1000 usec, rely 255/255, load 1/255
  Encapsulation ARPA, loopback not set, keepalive set (10 sec)
  ARP type: ARPA, ARP Timeout 04:00:00
...
```

The bandwidth, delay, reliability, load, and MTU for a media are defined as follows:

Bandwidth
> The bandwidth for a link represents how fast the physical media can transmit bits onto a wire. Thus, an HSSI link transmits approximately 45,000 kbits every second, Ethernet runs at 10,000 kbps, a T-1 link transmits 1,544 kbits every second, and a 56-kbps link transmits 56 kbits every second.
>
> *Ethernet0* on *router1* is configured with a bandwidth of 10,000 kbps.

Delay
> The delay for a link represents the time to traverse the link in an unloaded network and includes the propagation time for the media. Ethernet has a delay value of 1 ms; a satellite link has a delay value in the neighborhood of 1 second.
>
> *Ethernet0* on *router1* is configured with a delay of 1,000 ms.

Reliability
> Link reliability is dynamically measured by the router and is expressed as a numeral between 1 and 255. A reliability of 255 indicates a 100% reliable link.
>
> *Ethernet0* on *router1* is 100% reliable.

Load

Link utilization is dynamically measured by the router and is expressed as a numeral between 1 and 255. A load of 255 indicates 100% utilization.

Ethernet0 on *router1* has a load of 1/255.

MTU

The MTU, or Maximum Transmission Unit, represents the largest frame size the link can handle.

Ethernet0 on *router1* has an MTU size of 1,500 bytes.

The MTU, bandwidth, and delay values are static parameters that Cisco routers derive from the media type. Table 3-1 shows some common values for bandwidth and delay. These default values can be modified using the commands shown in the next section.

Table 3-1. Default bandwidth and delay values

Media type	Default bandwidth	Default delay
Ethernet	10 Mbps	1,000 ms
Fast Ethernet	100 Mbps	100 ms
FDDI	100 Mbps	100 ms
T-1 (serial interface)[a]	1,544 kbps	20,000 ms
56 kbps (serial interface)	1,544 kbps	20,000 ms
HSSI	45,045 kbps	20,000 ms

[a] All serial interfaces on Cisco routers are configured with the same *default* bandwidth (1,544 kbits/s) and delay (20,000 ms) parameters.

The reliability and load values are dynamically computed by the router as five-minute exponentially weighted averages.

Modifying interface bandwidth, delay, and MTU

The default bandwidth and delay values may be overridden by the following interface commands:

```
bandwidth kilobits
delay tens-of-microseconds
```

So, the following commands will define a bandwidth of 56,000 bps and a delay of 10,000 ms on interface *Serial0*:

```
interface Serial0
bandwidth 56
delay 1000
```

These settings affect only IGRP routing parameters. The actual physical characteristics of the interface—the clock-rate on the wire and the media delay—have no relationship to the bandwidth or delay values configured as in this example or seen as output of the *show interface* command. Thus, interface *Serial0* in the previous example may actually be clocking data at 128,000 bps, a rate that will be governed by the configuration of the modem or the CSU/DSU attached to *Serial0*. Note that, by default, Cisco sets the bandwidth and delay on all serial interfaces to be 1,544 kbps and 20,000 ms, respectively (see Table 3-1).

Note that delay on an interface is specified in *tens of microseconds*. Thus:

```
delay 1000
```

describes a delay of 10,000 ms.

The MTU on an interface can be modified using the following command:

```
mtu bytes
```

However, the MTU size has no bearing on IGRP route selection. The MTU size should not be modified to affect routing behavior. The default MTU values represent the maximum allowed for the media type; lowering the MTU size can impair performance by causing needless fragmentation of IP datagrams.

Later in this chapter we will see how modifications to the bandwidth and delay parameters on an interface can affect route selection.

IGRP routing update

IGRP updates are directly encapsulated in IP with the protocol field (in the IP header) set to 9. The format of an IGRP packet is shown in Figure 3-3.

Just like RIP, IGRP allows a station to request routes. This allows a router that has just booted up to request the routing table from its neighbors instead of waiting for the next cycle of updates, which could be as much as 90 seconds later for IGRP.

The destination IP address in IGRP updates is 255.255.255.255. The source IP address is the IP address of the interface from which the update is issued.

Each update packet contains three types of routes:

Interior routes
> Contain subnet information for the major network number associated with the address of the interface to which the update is being sent. If the IGRP update is being sent on a broadcast network, the internal routes are subnet numbers from the same major network number that is configured in the broadcast media.

System routes
> Contain major network numbers that may have been summarized when a network-number boundary was crossed.

Exterior routes
> Represent candidates for the default route. Unlike RIP, which uses 0.0.0.0 to represent the default, IGRP uses specific network numbers as candidates for the default by tagging the routes as exterior.

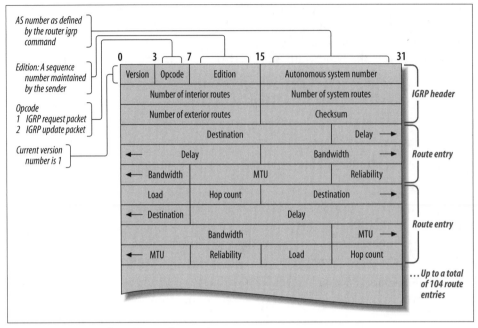

Figure 3-3. Format of an IGRP update packet

Interior, system, and exterior routes appear in order in each update packet. The count of interior, system, and exterior routes identifies the route type for each route entry.

Note that the IGRP update has only three octets for the destination network-number field, whereas IP addresses are four octets in length. IGRP extracts the four-octet IP address using the heuristic shown in Table 3-2.

Table 3-2. Deriving the four-octet IP destination address from the three-octet destination field

Route type	Heuristic to derive four-octet IP destination address
Interior route	The first octet is derived from the IP address of the interface that received the update; the last three octets are derived from the IGRP update.
System route	The route is assumed to have been summarized. The last octet of the IP destination address is 0.
Exterior route (default route)	The route is assumed to have been summarized. The last octet of the IP destination address is 0.

Just like RIP, IGRP updates do not contain subnet mask information. This classifies both RIP and IGRP as *classful* routing protocols. Subnet mask information for routes received in IGRP updates is derived using the same rules as in RIP.

When an update is received for a route, it contains the bandwidth, delay, reliability, load, and MTU values for the path to the destination network via the source of the update. I already defined bandwidth, delay, reliability, load, and MTU for an interface. Now let's define these parameters again for a path.

Path bandwidth, delay, reliability, load, and MTU

The following list defines bandwidth, delay, reliability, load, and MTU for a path:

Bandwidth
> The bandwidth for a path is the minimum bandwidth in the path to the destination network. Compare a network to a sequence of pipes for the transmission of a fluid; the slowest pipe (or the thinnest pipe) will dictate the rate of flow of the fluid. Thus, if a path to a network is through an Ethernet segment, a T-1 line, and another Ethernet segment, the path bandwidth will be 1,544 kbps (see Table 3-1).

Delay
> The delay for a path is the sum of all delay values on the path to the destination network. The IGRP unit of delay is in tens of microseconds. A path through a network via an Ethernet segment, a T-1 line, and another Ethernet segment will have a path delay of 22,000 ms or 2,200 IGRP delay units (see Table 3-1).
>
> The IGRP update packet has three octets to represent delay (in units of tens of microseconds). The largest value of delay that can be represented is $2^{24} \times 10$ ms, which is roughly 167.7 seconds. 167.7 seconds is thus the maximum possible delay value for an IGRP network. All ones in the delay field are also used to indicate that the network indicated is *unreachable*.

Reliability
> The reliability for a path is the reliability of the least reliable link in the path.

Load
> The load for a path is the load on the most heavily loaded link in the path.

MTU
> The MTU represents the smallest MTU along the path. MTU is currently not used in computing the metric.

Note that, in addition to these parameters, the update packet includes the hop count to the destination. The default maximum hop count for IGRP is 100. This default can be modified with the command:

```
metric maximum-hops hops
```

The maximum value for *hops* is 255. A network with a diameter over 100 is very large indeed, especially for a network running IGRP. Do not expect to modify the maximum hop count for IGRP, even if you are working for an interstellar ISP. Large networks will usually require routing features that do not exist in IGRP.

The bandwidth, delay, reliability, load, and MTU values for the path selected by a router can be seen as output of the *show ip route* command:

```
NewYork#show ip route 172.16.100.0
Routing entry for 172.16.100.0 255.255.255.0
  Known via "igrp 10", distance 100, metric 8576
  Redistributing via igrp 10
  Advertised by igrp 10 (self originated)
```

```
Last update from 172.16.251.2 on Serial1, 00:00:29 ago
Routing Descriptor Blocks:
* 172.16.251.2, from 172.16.251.2, 00:00:29 ago, via Serial1
      Route metric is 8576, traffic share count is 1
      Total delay is 21000 microseconds, minimum bandwidth is 1544 Kbit
      Reliability 255/255, minimum MTU 1500 bytes
      Loading 1/255, Hops 2
```

IGRP composite metric

The path metric of bandwidth, delay, reliability, load, and MTU needs to be expressed as a composite metric for you to be able to compare paths. The default behavior of Cisco routers considers only bandwidth and delay in computing the composite metric (the parameters reliability, load, and MTU are ignored):

Metric = BandW + Delay

BandW is computed by taking the smallest bandwidth (expressed in kbits/s) from all outgoing[*] interfaces to the destination (including the destination) and dividing 10,000,000 by this number (the smallest bandwidth). For example, if the path from a router to a destination Ethernet segment is via a T-1 link, then:

BandW = 10,000,000/1,544 = 6,476

Delay is computed by adding the delays from all outgoing interfaces to the destination (including the delay on the interface connecting to the destination network) and dividing by 10:

Delay = (20,000 + 1,000)/10 = 2,100

And then the composite metric for the path to the Ethernet segment would be:

Metric = BandW + Delay = 1,000 + 2,100 = 3,100

Let's now go back to TraderMary's network to see why router *NewYork* selected the direct 56-kbps link to route to 172.16.100.0 and not the two-hop T-1 path via *Chicago*:

```
NewYork>sh ip route
...
I       172.16.100.0 [100/8576] via 172.16.251.2, 0:00:31, Serial0
...
```

The values of the IGRP metrics for these paths can be seen here:

```
Ames#sh interface Ethernet 0
Ethernet0 is up, line protocol is up
```

---

[*] The concept of an *outgoing* interface is best illustrated with an example. In TraderMary's network, the outgoing interfaces from *NewYork* to 172.16.100.0 will be *NewYork* interface *Serial0*, *Chicago* interface *Serial*, and *Ames* interface *Ethernet0*. When computing the metric for *NewYork* to 172.16.100.0, we will use the IGRP parameters of bandwidth, delay, load, reliability, and MTU for these interfaces. We will not use the IGRP parameters from interfaces. However, unless they have been modified, the parameters on this second set of interfaces would be identical to the first.

```
Hardware is Lance, address is 00e0.b056.1b8e (bia 00e0.b056.1b8e)
Description: Lab Test
Internet address is 172.16.100.1/24
MTU 1500 bytes, BW 10000 Kbit, DLY 1000 usec, rely 255/255, load 1/255
Encapsulation ARPA, loopback not set, keepalive set (10 sec)
...

NewYork# show interfaces serial 0
Serial 0 is up, line protocol is up
Hardware is MCI Serial
Internet address is 172.16.250.1, subnet mask is 255.255.255.0
MTU 1500 bytes, BW 1544 Kbit, DLY 20000 usec, rely 255/255, load 1/255
Encapsulation HDLC, loopback not set, keepalive set (10 sec)
...
```

There are two paths to consider:

1. *NewYork* → *Ames* → 172.16.100.0.

   Bandwidth values in the path: (serial link) 1,544 kbits/s, (Ethernet segment) 10,000 kbits/s

   Delay values in the path: (serial link) 2,000, (Ethernet segment) 100

   Smallest bandwidth in the path: 1,544

   > $BandW = 10,000,000/1,544 = 6,476$
   > $Delay = 2,000 + 100 = 2,100$
   > $Metric = BandW + Delay = 8,576$

2. *NewYork* → *Chicago* → *Ames* to 172.16.100.0.

   Bandwidth values in the path: (serial link) 1,544 kbits/s, (serial link) 1,544 kbits/s, (Ethernet segment) 10,000 kbits/s

   Delay values in the path: (serial link) 2,000, (serial link) 2,000, (Ethernet segment) 100

   Smallest bandwidth in the path: 1,544

   > $BandW = 10,000,000/56 = 6,476$
   > $Delay = 2,000 + 2,000 + 100 = 4,100$
   > $Metric = BandW + Delay = 10,576$

NewYork will prefer to route via the first path because the metric is smaller. Why does *NewYork* use a bandwidth of 1,544 for the 56-kbps link to *Ames*? Go back to Table 3-1 and you will see that the default bandwidth and delay values of 1,544 kbps and 20,000 ms apply to all serial interfaces, regardless of the speed of the modem device attached to the router port.

The IGRP metric can be customized to use reliability and load with the following formula (Equation 1):

$$Metric = k1 \times BandW + k2 \times BandW/(256 - load) + k3 \times Delay$$

where the default values of the constants are k1 = k3 = 1 and k2 = k4 = k5 = 0.

If k5 is not equal to zero, an additional operation is done:

$$Metric = Metric \times [k5/(reliability + k4)]$$

The constants k1, k2, k3, k4, and k5 can be modified with the command:

```
metric weights tos k1 k2 k3 k4 k5
```

where *tos* identifies the type of service and must be set to zero (because only one type of service has been defined).

Plugging the default values of k1, k2, k3, k4, and k5 into Equation 1 yields:

$$Metric = BandW + Delay$$

which we saw earlier.

To make the metric sensitive to the network load (in addition to bandwidth and delay), set k1 = k2 = k3 = 1 and k4 = k5 = 0. This yields:

$$Metric = BandW + BandW/(256-load) + Delay$$

The problem with using load in the metric computation is that it can make a route unstable. For example, a router may select a path through router *P* as its next hop to reach a destination. When the load on the path through *P* rises, in a few minutes (the value of load is computed as a five-minute exponentially weighted average) the metric for the path through *P* may become larger than the metric for an alternative path through router *Q*. The traffic then shifts to *Q*; this causes the load to increase on the path through *Q* and the path through *P* becomes more attractive. Thus, setting k2 = 1 can make a route unstable and cause traffic to bounce between two paths. Further, abrupt changes in metric cause flash updates; the route may also go into hold-down.

Instead of selecting the best path based on load, you may consider load balancing over several paths. Load balancing occurs automatically over equal-cost paths. If two or more paths have slightly different metrics, you may consider modifying the bandwidth and delay parameters to make the metrics equal and to utilize all the paths. See the example on modifying bandwidth and delay parameters in the next section.

To make the metric sensitive to network reliability (in addition to bandwidth and delay), set k1 = k3 = k5 =1 and k2 = k4 = 0. In the event of link errors, this will cause the metric on the path to increase, and IGRP will select an alternative path when the metric has worsened enough. A typical action in today's networks is to turn a line down until the transmission problem is resolved, not to base routing decisions on how badly the line is running.

 Cisco strongly recommends *not* modifying the k1, k2, k3, k4, and k5 values for IGRP.

Modifying IGRP metrics

TraderMary's network was still using the 56-kbps path between *NewYork* and *Ames*, even when IGRP was running on the routers (refer to "Getting IGRP Running"). Why is it that *NewYork* and *Ames* did not pick up the lower bandwidth for the 56-kbps link?

Table 3-1 contains the key to our question. All serial interfaces on a Cisco router are configured with the same bandwidth (1,544 kbps) and delay (20,000 ms) values. Thus, IGRP sees the 56-kbps line with the same bandwidth and delay parameters as a T-1 line.

In order to utilize the 56-kbps link only as backup, we need to modify TraderMary's network as follows:

```
hostname NewYork
...
interface Ethernet0
ip address 172.16.1.1 255.255.255.0
!
interface Ethernet1
ip address 192.168.1.1 255.255.255.0
!
interface Serial0
description New York to Chicago link
ip address 172.16.250.1 255.255.255.0
!
interface Serial1
description New York to Ames link
bandwidth 56
ip address 172.16.251.1 255.255.255.0
...
router igrp 10
network 172.16.0.0


hostname Chicago
...
interface Ethernet0
ip address 172.16.50.1 255.255.255.0
!
interface Serial0
description Chicago to New York link
ip address 172.16.250.2 255.255.255.0
!
interface Serial1
description Chicago to Ames link
ip address 172.16.252.1 255.255.255.0
...

router igrp 10
network 172.16.0.0
```

```
hostname Ames
...
interface Ethernet0
ip address 172.16.100.1 255.255.255.0
!
interface Serial0
description Ames to Chicago link
ip address 172.16.252.2 255.255.255.0
!
interface Serial1
description Ames to New York link
bandwidth 56
ip address 172.16.251.2 255.255.255.0
...

router igrp 10
network 172.16.0.0
```

The new routing tables look like this:

```
NewYork#show ip route
...
Gateway of last resort is 0.0.0.0 to network 0.0.0.0

     172.16.0.0/24 is subnetted, 6 subnets
I       172.16.252.0 [100/10476] via 172.16.250.2, 00:00:43, Serial0
C       172.16.250.0 is directly connected, Serial0
C       172.16.251.0 is directly connected, Serial1
I       172.16.50.0 [100/8576] via 172.16.250.2, 00:00:43, Serial0
C       172.16.1.0 is directly connected, Ethernet0
I       172.16.100.0 [100/10576] via 172.16.250.2, 00:00:43, Serial0
C     192.168.1.0/24 is directly connected, Ethernet1


Chicago#sh ip route
...
Gateway of last resort is not set

     172.16.0.0/24 is subnetted, 6 subnets
C       172.16.252.0 is directly connected, Serial1
C       172.16.250.0 is directly connected, Serial0
I       172.16.251.0 [100/182571] via 172.16.250.1, 00:00:01, Serial0
                     [100/182571] via 172.16.252.2, 00:01:01, Serial1
C       172.16.50.0 is directly connected, Ethernet0
I       172.16.1.0 [100/8576] via 172.16.250.1, 00:00:01, Serial0
I       172.16.100.0 [100/8576] via 172.16.252.2, 00:01:01, Serial1


Ames#sh ip route
...
Gateway of last resort is not set

     172.16.0.0/24 is subnetted, 6 subnets
C       172.16.252.0 is directly connected, Serial0
I       172.16.250.0 [100/10476] via 172.16.252.1, 00:00:24, Serial0
```

```
C        172.16.251.0 is directly connected, Serial1
I        172.16.50.0 [100/8576] via 172.16.252.1, 00:00:24, Serial0
I        172.16.1.0 [100/10576] via 172.16.252.1, 00:00:24, Serial0
C        172.16.100.0 is directly connected, Ethernet0
```

Let's now go back to TraderMary's network and corroborate the metric values seen for 172.16.100.0 in router *NewYork's* routing table. The following calculations show TraderMary's network as in Figure 3-1 but with IGRP bandwidth and delay values for each interface. There are two paths to consider:

1. *NewYork → Ames →* 172.16.100.0.

   Bandwidth values in the path: (serial link) 56 kbits/s, (Ethernet segment) 10,000 kbits/s

   Smallest bandwidth in the path: 56

   > $BandW = 10,000,000/56 = 178,571$
   > $Delay = 2,000 + 100 = 2100$
   > $Metric = BandW + Delay = 180,671$

2. *NewYork → Chicago → Ames →* 172.16.100.0

   Bandwidth values in the path: (serial link) 1,544 kbits/s, (serial link) 1,544 kbits/s, (Ethernet segment) 10,000 kbits/s

   Smallest bandwidth in the path: 1,544

   > $BandW = 10,000,000/1,544 = 6,476$
   > $Delay = 2,000 + 2,000 + 100 = 4,100$
   > $Metric = BandW + Delay = 10,576$

Using the lower metric for the path via *Chicago*, *NewYork's* route to 172.16.100.0 shows as:

```
NewYork>sh ip route
...
I        172.16.50.0 [100/1] via 172.16.250.2, 0:00:31, Serial0
I        172.16.100.0 [100/10576] via 172.16.250.2, 0:00:31, Serial0
I        172.16.252.0 [100/1] via 172.16.250.2, 0:00:31, Serial0
```

Let's corroborate IGRP's selection of the two-hop T-1 path in preference to the one-hop 56-kbps link by comparing the transmission delay for a 1,000-octet packet. A 1,000-octet packet will take 143 ms ($1,000 \times 8/56,000$ second) over a 56-kbps link and 5 ms ($1,000 \times 8/1,544,000$ second) over a T-1 link. Neglecting buffering and processing delays, two T-1 hops will cost 10 ms in comparison to 143 ms via the 56-kbps link.

Processing IGRP updates

The processing of IGRP updates is very similar to the processing of RIP updates, described in the previous chapter. The IGRP update comes with an autonomous system number. If this does not match the IGRP AS number configured on the router receiving the update, the entire upgrade is disregarded. Thus, routers *NewYork* and

Nairobi in TraderMary's network will receive updates from each other but will discard them.

Each network number received in the update is checked for validity. Illegal network numbers such as 0.0.0.0/8, 127.0.0.0/8, and 128.0.0.0/16 are sometimes referred to as "Martian Network Numbers" and will be disregarded when received in an update (RFCs 1009, 1122).

The rules for processing IGRP updates are:

1. If the destination network number is unknown to the router, install the route using the source IP address of the update (provided the route is not indicated as unreachable).

2. If the destination network number is known to the router but the update contains a smaller metric, modify the routing table entry with the new next hop and metric.

3. If the destination network number is known to the router but the update contains a larger metric, ignore the update.

4. If the destination network number is known to the router and the update contains a higher metric that is from the same next hop as in the table, update the metric.

5. If the destination network number is known to the router and the update contains the same metric from a different next hop, install the route as long as the maximum number of paths to the same destination is not exceeded. These parallel paths are then used for load balancing. Note that the default maximum number of paths to a single destination is six in IOS Releases 11.0 or later.

Parallel Paths

For the routing table to be able to install multiple paths to the same destination, the IGRP metric for all the paths must be equal. The routing table will install several parallel paths to the same destination (the default maximum is six in current releases of IOS).

Load-sharing over parallel paths depends on the switching mode. If the router is configured for *process switching*, load balancing will be on a packet-by-packet basis. If the router is configured for *fast switching*, load balancing will be on a per-destination basis. For a more detailed discussion of switching mode and load balancing, see Chapter 2.

Unequal metric (cost) load balancing

The default behavior of IGRP installs parallel routes to a destination only if all routes have identical metric values. Traffic to the destination is load-balanced over all installed routes, as described earlier.

Equal-cost load balancing works well almost all the time. However, consider Trader-Mary's network again. Say that TraderMary adds a node in London. Since traffic to London is critical, the network is engineered with two links from New York: one running at 128 kbps and another running at 56 kbps. Figure 3-4 shows unequal-cost load balancing.

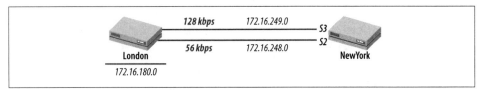

Figure 3-4. Unequal-cost load balancing

The routers are first configured as follows:

```
hostname NewYork
...
interface Ethernet0
ip address 172.16.1.1 255.255.255.0
!
interface Ethernet1
ip address 192.168.1.1 255.255.255.0
...
interface Serial2
bandwidth 128
ip address 172.16.249.1 255.255.255.0
!
interface Serial3
bandwidth 56
ip address 172.16.248.1 255.255.255.0
...
router igrp 10
network 172.16.0.0


hostname London
...
interface Ethernet0
ip address 172.16.180.1 255.255.255.0
!
interface Serial0
bandwidth 128
ip address 172.16.249.2 255.255.255.0
!
interface Serial1
bandwidth 56
ip address 172.16.284.2 255.255.255.0
...
router igrp 10
network 172.16.0.0
```

However, if you check *NewYork*'s routing table you will see that all traffic to London is being routed via the 128-kbps link:

```
NewYork>sh ip route
...
172.16.0.0/24 is subnetted, ...
I        172.16.180.0 [100/80225] via 172.16.249.2, 00:01:07, Serial2
...
```

This is because the *NewYork → London* metric is 80,225 via the 128-kbps path and 180,671 via the 56-kbps path.

The problem with this routing scenario is that the 56-kbps link is entirely unused, even when the 128-kbps link is congested. Overseas links are expensive: the network design ought to try to utilize all links. One way around this problem is to modify the IGRP parameters to make both links look equally attractive. This can be accomplished by modifying the 56-kbps path as follows:

```
hostname NewYork
...
interface Serial3
bandwidth 128
ip address 172.16.248.1 255.255.255.0
...
```

With this approach, both links would appear equally attractive. The routing table for *NewYork* will look like this:

```
NewYork>sh ip route
...
172.16.0.0/24 is subnetted, ...
I        172.16.180.0 [100/80225] via 172.16.249.2, 00:01:00, Serial2
                      [100/80225] via 172.16.248.2, 00:01:00, Serial3
```

However, traffic will now be evenly distributed over the two links, which may congest the 56-kbps link while leaving the 128-kbps link underutilized.

Another solution is to modify IGRP's default behavior and have it install unequal-cost links in its table, balancing traffic over the links in proportion to the metrics on the links. The variance that is permitted between the lowest and highest metrics is specified by an integer in the *variance* command. For example:

```
router igrp 10
network 172.16.0.0
variance 2
```

specifies that IGRP will install routes with different metrics as long as the largest metric is less than twice the lowest metric. In other words, if the variance is v, then:

$$\text{highest metric} \ge \text{lowest metric} \times v$$

The maximum number of routes that IGRP will install will still be four, by default. This maximum can be raised to six when running IOS 11.0 or later.

Going back to TraderMary's network, the metric value for the 128-kbps path to London is 80,225 while the metric value for the 56-kbps path is 180,671. The ratio 180,671/80,225 is 2.25; hence, a variance of 3 will be adequate. *NewYork* may now be configured as follows:

```
hostname NewYork
...
interface Ethernet0
ip address 172.16.1.1 255.255.255.0
!
interface Ethernet1
ip address 192.168.1.1 255.255.255.0
...
interface Serial2
bandwidth 128
ip address 172.16.249.1 255.255.255.0
!
interface Serial3
bandwidth 56
ip address 172.16.248.1 255.255.255.0
...
router igrp 10
network 172.16.0.0
variance 3
```

And the routing table for *NewYork* will look like this:

```
NewYork>sh ip route
...
172.16.0.0/24 is subnetted, ...
I      172.16.180.0 [100/80225] via 172.16.249.2, 00:01:00, Serial2
                    [100/180671] via 172.16.248.2, 00:01:00, Serial3
```

Traffic from *NewYork* to *London* will be divided between *Serial2* and *Serial3* in the inverse ratio of their metrics: *Serial2* will receive 2.25 times as much traffic as *Serial3*.

The default value of variance is 1. A danger with using a variance value of greater than 1 is the possibility of introducing a routing loop. Thus, *NewYork* may start routing to *London* via *Chicago* if the variance is made sufficiently large. IGRP checks that the paths it chooses to install are always downstream (toward the destination) by choosing only next hops with lower metrics to the destination.

Steady State

It is important for you as the network administrator to be familiar with the state of the network during normal conditions. Deviations from this state will be your clue to troubleshooting the network during times of network outage. This output shows the values of the IGRP timers:

```
NewYork#sh ip protocol
Routing Protocol is "igrp 10"
```

```
Sending updates every 90 seconds, next due in 61 seconds
Invalid after 270 seconds, hold down 280, flushed after 630
Outgoing update filter list for all interfaces is
Incoming update filter list for all interfaces is
Default networks flagged in outgoing updates
Default networks accepted from incoming updates
IGRP metric weight K1=1, K2=0, K3=1, K4=0, K5=0
IGRP maximum hopcount 100
IGRP maximum metric variance 1
Redistributing: igrp 10
Routing for Networks:
   172.16.0.0
Routing Information Sources:
   Gateway         Distance       Last Update
1  172.16.250.2         100       00:00:40
2  172.16.251.2         100       00:00:09
Distance: (default is 100)
```

Note that IGRP updates are sent every 90 seconds and the next update is due in 61 seconds, which means that an update was issued about 29 seconds ago.

Further, lines 1 and 2 show the gateways from which router *NewYork* has been receiving updates. This list is valuable in troubleshooting—missing routes from a routing table could be because the last update from a gateway was too long ago. Check the time of the last update to ensure that it is within the IGRP update timer:

```
NewYork#show ip route
...
Gateway of last resort is not set

     172.16.0.0/24 is subnetted, 6 subnets
I       172.16.252.0 [100/10476] via 172.16.251.2, 00:00:26, Serial1
                     [100/10476] via 172.16.250.2, 00:00:37, Serial0
C       172.16.250.0 is directly connected, Serial0
C       172.16.251.0 is directly connected, Serial1
I       172.16.50.0 [100/8576] via 172.16.250.2, 00:00:37, Serial0
C       172.16.1.0 is directly connected, Ethernet0
I       172.16.100.0 [100/8576] via 172.16.251.2, 00:00:26, Serial1
C    192.168.1.0/24 is directly connected, Ethernet1
```

One key area to look at in the routing table is the timer values. The format that Cisco uses for timers is *hh:mm:ss* (hours:minutes:seconds). You would expect the time against each route to be between 00:00:00 (0 seconds) and 00:01:30 (90 seconds). If a route was received more than 90 seconds ago, that indicates a problem in the network. You should begin by checking to see if the next hop for the route is reachable.

You should also be familiar with the number of major network numbers (two in the previous output—172.16.0.0 and 192.168.1.0) and the number of subnets in each (six in 172.16.0.0 and one in 192.168.1.0). In most small to mid-sized networks, these counts will change only when networks are added or subtracted.

Speeding Up Convergence

Like RIP, IGRP implements hold-downs, split horizon, triggered updates, and poison reverse (see Chapter 2 for details on these convergence methods). Like RIP, IGRP also maintains an update timer, an invalid timer, a hold-down timer, and a flush timer for every route in the routing table:

Update timer (default value: 90 seconds)
> After sending a routing update, IGRP sets the update timer to 0. When the timer expires, IGRP issues another routing update.

Invalid timer (default value: 270 seconds)
> Every time a router receives an update for a route, it sets the invalid timer to 0. The expiration of the invalid timer indicates that the source of the routing information is suspect. Even though the route is declared invalid, packets are still forwarded to the next hop specified in the routing table. Note that prior to the expiration of the invalid timer, IGRP would process any updates received by updating the route's timers.

Hold-down timer (default value: 280 seconds)
> When the invalid timer expires, the route automatically enters the hold-down phase. During hold-down all updates regarding the route are disregarded—it is assumed that the network may not have converged and that there may be bad routing information circulating in the network. The hold-down timer is started when the invalid timer expires.

Flush timer (default value: 630 seconds)
> Every time a router receives an update for a route, it sets the flush timer to 0. When the flush timer expires, the route is removed from the routing table and the router is ready to receive a new route update. Note that the flush timer overrides the hold-down timer.

Setting Timers

IGRP timers can be modified to allow faster convergence. The configuration:

```
router igrp 10
timers basic 30 90 90 180
```

would generate IGRP updates every 30 seconds, mark a route invalid in 90 seconds, keep the route in hold-down for 90 seconds, and flush the route in 180 seconds.

However, IGRP timers should not be modified without a detailed understanding of route convergence in Distance Vector protocols (see Chapter 2). Selecting too short a hold-down period, for example, may cause bad routing information to persist in a network. Selecting too long a hold-down period would increase the time it takes to learn a route via a different path after a failure.

Changing timers also presents the danger that sooner or later someone will configure a router with default timers. This may cause *route flapping*; i.e., routes to some network numbers may become intermittently invisible.

 Do not modify IGRP timers unless absolutely necessary. If you modify IGRP timers, make sure that all routers have the same timers.

Disabling IGRP Hold-Downs

IGRP hold-downs can be disabled with the command:

```
router igrp 10
no metric holddown
```

thus speeding up convergence when a route fails. However, the problem with turning off hold-downs is that if a triggered update regarding the failure does not reach some router, that router could insert bad routing information into the network. Doesn't this seem like a dangerous thing to do?

Split horizon, triggered updates, and poison reverse are implemented in IGRP much like they are in RIP.

Route Summarization

IGRP summarizes network numbers when crossing a major network-number boundary, just like RIP does. Route summarization reduces the number of routes that need to be exchanged, processed, and stored.

However, route summarization does not work well in discontiguous networks. Consider the discontiguous network in Figure 3-5. Router *X* will receive advertisements for 10.0.0.0 from both routers *A* and *B*. If *X* sent packets with the destination 10.1.1.1 to *B*, the packet would be lost—*B* would have to drop the packet because it would not have a route for 10.1.1.1 in its table. Likewise, if *X* sent packets with the destination 10.2.1.1 to *A*, the packet would be lost—*A* would have to drop the packet because it would not have a route for 10.2.1.1.

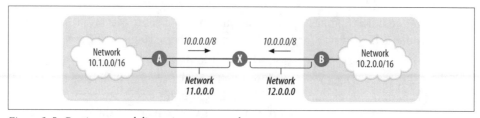

Figure 3-5. Contiguous and discontiguous networks

Both IGRP and RIP networks must be designed in contiguous blocks of major network numbers.

Default Routes

IGRP tracks default routes in the exterior section of its routing updates. A router receiving 10.0.0.0 in the exterior section of a routing update would mark 10.0.0.0 as a default route and install its next hop to 10.0.0.0 as the *gateway of last resort*. Consider the network in Figure 3-6 as an example in which a core router connects to several branch routers in remote sites.

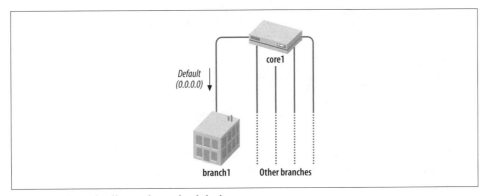

Figure 3-6. Branch offices only need a default route

The core router is configured as follows:

```
    hostname core1
    !
    interface Ethernet0
     ip address 192.168.1.1 255.255.255.0
    ...
    interface Serial0
    ip address 172.16.245.1 255.255.255.0
    ...
    router igrp 10
3     redistribute static
    network 172.16.0.0
4     default-metric 10000 100 255 1 1500
    !
    no ip classless
5   ip default-network 10.0.0.0
6   ip route 10.0.0.0 255.0.0.0 Null0
```

The branch router is configured as follows:

```
    hostname branch1
    ...
```

```
interface Serial0
ip address 172.16.245.2 255.255.255.0
...
router igrp 10
redistribute static
network 172.16.0.0
!
no ip classless
```

An examination of *branch1*'s routing table would show:

```
branch1#sh ip route
Codes: C - connected, S - static, I - IGRP, R - RIP, M - mobile, B - BGP
       D - EIGRP, EX - EIGRP external, O - OSPF, IA - OSPF inter area
       N1 - OSPF NSSA external type 1, N2 - OSPF NSSA external type 2
       E1 - OSPF external type 1, E2 - OSPF external type 2, E - EGP
       i - IS-IS, L1 - IS-IS level-1, L2 - IS-IS level-2, * - candidate default

Gateway of last resort is 172.16.245.1 to network 10.0.0.0

      172.16.0.0/24 is subnetted, 1 subnets
C        172.16.245.0 is directly connected, Serial0
I*    10.0.0.0/8 [100/8576] via 172.16.245.1, 00:00:26, Serial0
```

Note that network 10.0.0.0 has been flagged as a default route (*). To ensure that the default route works, let's do a test to see if *branch1* can ping 192.168.1.1, even though 192.168.1.0 is not in *branch1*'s routing table:

```
branch1#ping 192.168.1.1

Type escape sequence to abort.
Sending 5, 100-byte ICMP Echos to 192.168.1.1, timeout is 2 seconds:
!!!!!
Success rate is 100 percent (5/5), round-trip min/avg/max = 40/50/80 ms
```

Here are the steps we followed in the creation of the default route:

1. Network 10.0.0.0 was flagged as a default route by *core1* (line 5).

2. Network 10.0.0.0 was defined via a static route (line 6).

3. The default route was redistributed into IGRP, which then placed the route in the exterior section of its update message to *branch1* (line 3).

4. A default metric was attached to the redistribution (line 4).

There are a few things to note when creating default routes in IGRP. First, IGRP does not use 0.0.0.0 as a default route. Thus, if 0.0.0.0 were defined in place of 10.0.0.0, IGRP would not convey it. Second, how should one choose which network number to flag as a default route? In the previous example, the network 10.0.0.0 does not need to be a real network number configured on an interface; it could just be a fictitious number (that does not exist as a real number in the network) to which all default traffic will be sent. Using a fictitious number instead of a real network number as the default route can have certain advantages. For example, a fictitious network number will not go down if an interface goes down. Further, changing the ideal candidate for the default route can be much easier with fictitious network numbers than with real network numbers.

Multiple Default Routes

To increase the reliability of the connection to branches, each branch may be connected to two core routers:

```
hostname core2
!
interface Ethernet0
 ip address 192.168.1.1 255.255.255.0
...
interface Serial0
ip address 172.16.246.1 255.255.255.0
...
router igrp 10
 redistribute static
 network 172.16.0.0
 default-metric 10000 100 255 1 1500
!
no ip classless
ip default-network 10.0.0.0
ip route 10.0.0.0 255.0.0.0 Null0
```

branch1 will now receive two default routes:

```
branch1>sh ip route
...
Gateway of last resort is 172.16.250.1 to network 10.0.0.0

     172.16.0.0/24 is subnetted, 2 subnets
C       172.16.245.0 is directly connected, Serial1
C       172.16.246.0 is directly connected, Serial0
I*   10.0.0.0/8 [100/8576] via 172.16.245.1, 00:00:55, Serial0
                 [100/8576] via 172.16.246.1, 00:00:55, Serial1
```

Note that it is also possible to set up one router (say, *core1*) as primary and the second router (*core2*) as backup. To do this, set up the default from *core2* with a *worse* metric, as shown in line 7:

```
  hostname core2
  !
  interface Ethernet0
   ip address 192.168.1.1 255.255.255.0
  ...
  interface Serial0
  ip address 172.16.246.1 255.255.255.0
  ...
  router igrp 10
   redistribute static
   network 172.16.0.0
7  default-metric 1544 2000 255 1 1500
  !
```

```
no ip classless
ip default-network 10.0.0.0
ip route 10.0.0.0 255.0.0.0 Null0
```

Classful Route Lookups

Router *branch1* is configured to perform classful route lookups (see line 7 in the previous code block). A classful route lookup works as follows:

1. Upon receiving a packet, the router first determines the major network number for the destination. If the destination IP address is 172.16.1.1, the major network number is 172.16.0.0. If the destination IP address is 192.168.1.1, the major network number is 192.168.1.0.

2. Next, the router checks to see if this major network number exists in the routing table. If the major network number exists in the routing table (172.16.0.0 does), the router checks for the destination's subnet. In our example, *branch1* would look for the subnet 172.16.1.0. If this subnet exists in the table, the packet will be forwarded to the next hop specified in the table. If the subnet does not exist in the table, the packet will be dropped.

3. If the major network number does not exist in the routing table, the router looks for a default route. If a default route exists, the packet will be forwarded as specified by the default route. If there is no default route in the routing table, the packet will be dropped.

Router *branch1* is able to ping 192.168.1.1 as a consequence of rule 3:

```
branch1#ping 192.168.1.1

Type escape sequence to abort.
Sending 5, 100-byte ICMP Echos to 192.168.1.1, timeout is 2 seconds:
!!!!!
Success rate is 100 percent (5/5), round-trip min/avg/max = 40/50/80 ms
```

However, let's define a new subnet of 172.16.0.0 on *core1* (and then block the advertisement of this subnet with an access list on lines 8 and 9) and see if *branch1* can reach it using a default route:

```
hostname core1
!
interface Ethernet0
 ip address 192.168.1.1 255.255.255.0
!
interface Ethernet1
ip address 172.16.10.1 255.255.255.0
...
interface Serial0
ip address 172.16.245.1 255.255.255.0
...
router igrp 10
```

```
    redistribute static
    network 172.16.0.0
    default-metric 10000 100 255 1 1500
    distribute-list 1 out serial0
    !
    no ip classless
    ip default-network 10.0.0.0
    ip route 10.0.0.0 255.0.0.0 Null0
    !
8   access-list 1 deny 172.16.10.0 0.0.0.255
9   access-list 1 permit 0.0.0.0 255.255.255.255


    branch1#sh ip route
    ...
    Gateway of last resort is 172.16.245.1 to network 10.0.0.0

         172.16.0.0/24 is subnetted, 1 subnets
    C        172.16.245.0 is directly connected, Serial0
    I*   10.0.0.0/8 [100/8576] via 172.16.245.1, 00:00:26, Serial0


    branch1#ping 192.168.1.1

    Type escape sequence to abort.
    Sending 5, 100-byte ICMP Echos to 172.16.10.1, timeout is 2 seconds:
    !!!!!
    Success rate is 100 percent (5/5), round-trip min/avg/max = 40/50/80 ms
```

This demonstrates the use of rule 2, which causes the packet for 172.16.10.1 to be dropped. Note that in this example 172.16.10.1 did not match the default route, whereas 192.168.1.1 did match the default.

Classless route lookup, the other option, is discussed in Chapter 5.

Summing Up

IGRP has the robustness of RIP but adds a major new feature—route metrics based on bandwidth and delay. This feature—along with the ease with which it can be configured and deployed—has made IGRP tremendously popular for small* to mid-sized networks. However, IGRP does not address several problems that also affect RIP:

- The exchange of full routing updates does not scale for large networks—the overhead of generating and processing all routes in the AS can be high.

---

* The definition of small, medium, and large IP networks can be discussed ad nauseam because of the number of variables involved (number of routers and routes, network bandwidth/utilization, network delay/latency, etc.), but rough measures are as follows: small—a few dozen routers with up to a few hundred routes; medium—a few hundred routers with a few thousand routes; large—anything bigger than medium.

- IGRP convergence times can be too long.
- Subnet mask information is not exchanged in IGRP updates, so Variable Length Subnet Masks (VLSM) and discontiguous address spaces are not supported.

These issues may be too significant to overlook in large IP networks in which address-space conservation may necessitate VLSM, full route updates would be so large that they would consume significant network resources (serial links to branches tend to saturate quickly, and smaller routers may consume a lot of CPU power just to process all the routes at every update interval), and the convergence times may be too long because of the network diameter. Even small to mid-sized networks may choose not to implement IGRP if convergence time is an issue.

CHAPTER 4

Enhanced Interior Gateway Routing Protocol (EIGRP)

The Enhanced Interior Gateway Routing Protocol (EIGRP), referred to as an advanced Distance Vector protocol, offers radical improvements over IGRP. Traditional DV protocols such as RIP and IGRP exchange periodic routing updates with all their neighbors, saving the best distance (or metric) and the vector (or next hop) for each destination. EIGRP differs in that it saves not only the best (least-cost) route but all routes, allowing convergence to be much quicker. Further, EIGRP updates are sent only upon a network topology change; updates are not periodic.

Getting EIGRP running is not much more difficult than getting IGRP running, as we will see in the section "Getting EIGRP Running."

Even though EIGRP offers radical improvements over IGRP, there are similarities between the protocols. Like IGRP, EIGRP bases its metric on bandwidth, delay, reliability, load, and MTU (see the "EIGRP Metric" section).

The fast convergence feature in EIGRP is due to the Diffusing Update Algorithm (DUAL), discussed in "How EIGRP Works."

EIGRP updates carry subnet mask information. This allows EIGRP to summarize routes on arbitrary bit boundaries, support classless route lookups, and allow the support of Variable Length Subnet Masks (VLSM). This is discussed in "Variable Length Subnet Masks" and "Route Summarization."

Setting up default routes in EIGRP is discussed in "Default Routes."

Troubleshooting EIGRP can be tricky. This chapter ends with some troubleshooting tips in "Troubleshooting EIGRP."

EIGRP is a Cisco proprietary protocol; other router vendors do not support EIGRP. Keep this in mind if you are planning a multivendor router environment.

This chapter focuses on EIGRP's enhancements over IGRP: the use of DUAL; and the use of subnet masks in updates, which in turn allow VLSM and route summarization at arbitrary bit boundaries. This chapter does not cover router metrics in detail or the concept of parallel paths. Those concepts have not changed much in EIGRP. I assume that the reader is familiar with IGRP.

Getting EIGRP Running

TraderMary's network, shown in Figure 4-1, can be configured to run EIGRP as follows.

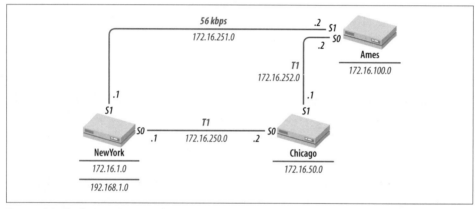

Figure 4-1. TraderMary's network

Just like RIP and IGRP, EIGRP is a distributed protocol that needs to be configured on every router in the network:

```
hostname NewYork
...
interface Ethernet0
ip address 172.16.1.1 255.255.255.0
!
interface Ethernet1
ip address 192.168.1.1 255.255.255.0
!
interface Serial0
description New York to Chicago link
ip address 172.16.250.1 255.255.255.0
!
interface Serial1
description New York to Ames link
bandwidth 56
ip address 172.16.251.1 255.255.255.0
```

```
...
router eigrp 10
network 172.16.0.0


hostname Chicago
...
interface Ethernet0
ip address 172.16.50.1 255.255.255.0
!
interface Serial0
description Chicago to New York link
ip address 172.16.250.2 255.255.255.0
!
interface Serial1
description Chicago to Ames link
ip address 172.16.252.1 255.255.255.0
...

router eigrp 10
network 172.16.0.0


hostname Ames
...
interface Ethernet0
ip address 172.16.100.1 255.255.255.0
!
interface Serial0
description Ames to Chicago link
ip address 172.16.252.2 255.255.255.0
!
interface Serial1
description Ames to New York link
bandwidth 56
ip address 172.16.251.2 255.255.255.0
...

router eigrp 10
network 172.16.0.0
```

The syntax of the EIGRP command is:

```
router eigrp autonomous-system-number
```

in global configuration mode. The networks that will be participating in the EIGRP process are then listed:

```
network 172.16.0.0
```

What does it mean to list the network numbers participating in EIGRP?

1. Router *NewYork* will include directly connected `172.16.0.0` subnets in its updates to neighboring routers. For example, `172.16.1.0` will now be included in updates to the routers *Chicago* and *Ames*.

2. *NewYork* will receive and process EIGRP updates on its `172.16.0.0` interfaces from other routers running EIGRP 10. For example, *NewYork* will receive EIGRP updates from *Chicago* and *Ames*.

3. By exclusion, network `192.168.1.0`, connected to *NewYork*, will not be advertised to *Chicago* or *Ames*, and *NewYork* will not process any EIGRP updates received on *Ethernet0* (if there is another router on that segment).

The routing tables for *NewYork*, *Chicago*, and *Ames* will show all `172.16.0.0` subnets. Here is *NewYork*'s table:

```
NewYork#sh ip route
Codes: C - connected, S - static, I - IGRP, R - RIP, M - mobile, B - BGP
       D - EIGRP, EX - EIGRP external, O - OSPF, IA - OSPF inter area
       N1 - OSPF NSSA external type 1, N2 - OSPF NSSA external type 2
       E1 - OSPF external type 1, E2 - OSPF external type 2, E - EGP
       i - IS-IS, L1 - IS-IS level-1, L2 - IS-IS level-2, * - candidate default

Gateway of last resort is not set

     172.16.0.0/24 is subnetted, 6 subnets
D       172.16.252.0 [90/2681856] via 172.16.250.2, 00:18:54, Ethernet0/0
C       172.16.250.0 is directly connected, Ethernet0/0
C       172.16.251.0 is directly connected, Ethernet0/1
D       172.16.50.0 [90/2195456] via 172.16.250.2, 00:18:54, Ethernet0/0
C       172.16.1.0 is directly connected, Loopback0
D       172.16.100.0 [90/2707456] via 172.16.250.2, 00:18:54, Ethernet0/0
C    192.168.1.0/24 is directly connected, Loopback1
```

The EIGRP-derived routes in this table are labeled with a "D" in the left margin. Note that the routing table provides summary information (as in line 1). Line 1 contains subnet mask information (24 bits, or `255.255.255.0`) and the number of subnets in `172.16.0.0` (6).

In addition to the routing table, EIGRP builds another table called the *topology table*:

```
NewYork#sh ip eigrp topology
IP-EIGRP Topology Table for process 10

Codes: P - Passive, A - Active, U - Update, Q - Query, R - Reply,
       r - Reply status

P 172.16.252.0/24, 1 successors, FD is 2681856
        via 172.16.250.2 (2681856/2169856), Serial0
        via 172.16.251.2 (46738176/2169856), Serial1
P 172.16.250.0/24, 1 successors, FD is 2169856
        via Connected, Serial0
P 172.16.251.0/24, 1 successors, FD is 46226176
        via Connected, Serial1
P 172.16.50.0/24, 1 successors, FD is 2195456
        via 172.16.250.2 (2195456/281600), Serial0
P 172.16.1.0/24, 1 successors, FD is 128256
        via Connected, Ethernet0
P 172.16.100.0/24, 1 successors, FD is 2707456
```

```
3           via 172.16.250.2 (2707456/2195456), Serial0
4           via 172.16.251.2 (46251776/281600), Serial1
```

This topology table shows two entries for *Ames*'s subnet, 172.16.100.0 (line 2). Only the lower-cost route (line 3) is installed in the routing table, but the second entry in the topology table (line 4) allows *NewYork* to quickly converge on the less preferred path if the primary path fails.

Note that network 192.168.1.0, defined on *NewYork* interface *Ethernet1*, did not appear in the routing tables of *Chicago* and *Ames*. To be propagated, 192.168.1.0 would have to be defined in a network statement under the EIGRP configuration on *NewYork*:

```
hostname NewYork
...
router eigrp 10
network 172.16.0.0
network 192.168.1.0
```

Each EIGRP process is identified by an autonomous system (AS) number, just like IGRP processes. Routers with the *same* AS numbers will exchange routing information with each other, resulting in a *routing domain*. Routers with dissimilar AS numbers will not exchange any routing information by default. However, routes from one routing domain can be leaked into another domain through the redistribution commands—this is covered in Chapter 8.

Compare the routing table in this section with the corresponding table for IGRP in Chapter 3. The essential contents are identical: the same routes with the same next hops. However, the route metrics look much bigger and the route update times are very high. IGRP routes would have timed out a while ago.

EIGRP metrics are essentially derived from IGRP metrics. The following section provides a quick summary.

EIGRP Metric

The EIGRP composite metric is computed exactly as the IGRP metric is and then multiplied by 256. Thus, the default expression for the EIGRP composite metric is:

$$Metric = [BandW + Delay] \times 256$$

where *BandW* and *Delay* are computed exactly as for IGRP (see the section "IGRP Metric" in Chapter 3). In summary, *BandW* is computed by taking the smallest bandwidth (expressed in kbits/s) from all outgoing interfaces to the destination (including the destination) and dividing 10,000,000 by this number (the smallest bandwidth), and *Delay* is the sum of all the delay values to the destination network (expressed in tens of microseconds).

Further, note that the total delay (line 6), minimum bandwidth (line 6), reliability (line 7), minimum MTU (line 7), and load (line 8) for a path, which are used to compute the composite metric (line 5), are shown as output of the *show ip route destination-network-number* command:

```
NewYork#sh ip route 172.16.50.0
Routing entry for 172.16.50.0 255.255.255.0
  Known via "eigrp 10", distance 90, metric 2195456, type internal
  Redistributing via eigrp 10
  Last update from 172.16.250.2 on Serial0, 00:00:21 ago
  Routing Descriptor Blocks:
  * 172.16.50.0, from 172.16.250.2, 00:00:21 ago, via Serial0
5       Route metric is 2195456, traffic share count is 1
6       Total delay is 21000 microseconds, minimum bandwidth is 1544 Kbit
7       Reliability 255/255, minimum MTU 1500 bytes
8       Loading 1/255, Hops 1
```

Converting route metrics between EIGRP and IGRP is very straightforward: EIGRP metrics are 256 times larger than IGRP metrics. This easy conversion becomes important when a network is running both IGRP and EIGRP, such as during a migration from IGRP to EIGRP.

Just like IGRP, EIGRP can be made to use load and reliability in its metric by modifying the parameters k1, k2, k3, k4, and k5 (see the "IGRP Metric" section in the previous chapter).

The constants k1, k2, k3, k4, and k5 can be modified with the following command:

```
metric weights tos k1 k2 k3 k4 k5
```

 Cisco strongly recommends *not* modifying the k1, k2, k3, k4, and k5 values for EIGRP.

How EIGRP Works

Unlike traditional DV protocols such as RIP and IGRP, EIGRP does not rely on *periodic* updates: routing updates are sent only when there is a change. Remember that RIP and IGRP reset the invalid and flush timers upon receiving a route update. When a route is lost, the updates stop; the invalid and flush timers grow and grow (the timers are not reset), and, ultimately, the route is flushed from the routing table. This process of convergence assumes periodic updates. EIGRP's approach has the advantage that network resources are not consumed by periodic updates. However, if a router dies, taking away all its downstream routes, how would EIGRP detect the loss of these routes? EIGRP relies on small *hello packets* to establish neighbor relationships and to detect the loss of a neighbor. Neighbor relationships are discussed in detail in the next section.

RIP and IGRP suffer from a major flaw: *routing loops*. Routing loops happen when information about the loss of a route does not reach all routers in the network because an update packet gets dropped or corrupted. These routers (that have not received the information about the loss of the route) inject bad routing information back into the network by telling their neighbors about the route they know. EIGRP uses *reliable* transmission for all updates between neighbors. Neighbors acknowledge the receipt of updates, and if an acknowledgment is not received, EIGRP retransmits the update.

RIP and IGRP employ a battery of techniques to reduce the likelihood of routing loops: split horizon, hold-down timers, and poison reverse. These techniques do not guarantee that loops will not occur and, in any case, result in long convergence times. EIGRP uses the Diffusing Update Algorithm (DUAL) for all route computations. DUAL's convergence times are an order of magnitude lower than those of traditional DV algorithms. DUAL is able to achieve such low convergence times by maintaining a table of loop-free paths to every destination, in addition to the least-cost path. DUAL is described in more detail later in this chapter.

DUAL can support IP, IPX, and AppleTalk. A protocol-dependent module encapsulates DUAL messages and handles interactions with the routing table. In summary, DUAL requires:

1. A method for the discovery of new neighbors and their loss (see the next section, "Neighbor Relationship").
2. Reliable transmission of update packets between neighbors (see the later section "Reliable Transport Protocol").
3. Protocol-dependent modules that can encapsulate DUAL traffic in IP, IPX, or AppleTalk. This text will deal only with EIGRP in IP networks (see the later section "Protocol-Dependent Module").

I'll end this section with a discussion of EIGRP packet formats.

Neighbor Relationship

A router discovers a neighbor when it receives its first hello packet on a directly connected network. The router requests DUAL to send a full route update to the new neighbor. In response, the neighbor sends its full route update. Thus, a new neighbor relationship is established in the following steps:

1. When a router *A* receives a hello packet from a new neighbor *B*, *A* sends its topology table to router *B* in unicast updates with the *initialization bit* turned on.
2. When router *B* receives a packet with the initialization bit on, it sends its topology table to router *A*.

The interval between hello packets from any EIGRP-speaking router on a network is five seconds (by default) on most media types. Each hello packet advertises *hold-time*—the length of time the neighbor should consider the sender up. The default hold-time is 15 seconds. If no hellos are received for the duration of the hold-time, DUAL is informed that the neighbor is down. Thus, in addition to detecting a new neighbor, hello packets are also used to detect the loss of a neighbor.

The hello-interval can be changed with the following command in interface configuration mode:

```
ip hello-interval eigrp autonomous-system-number seconds
```

Lengthening the hello-interval will also lengthen the route convergence time. However, a longer hello-interval may be desirable on a congested network with many EIGRP routers.

If the hello-interval is changed, the hold-time should also be modified. A rule of thumb is to keep the hold-time at three times the hello-interval.

```
ip hold-time eigrp autonomous-system-number seconds
```

Note that the hello-interval and hold-time need *not* be the same for all routers on a network. Each router advertises its own hold-time, which is recorded in the neighbor's neighbor table.

The default hello-interval is 60 seconds (with a hold-time of 180 seconds) on multipoint interfaces (such as ATM, Frame Relay, and X.25) with link speeds of T-1 or less. Hello packets are multicast; no acknowledgments are expected.

The following output shows *NewYork*'s neighbors. The first column—labeled H—is the order in which the neighbors were learned. The hold-time for 172.16.251.2 (*Ames*) is 10 seconds, from which we can deduce that the last hello was received 5 seconds ago. The hold-time for 172.16.250.2 (*Chicago*) is 13 seconds, from which we can deduce that the last hello was received 2 seconds ago. The hold-time for a neighbor should not exceed 15 seconds or fall below 10 seconds (if the hold-time fell below 10 s, that would indicate the loss of one or more hello packets).

```
NewYork#sh ip eigrp neighbor
IP-EIGRP neighbors for process 10
H   Address              Interface   Hold Uptime   SRTT   RTO  Q   Seq
                                     (sec)         (ms)        Cnt Num
1   172.16.251.2         Se0/1        10 00:17:08   28   2604  0   7
0   172.16.250.2         Se0/0        13 00:24:43   12   2604  0   14.
```

After a neighbor relationship has been established between A and B the only EIGRP overhead is the exchange of hello packets, unless there is a topological change in the network.

Reliable Transport Protocol

The EIGRP transport mechanism uses a mix of multicast and unicast packets, using reliable delivery when necessary. All transmissions use IP with the protocol type field set to 88. The IP multicast address used is 224.0.0.10.

DUAL requires guaranteed and sequenced delivery for some transmissions. This is achieved using acknowledgments and sequence numbers. So, for example, *update packets* (containing routing table data) are delivered reliably (with sequence numbers) to all neighbors using multicast. *Acknowledgment packets*—with the correct sequence number—are expected from every neighbor. If the correct acknowledgment number is not received from a neighbor, the update is retransmitted as a unicast.

The sequence number (seq num) in the last packet from the neighbor is recorded to ensure that packets are received in sequence. The number of packets in the queue that might need retransmission is shown as a queue count (QCnt), and the smoothed round trip time (SRTT) is used to estimate how long to wait before retransmitting to the neighbor. The retransmission timeout (RTO) is the time the router will wait for an acknowledgment before retransmitting the packet in the queue.

Some transmissions do not require reliable delivery. For example, hello packets are multicast to all neighbors on an Ethernet segment, whereas acknowledgments are unicast. Neither hellos nor acknowledgments are sent reliably.

EIGRP also uses *queries* and *replies* as part of DUAL. Queries are multicast or unicast using reliable delivery, whereas replies are always reliably unicast. Query and reply packets are discussed in more detail in the next section.

Diffusing Update Algorithm (DUAL)

All route computations in EIGRP are handled by DUAL. One of DUAL's tasks is maintaining a table of loop-free paths to every destination. This table is referred to as the *topology table*. Unlike traditional DV protocols that save only the best (least-cost) path for every destination, DUAL saves all paths in the topology table. The least-cost path(s) is copied from the topology table to the routing table. In the event of a failure, the topology table allows for very quick convergence if another loop-free path is available. If a loop-free path is not found in the topology table, a route recomputation must occur, during which DUAL queries its neighbors, who, in turn, may query their neighbors, and so on... hence the name "Diffusing" Update Algorithm.

These processes are described in detail in the following sections.

Reported distance

Just like RIP and IGRP, EIGRP calculates the lowest cost to reach a destination based on updates[*] from neighbors. An update from a router *R* contains the cost to reach the destination network *N* from *R*. This cost is referred to as the *reported distance* (RD). *NewYork* receives an update from *Ames* with a cost of 281,600, which is *Ames*'s cost to reach `172.16.100.0`. In other words, the RD for *Ames* to reach `172.160.100.0` as reported to *NewYork* is 281,600. Just like *Ames*, *Chicago* will report its cost to reach `172.16.100.0`. *Chicago*'s RD is 2,195,456 (see Figure 4-2).

---

[*] Unlike RIP and IGRP, EIGRP updates are *not* periodic. EIGRP updates are sent only when there is a topological change in the network.

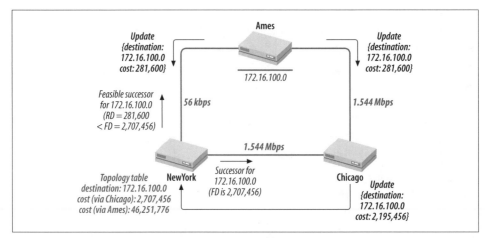

Figure 4-2. Ames is a feasible successor for 172.16.100.0

Feasible distance and successor

NewYork will compute its cost to reach 172.16.100.0 via *Ames* and *Chicago*. *New-York* will then compare the metrics for the two paths. *NewYork*'s cost via *Ames* is 46,251,776. *NewYork*'s cost via *Chicago* is 2,707,456. The lowest cost to reach a destination is referred to as the *feasible distance* (FD) for that destination. *NewYork*'s FD to 172.16.100.0 is 2,707,456 (*BandW* = 1,544 and *Delay* = 4,100). The next-hop router in the lowest-cost path to the destination is referred to as the *successor*. *New-York*'s successor for 172.16.100.0 is 172.16.50.1 (*Chicago*).

Feasibility condition and feasible successor

If a reported distance for a destination is less than the feasible distance for the same destination, the router that advertised the RD is said to satisfy the *feasibility condition* (FC) and is referred to as a *feasible successor* (FS). *NewYork* sees an RD of 281,600 via *Ames*, which is lower than *NewYork*'s FD of 2,707,456. *Ames* satisfies the FC. *Ames* is an FS for *NewYork* to reach 172.16.100.0.

Loop freedom

The feasibility condition is a test for *loop freedom*: if the FC is met, the router advertising the RD must have a path to the destination not through the router checking the FC—if it did, the RD would have been higher than the FD.

Let's illustrate this concept with another example. Consider the network in Figure 4-3. The metric values used in this example have been simplified to small numbers to make it easier to follow the concept.

Router *A*'s best route to network *N* is via router *B*, and the cost of this path is 100 (*A*'s FD to *N* is 100). Router *X* also knows how to get to network *N*; *X* advertises *N*

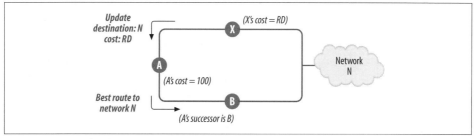

Figure 4-3. Loop freedom

to *A* in an update packet (*A* copies this information into its topology table). In the event that *A*'s link to *B* fails, *A* can use the route to *N* via *X* if *X* does not use *A* to get to *N* (in other words, if the path is loop-free). Thus, the key question for *A* to answer is whether or not the path that *X* advertises is loop-free.

Here is how *A* answers this question. Let's say that *X* advertises *N* with a metric of 90 (*X*'s RD for *N*). *A* compares 90 (RD) with 100 (FD). Is RD < FD? This comparison is the FC check. Since *A*'s FD is 100, *X*'s path to *N* must not be via *A* (and is loop-free). If *X* advertises *N* with a metric of 110, *X*'s path to *N* could be via *A* (the RD is not less than the FD, so the FC check fails)—110 could be *A*'s cost added to the metric of the link between *A* and *X* (and, hence, is not guaranteed to be free of a loop).

Topology table

All destinations advertised by neighbors are copied into the topology table. Each destination is listed along with the neighbors that advertised the destination, the RD, and the metric to reach the destination via that neighbor. Let's look at *NewYork*'s topology table and zoom in on destination 172.16.100.0. There are two neighbors that sent updates with this destination: *Chicago* (172.16.250.2) and *Ames* (172.16.251.2), as shown on lines 9 and 10, respectively:

```
NewYork#sh ip eigrp topology
IP-EIGRP Topology Table for process 10

Codes: P - Passive, A - Active, U - Update, Q - Query, R - Reply,
       r - Reply status

...
  P 172.16.100.0/24, 1 successors, FD is 2,707,456
9         via 172.16.250.2 (2,707,456/2,195,456), Serial0
10        via 172.16.251.2 (46,251,776/281,600), Serial1
```

Chicago sent an update with an RD of 2,195,456, and *Ames* sent an update with an RD *of* 281,600. *NewYork* computes its own metric to 172.16.100.0: 2,707,456 and 46,251,776 via *Chicago* and *Ames*, respectively. *NewYork* uses the lower-cost path via *Chicago*. *NewYork*'s FD to 172.16.100.0 is thus 2,707,456, and *Chicago* is the successor. Next *NewYork* checks to see if *Ames* qualifies as a feasible successor. *Ames*'s RD is 281,600. This is checked against the FD. Since the RD < FD (281,600 < 2,707,456), *Ames* is a feasible successor (see Figure 4-2).

Note that not all loop-free paths satisfy the FC. Thus, *NewYork*'s topology table does not contain the alternate path to 172.16.50.0 (via *Ames*). The FC guarantees that the paths that satisfy the condition are loop-free; however, not all loop-free paths satisfy the FC.

Let's take a closer look at 172.16.50.0 (*Chicago*) in *NewYork*'s topology table:

```
NewYork#sh ip eigrp topology
IP-EIGRP Topology Table for process 10

Codes: P - Passive, A - Active, U - Update, Q - Query, R - Reply,
       r - Reply status

...
P 172.16.50.0/24, 1 successors, FD is 2195456
        via 172.16.250.2 (2195456/281600), Serial0
```

Notice that *Ames* (172.16.251.2) did not become a feasible successor, even though *Ames* offers a valid loop-free path. The condition that *Ames* would have to satisfy to become a feasible successor is for its RD to be less than *NewYork*'s FD to 172.16.50.0. *Ames*'s RD can be seen from *Ames*'s routing table:

```
Ames#sh ip route
...
     172.16.0.0/24 is subnetted, 6 subnets
C       172.16.252.0 is directly connected, Serial0
D       172.16.250.0 [90/2681856] via 172.16.252.1, 00:21:10, Serial0
C       172.16.251.0 is directly connected, Serial1
11  D   172.16.50.0 [90/2195456] via 172.16.252.1, 00:21:10, Serial0
D       172.16.1.0 [90/2707456] via 172.16.252.1, 00:15:36, Serial0
C       172.16.100.0 is directly connected, Ethernet0
```

Ames's metric to 172.16.50.0 is 2,195,456 (line 11). This will be the metric that *Ames* reports to *NewYork*. The RD is thus 2,195,456. *NewYork*'s FD to 172.16.50.0 is 2,195,456. The RD and the FD are equal, which is not surprising given the topology: both *NewYork* and *Ames* have identical paths to 172.16.50.0—a T-1 link, a router, and the destination Ethernet segment. Since the condition for feasible successor is that RD < FD, *Ames* is not an FS for 172.16.50.0 (see Figure 4-4).

The output of *show ip eigrp topology* shows only feasible successors. The output of *show ip eigrp topology all-links* shows all neighbors, whether feasible successors or not.

Note the "P" for "passive state" in the left margin of each route entry in *NewYork*'s topology table. *Passive state* indicates that the route is in quiescent mode, implying that the route is known to be good and that no activities are taking place with respect to the route.

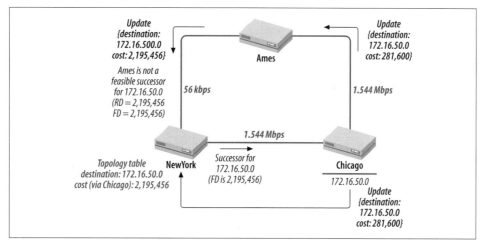

Figure 4-4. Ames is not a feasible successor for 172.16.50.0

Any of the following events can cause DUAL to reevaluate its feasible successors:

- The transition in the state of a directly connected link
- A change in the metric of a directly connected link
- An update from a neighbor

If DUAL finds a feasible successor in its own topology table after one of these events, the route remains in passive state. If DUAL cannot find a feasible successor in its topology table, it will send a query to all its neighbors and the route will transition to *active state*.

The next section contains two examples of DUAL reevaluating its topology table. In the first example, the route remains passive; in the second example, the route becomes active before returning to the passive state.

Convergence in DUAL— local computation

Let's say that the *NewYork → Chicago* link fails (Figure 4-5).

NewYork's routing table shows that 172.16.100.0 and 172.16.50.0 are learned via this link (*Serial0*):

```
NewYork#sh ip route
...
     172.16.0.0/24 is subnetted, 6 subnets
...
D       172.16.50.0 [90/2195456] via 172.16.250.2, 00:18:54, Serial0
D       172.16.100.0 [90/2707456] via 172.16.250.2, 00:18:54, Serial0
...
```

These routes become invalid. DUAL attempts to find new successors for both destinations—172.16.50.0 and 172.16.100.0.

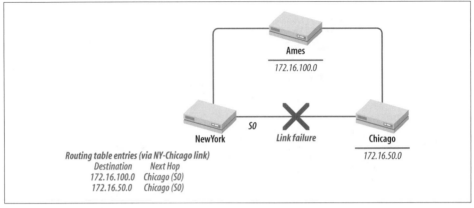

Ames
172.16.100.0

NewYork
S0   Link failure   Chicago
172.16.50.0

Routing table entries (via NY-Chicago link)
Destination   Next Hop
172.16.100.0   Chicago (S0)
172.16.50.0   Chicago (S0)

Figure 4-5. Link failure

Let's start with 172.16.100.0. DUAL checks the topology table for 172.16.100.0:

```
NewYork#sh ip eigrp topology
...
P 172.16.100.0/24, 1 successors, FD is 2707456
12          via 172.16.250.2 (2707456/2195456), Serial0
13          via 172.16.251.2 (46251776/281600), Serial1
```

Since *Serial0* is down, the only feasible successor is 172.16.251.2 (*Ames*). Let's review how *Ames* qualifies as an FS. The FS check is:

- RD < FD.
- RD=281,600 (line 13).
- FD=2,707,456 (line 12).
- Since 281,600 < 2,707,456, *Ames* qualifies as an FS.

In plain words, this implies that the path available to *NewYork* via *Ames* (the FS) is independent of the primary path that just failed. DUAL installs *Ames* as the new successor for 172.16.100.0.

In our case study, only one FS was available. In general, multiple FSs may be available, all of which satisfy the condition that their RD < FD, where FD is the cost of the route to the destination via the successor that was just lost.

DUAL will compute its metric to reach the destination via each FS. Since DUAL is searching for the successor(s) for this destination, it will choose the minimum from this set of metrics via each FS. Let the lowest metric be *Dmin*. If only one FS yields this metric of *Dmin*, that FS becomes the new successor. If multiple FSs yield metrics equal to *Dmin*, they all become successors (subject to the limitation in the maximum number of parallel paths allowed—four or six, depending on the IOS version number). Since the new successor(s) is found locally (without querying any other router), the route stays in passive state. After DUAL has installed the new successor, it sends an update to all its neighbors regarding this change.

How long does this computation take? We simulated the failure of the *NewYork → Chicago* link in our laboratory. To measure how long EIGRP would take to converge after the failure of the link, we started a long ping test just before failing the *New-York → Chicago* link:

```
NewYork#ping
Protocol [ip]:
Target IP address: 172.16.100.1
Repeat count [5]: 1000
...
Sending 1000, 100-byte ICMP Echos to 172.16.100.1, timeout is 2 seconds:

!!!!!!!!!!!!!!!!!!!!!!!!!!!!!!!!!!!!!!!!!!!!.!!!!!!!!!!!!!!!!!!!!!!!!!!!!!!!!!
!!!!!!!!!!!!!!!!!!!!!!!!!!!!!!!!!!!!!!!!!!!!!!!!!!!!!!!!!!!!!!!!!!!!!!

Success rate is 99 percent (999/1000), round-trip min/avg/max = 1/3/92 ms
```

Note that only one ping packet was lost during this computation, implying that the convergence time (including the time to detect the failure of the link) was in the range of two to four seconds.

Convergence in DUAL—diffusing computation

Let's next follow the steps that DUAL would take for 172.16.50.0. Notice that this is a different case in that when *Serial0* is down, *NewYork* has no feasible successors in its topology table (see line 14).

```
NewYork#sh ip eigrp topology
...
   P 172.16.50.0/24, 1 successors, FD is 2195456
14          via 172.16.250.2 (2195456/281600), Serial0
...
```

DUAL knows of no feasible successors, but *NewYork* has a neighbor that may know of a feasible successor. DUAL places the route in active state (see line 15) and sends a query to all its neighbors:

```
NewYork#sh ip eigrp topology
IP-EIGRP Topology Table for process 10

Codes: P - Passive, A - Active, U - Update, Q - Query, R - Reply,
       r - Reply status

...
15 A 172.16.50.0/24, 0 successors, FD is 2195456, Q
          1 replies, active 00:00:06, query-origin: Local origin
          Remaining replies:
16          via 172.16.251.2, r, Serial1
```

which in this case is only 172.16.251.2 (*Ames*, as in line 16). *NewYork* sets the reply flag on (line 16), which indicates that *NewYork* expects a reply to the query. *Ames* receives the query and marks its topology table entry for 172.16.50.0 via *NewYork* as down. Next, *Ames* checks its topology table for a feasible successor:

```
Ames#sh ip eigrp topology
IP-EIGRP Topology Table for process 10

Codes: P - Passive, A - Active, U - Update, Q - Query, R - Reply,
       r - Reply status

   ...
17 P 172.16.50.0/24, 1 successors, FD is 2195456
         via 172.16.252.1 (2195456/281600), Serial0
   ...
```

and finds that it has a successor (172.16.252.1). *Ames* sends a reply packet to *New-York* with an RD of 2,195,456 (line 17). *NewYork* marks the route as passive and installs a route for 172.16.50.0 via 172.16.251.2 (*Ames*).

In general, if DUAL does not find a feasible successor, it forwards the query to its neighbors. The query thus propagates ("diffuses") until a reply is received. Routers that did not find a feasible successor would return an unreachable message. So, if *Ames* did not have a feasible successor in its topology table, it would mark the route as active and propagate the query to its neighbor, if it had another neighbor. If *Ames* had no other neighbor (and no feasible successor) it would return an unreachable message to *NewYork* and mark the route as unreachable in its own table.

When DUAL marks a route as active and sets the *r* flag on, it sets a timer for how long it will wait for a reply. The default value of the timer is three minutes. DUAL waits for a reply from all the neighbors it queries. If a neighbor does not respond to a query, the route is marked as *stuck-in-active* and DUAL deletes all routes in its topology table that point to the unresponsive neighbor as a feasible successor.

Protocol-Dependent Module

The successors in the DUAL topology table are eligible for installation in the routing table. Successors represent the best path to the destination known to DUAL. However, whether the successor is copied into the routing table is another matter. The router may be aware of a route to the same destination from another source (such as another routing protocol or via a static route) with a lower *distance*. The IP protocol-dependent module (PDM) handles this task. The PDM may also carry information in the reverse direction—from the routing table to the topology table. This will occur if routes are being redistributed into EIGRP from another protocol.

The PDM is also responsible for encapsulating EIGRP messages in IP packets.

EIGRP Packet Format

EIGRP packets are encapsulated directly in IP with the protocol field set to 88. The destination IP address in EIGRP depends on the packet type—some packets are sent as multicast (with an address of 224.0.0.10) and others are sent as unicast (see the earlier section "Reliable Transport Protocol" for more details). The source IP address is the IP address of the interface from which the packet is issued.

Following the IP header is an EIGRP header. Key fields in the EIGRP header are as follows, and are also shown in Figure 4-6:

- The *opcode* field specifies the EIGRP packet type (update, query, reply, hello).
- The *checksum* applies to the entire EIGRP packet, excluding the IP header.
- The rightmost bit in the *flags* field is the initialization bit and is used in establishing a new neighbor relationship (see "Neighbor Relationship" earlier in this chapter).
- The *sequence* and *ack* fields are used to send messages reliably (see "Reliable Transport Protocol" earlier in this chapter).
- The *AS number* identifies the EIGRP process issuing the packet. The EIGRP process receiving the packet will process the packet only if the receiving EIGRP process has the same AS number; otherwise, the packet will be discarded.

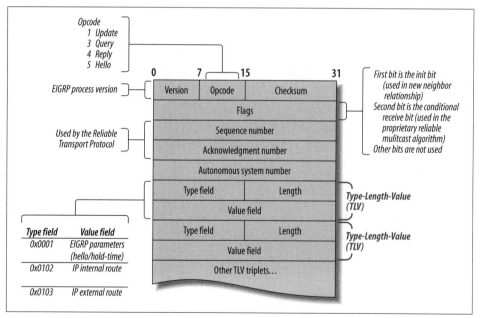

Figure 4-6. Format of EIGRP packets

The fields following the EIGRP header depend on the opcode field. Of particular interest to routing engineers is the information in updates. We will ignore the other types of EIGRP messages and focus on IP internal route updates and IP external route updates.

Internal routes contain destination network numbers learned within this EIGRP AS. For example, *NewYork* learns 172.16.50.0 from EIGRP 10 on *Chicago* as an internal route.

External routes contain destination network numbers that were not learned within this EIGRP AS but rather derived from another routing process and redistributed into this EIGRP AS.

Internal and external routes are represented differently in the EIGRP update.

Internal routes

Internal routes have a *type* field of 0x0102. The metric information contained with the route is much like IGRP's (see Chapter 3). However, there are two new fields: *next hop* and *prefix length*. Figure 4-7 shows the value field for the IP internal route.

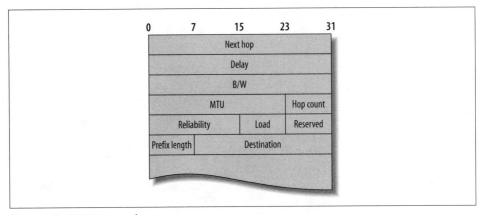

Figure 4-7. EIGRP internal route

The next hop identifies the router to send packets destined for *destination*, the network number of the destination. In general, the next hop field for internal routes will be the IP address of the router on the interface on which it is issuing the update.

The prefix length field signifies the subnet mask to be associated with the network number specified in the destination field. Thus, if an EIGRP router is configured as follows:

```
ip address 172.16.1.1 255.255.255.0
```

it will advertise 172.16.1.0 with a prefix length of 24.

Likewise, if the router is configured as follows:

```
ip address 172.16.250.1 255.255.255.252
```

it will advertise 172.16.250.0 with a prefix length of 30.

External routes

Additional fields are required to represent the source from which external routes are derived, as shown in Figure 4-8.

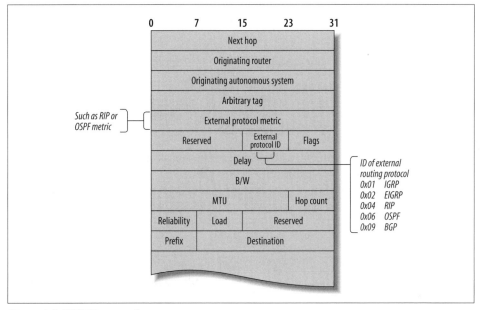

Figure 4-8. EIGRP external route

The next hop field identifies the router to send packets destined for *destination*, the network number of the destination. This field was absent in the IGRP update. Let's look at what this field signifies.

In IGRP, if router X sends an update to router A with a destination network number of N, router A's next hop for packets to N will be X. In EIGRP, router X can send an update to router A with a destination network number of N and a next hop field of Y. This is useful, say, in a scenario where X and Y are running RIP and X is redistributing routes from RIP to IGRP. When X sends an update to its neighbors on a shared network, X can tell them to send traffic for network N directly to Y and not to X. This saves X from having to accept traffic on a shared network and then reroute it to Y.*

---

* You may ask why this cannot be handled by ICMP redirects. Cisco does not support redirects between routers.

The *originating router, originating AS, external protocol metric*, and *external protocol ID* fields specify information about the router and the routing process from which this route was derived. The external protocol ID specifies the routing protocol from which this route was derived. Here is a partial list of external protocol IDs: IGRP—0x01; EIGRP—0x02; RIP—0x04; OSPF—0x06; BGP—0x09. Thus, if a route was learned from RIP with a hop count of 3 and redistributed into EIGRP, the originating router field would contain the address of the RIP router, the originating AS field would be empty, the external protocol metric would be 3, and the external protocol ID would be 0x04.

The *arbitrary tag* field is used to carry route maps.

Candidate default routes are marked by setting the flags field to 0x02. A flags field of 0x01 indicates an external route (but not a candidate default route).

The other parameters in the external route packet are similar to those in IGRP.

Variable Length Subnet Masks

Unlike RIP and IGRP, EIGRP updates carry subnet mask information. The network architect now has the responsibility of using addresses wisely. Reviewing Trader-Mary's configuration, a mask of 255.255.255.0 on the serial links is wasteful: there are only two devices on the link, so a 24-bit mask will waste 252 addresses. A 30-bit mask (255.255.255.252) allows two usable IP addresses in each subnet, which fits a serial line exactly.

Let's say that the network architect decided to subdivide 172.16.250.0 using a 30-bit mask for use on up to 64 possible subnets. The subnets that thus become available are:

1. 172.16.250.0
2. 172.16.250.4
3. 172.16.250.8
4. ...
64. 172.16.250.252

The serial links in TraderMary's network can be readdressed using these subnets:

```
hostname NewYork
...
interface Ethernet0
ip address 172.16.1.1 255.255.255.0
!
interface Ethernet1
ip address 192.168.1.1 255.255.255.0
!
interface Serial0
description New York to Chicago link
```

```
ip address 172.16.250.1 255.255.255.252
!
interface Serial1
description New York to Ames link
bandwidth 56
ip address 172.16.250.5 255.255.255.252
...
router eigrp 10
network 172.16.0.0


hostname Chicago
...
interface Ethernet0
ip address 172.16.50.1 255.255.255.0
!
interface Serial0
description Chicago to New York link
ip address 172.16.250.2 255.255.255.252
!
interface Serial1
description Chicago to Ames link
ip address 172.16.250.9 255.255.255.0
...

router eigrp 10
network 172.16.0.0


hostname Ames
...
interface Ethernet0
ip address 172.16.100.1 255.255.255.0
!
interface Serial0
description Ames to Chicago link
ip address 172.16.250.10 255.255.255.0
!
interface Serial1
description Ames to New York link
bandwidth 56
ip address 172.16.250.6 255.255.255.0
...

router eigrp 10
network 172.16.0.0
```

New York's routing table now looks like this:

```
NewYork#sh ip route
...
     172.16.0.0/16 is variably subnetted, 6 subnets, 2 masks
D        172.16.250.8/30 [90/2681856] via 172.16.250.2, 00:18:54, Serial0
C        172.16.250.0/30 is directly connected, Serial0
```

```
C       172.16.250.4/30 is directly connected, Serial1
D       172.16.50.0/24 [90/2195456] via 172.16.250.2, 00:18:54, Serial00
C       172.16.1.0/24 is directly connected, Ethernet0
D       172.16.100.0/24 [90/2707456] via 172.16.250.2, 00:18:54, Serial0
C     192.168.1.0/24 is directly connected, Ethernet1
```

Note that each route is now accompanied by its mask. When 172.16.0.0 had uniform masking, the routing table did not show the mask.

Further, let's say that Casablanca is a small office with only a dozen people on the staff. We may safely assign Casablanca a mask of 255.255.255.192 (a limit of 62 usable addresses). Forward-thinking is important when assigning addresses. When running IGRP, the network architect may have had the foresight to assign addresses from the beginning of the range. Excess addresses should not be squandered, such as by randomly choosing addresses for hosts. A general rule is to start assigning addresses from the beginning or the bottom of an address range. When a site is shrinking, again keep all addresses at one end.

Using subnet masks that reflect the size of the host population conserves addresses. Put on your plate only as much as you will eat.

Route Summarization

The default behavior of EIGRP is to summarize on network-number boundaries. This is similar to RIP and IGRP and is a prudent way for a routing protocol to reduce the number of routes that are propagated between routers. However, there are some enhancements in the way EIGRP summarizes routes that merit a closer look.

Automatic Summarization

Say TraderMary's network expands again, this time with a node in Shannon. Shannon gets connected to the London office via a 56-kbps link, as shown in Figure 4-9.

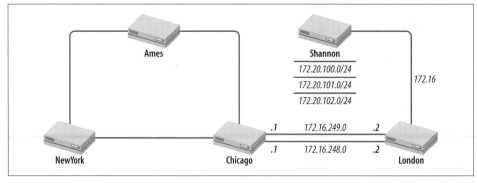

Figure 4-9. Route summarization

Shannon has three Ethernet segments with an IP subnet on each: 172.20.100.0/24, 172.20.101.0/24, and 172.20.102.0/24. The routers in London and Shannon are configured to run EIGRP 10 in keeping with the routing protocol in use in the U.S. *Shannon* will advertise 172.20.0.0/16 to *London* because the serial link from *London* to *Shannon* represents a network-number boundary (172.20.0.0/172.16.0.0). *Shannon* itself will see all 172.16.0.0 subnets (without summarization) because it has a directly connected 172.16.0.0 network.

In EIGRP, the router doing the summarization will build a route to *null0* (line 18) for the summarized address. Let's check *Shannon*'s routing table:

```
Shannon#sh ip route 172.20.0.0
...
     172.20.0.0/16 is subnetted, 6 subnets
C        172.20.100.0/24 is directly connected, Ethernet0
C        172.20.101.0/24 is directly connected, Ethernet1
18 D     172.20.0.0/16 is a summary, 00:12:11, Null0
C        172.20.102.0/24 is directly connected, Ethernet2
```

The route to *null0* ensures that if *Shannon* receives a packet for which it has no route (e.g., 172.20.1.1), it will route the packet using the null interface, thereby dropping the packet, rather than using some other route for the packet (such as a default route).

Now, let's muddy the picture up a bit. TraderMary acquires a small company in Ottawa which also happens to use a 172.20.0.0 subnet—172.20.1.0! The new picture looks something like Figure 4-10.

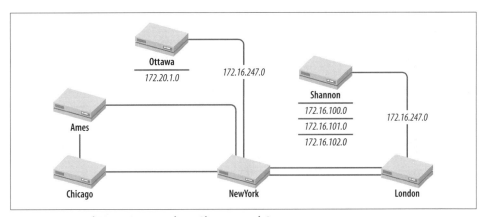

Figure 4-10. TraderMary's networks in Shannon and Ottawa

Ottawa is also configured to run EIGRP 10 with a link from *NewYork*. Since the IP address on the link is 172.16.0.0, *Ottawa* will send a summary update of 172.20.0.0 to *NewYork*.

We have a problem now. There are two sources advertising 172.20.0.0, and depending on where we are in the network, we will be able to route only to *Ottawa* or

Shannon. Thus, *NewYork* will install `172.20.0.0` only via *Ottawa*, and *London* will install `172.20.0.0` only via *Shannon.*

Unlike RIP and IGRP, EIGRP provides the option of disabling route summarization. Thus, *Shannon* and *Ottawa* can be configured as follows:

```
hostname Shannon
...
router eigrp 10
network 172.16.0.0
network 172.20.0.0
no auto-summary


hostname Ottawa
...
router eigrp 10
network 172.16.0.0
network 172.20.0.0
no auto-summary
```

When *no auto-summary* is turned on, *Shannon* and *Ottawa* will advertise their subnets to the rest of the network. The subnets happen to be unique, so any router will be able to route to any destination in the network.*

Note that *no auto-summary* was required only on the *Shannon* and *Ottawa* routers. *NewYork* and *London* and other routers will pass these subnets through (without summarizing them). Summarization happens only at a border between major network numbers, not at other routers.

The moral of this story is that EIGRP networks do not have to be contiguous with respect to major network numbers. However, I do not recommend deliberately building discontiguous networks. Summarizing on network-number boundaries is an easy way to reduce the size of routing tables and the complexity of the network. Disabling route summarization should be undertaken only when necessary.

Manual Summarization

EIGRP allows for the summarization of (external or internal) routes on any bit boundary. Manual summarization can be used to reduce the size of routing tables.

In our example, the network architect may decide to allocate blocks of addresses to *NewYork, Ames, Chicago,* etc. *NewYork* is allocated the block `172.16.1.0` through `172.16.15.0`. This may also be represented as `172.16.0.0/20`, signifying that the first four bits of the third octet in this range are all zeros, as is true for `172.16.1.0` through `172.16.15.0`.

---

* If the subnets overlapped, disabling route summarization would not do us any good. There are other methods to tackle duplicate address problems, such as Network Address Translation (NAT).

```
     hostname NewYork
     ...
19   interface Ethernet0
     ip address 172.16.1.1 255.255.255.0
     !
     interface Ethernet1
     ip address 192.168.1.1 255.255.255.0
     !
20   interface Ethernet2
     ip address 172.16.2.1 255.255.255.0
     !
     interface Serial0
     description New York to Chicago link
     ip address 172.16.250.1 255.255.255.0
     ip summary-address eigrp 10 172.16.0.0 255.255.240.0
     !
     interface Serial1
     description New York to Ames link
     bandwidth 56
     ip address 172.16.251.1 255.255.255.0
21   ip summary-address eigrp 10 172.16.0.0 255.255.240.0
     ...
     router eigrp 10
     network 172.16.0.0
```

NewYork now has two Ethernet segments (lines 19 and 20) from this block and has also been configured to send a summary route for this block (line 21) to its neighbors. The configuration of these routers is as shown in Figure 4-1. Here's *NewYork*'s routing table:

```
     NewYork#sh ip route
     ...
          172.16.0.0/16 is variably subnetted, 8 subnets, 2 masks
     D       172.16.252.0/24 [90/2681856] via 172.16.250.2, 00:01:44, Serial0
     C       172.16.250.0/24 is directly connected, Serial0
     C       172.16.251.0/24 is directly connected, Serial1
22   D       172.16.0.0/20 is a summary, 00:03:22, Null0
     C       172.16.1.0/24 is directly connected, Ethernet0
     C       172.16.2.0/24 is directly connected, Ethernet2
     D       172.16.50.0/20 [90/2195456] via 172.16.250.2, 00:01:45, Serial0
     D       172.16.100.0/20 [90/2707456] via 172.16.250.2, 00:01:45, Serial0
     C     192.168.1.0/24 is directly connected, Ethernet1
```

Note that *NewYork* installs a route to the null interface for the summarized address (172.16.0.0/20, as in line 22). Further, routers *Ames* and *Chicago* install this aggregated route (line 23) and not the individual 172.16.1.0/24 and 172.16.2.0/24 routes:

```
     Chicago#sh ip route
     ...
          172.16.0.0/16 is variably subnetted, 8 subnets, 2 masks
     C       172.16.252.0/24 is directly connected, Serial1
     C       172.16.250.0/24 is directly connected, Serial0
     D       172.16.251.0/24 [90/2681856] via 172.16.250.1, 00:02:30, Serial0
                              [90/2681856] via 172.16.252.2, 00:02:30, Serial1
```

```
        C       172.16.50.0/24 is directly connected, Ethernet0
    23  D       172.16.0.0/20 [90/2195456] via 172.16.250.1, 00:02:12, Serial0
        D       172.16.100.0/20 [90/2195456] via 172.16.252.2, 00:02:10, Serial1
```

The address aggregation commands on *NewYork* reduce the routing-table size in the rest of the network. Note that address aggregation plans need to be laid out ahead of time so that network numbers can be allocated accordingly. Thus, in the previous example, *NewYork* was allocated a block of 16 subnets:

> 172.16.96.0 through 172.16.15.0

Continuing this scheme, *Ames* may be allocated a block of 16 addresses that envelop the network number it is currently using (172.16.100.0):

> 172.16.96.0 through 172.16.111.0

and *Chicago* may be allocated a block of 16 addresses that envelop the network number it is currently using (172.16.50.0):

> 172.16.48.0 through 172.16.63.0

Ames could now be configured to summarize its block using the statement on its serial interfaces:

```
    ip summary-address eigrp 10 172.16.0.0 255.255.240.0
```

and *Chicago* could be configured to summarize its block using the statement on its serial interfaces:

```
    ip summary-address eigrp 10 172.16.0.0 255.255.240.0
```

Default Routes

EIGRP tracks default routes in the external section of its routing updates. Candidate default routes are marked by setting the flags field to 0x02.

Default routes are most often used to support branch offices that have only one or two connections to the core network (see Figure 4-11).

The core router is configured as follows:

```
    hostname core1
    !
    interface Ethernet0
     ip address 192.168.1.1 255.255.255.0
    ...
    interface Serial0
    ip address 172.16.245.1 255.255.255.0
    ...
    router eigrp 10
24   redistribute static metric 56 100 255 1 255
     network 172.16.0.0
    !
    ip classless
25  ip route 0.0.0.0 0.0.0.0 Null0
```

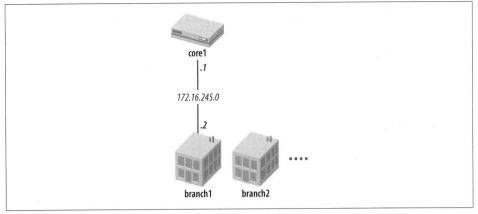

Figure 4-11. Branch offices only need a default route

The branch router is configured as follows:

```
hostname branch1
...
interface Serial0
ip address 172.16.245.2 255.255.255.0
...
26  router eigrp 10
    network 172.16.0.0
```

An examination of *branch1*'s routing table would show:

```
branch1#sh ip route
...
Gateway of last resort is 172.16.251.1 to network 0.0.0.0

     172.16.0.0/24 is subnetted, 6 subnets
C       172.16.245.0 is directly connected, Serial0
...
27  D*EX 0.0.0.0/0 [170/46251776] via 172.16.245.1, 00:01:47, Serial0
```

Since the default route is an external route, it is tagged with a distance of 170 (line 27).

The following steps were followed in the creation of this default route:

1. Network 0.0.0.0 was defined as a static route on *core1* (see line 25).
2. Network 0.0.0.0 was redistributed into EIGRP 10 (see line 24).
3. A default metric was attached to the redistribution (line 24).
4. EIGRP 10 was turned on in *branch1* (line 26).

To increase the reliability of the connection to branches, each branch may be connected to two core routers. *branch1* will now receive two default routes. One router (say, *core1*) may be set up as the primary, and the second router (*core2*) as backup. To do this, set up the default from *core2* with a *worse* metric, as we did for IGRP in Chapter 3.

Troubleshooting EIGRP

EIGRP can be difficult to troubleshoot because of its complexity. As a reminder, the best preparation for troubleshooting a network is to be familiar with the network and its state during normal (trouble-free) conditions. Become familiar with the routing tables, their sizes, the summarization points, routing timers, etc. Also, plan ahead with "what-if" scenarios. What if router *X* failed or link *Y* dropped? How would connectivity recover? Will all the routes still be in every router's table? Will the routes still be summarized?

Perhaps the second-best preparation for troubleshooting a network is the ability to track network implementations and changes. If network implementations/changes are made in a haphazard way with no central control, an implementation team may walk away from a change (unaware that their change caused an outage) and it may take the troubleshooting team hours, or even days, to unravel the events that led to the outage. Besides making the network more vulnerable, such loose methods of network operation create bad relationships between teams.

The following sections are a partial list of network states/conditions to check when looking for clues to routing problems in EIGRP.

Verifying Neighbor Relationships

If a router is unable to establish a stable relationship with its neighbors, it cannot exchange routes with those neighbors. The neighbor table can help check the integrity of neighbor relationships. Here is a sample of *NewYork*'s neighbor table:

```
NewYork#sh ip eigrp neighbor
IP-EIGRP neighbors for process 10
H   Address              Interface   Hold Uptime    SRTT   RTO   Q   Seq
                                     (sec)          (ms)         Cnt Num
1   172.16.251.2         Se0/1        10 00:17:08    28   2604   0   7
0   172.16.250.2         Se0/0        13 00:24:43    12   2604   0   14
```

First, check that the neighbor count matches the number of EIGRP speakers. If routers *A*, *B*, and *C* share an Ethernet segment and run EIGRP 10, all four routers should see each other in their neighbor tables. If router *C* is consistently missing from *A* and *B*'s tables, there may be a physical problem with *C* or *C* may be misconfigured (check *C*'s IP address and EIGRP configuration). Next, look for one-way neighbor relationships. Is *C* in *A* and *B*'s tables, but are *A* and *B* not in *C*'s table? This could indicate a physical problem with *C*'s connection or a filter that is blocking EIGRP packets.

If the hold-time exceeds 15 seconds (or the configured hold-time), the network may be congested and losing hellos. Increasing the hello-interval/hold-time may be a quick fix to the problem.

The uptime should reflect the duration that the routers have been up. A low uptime indicates that the neighbor relationship is being lost and reestablished.

The QCnt should be 0 (or at least should not exceed 0 on a consistent basis).

In summary, if a problem is found in the neighbor relationship, you should do the following:

1. Check for bad physical infrastructure.
2. Ensure that router ports are plugged into the correct hubs.
3. Check for filters blocking EIGRP packets.
4. Verify router configurations—check IP addresses, masks, EIGRP AS numbers, and the network numbers defined under EIGRP.
5. Increase the hello-interval/hold-time on congested networks.

The command to clear and reestablish neighbor relationships is:

```
clear ip eigrp neighbors [ip address | interface]
```

 Repeatedly clearing all neighbor relationships causes the loss of routes (and the loss of packets to those routes). Besides, repeatedly issuing *clear* commands usually does not fix the problem.

Stuck-in-Active

A route is regarded as stuck-in-active (SIA) when DUAL does not receive a response to a query from a neighbor for three minutes, which is the default value of the active timer. DUAL then deletes all routes from that neighbor, acting as if the neighbor had responded with an unreachable message for all routes.

Routers propagate queries through the network if feasible successors are not found, so it can be difficult to catch the culprit router (i.e., the router that is not responding to the query in time). The culprit may be running high on CPU utilization or may be connected via low-bandwidth links. Going back to TraderMary's network, when *NewYork* queries *Ames* for 172.16.50.0, it marks the route as active and lists the neighbor from which it is expecting a reply (line 28):

```
NewYork#sh ip eigrp topology
IP-EIGRP Topology Table for process 10

Codes: P - Passive, A - Active, U - Update, Q - Query, R - Reply,
       r - Reply status

...
A 172.16.50.0/24, 0 successors, FD is 2195456, Q
     1 replies, active 00:00:06, query-origin: Local origin
     Remaining replies:
28        via 172.16.251.2, r, Serial1
```

If this route were to become SIA, the network engineer should trace the path of the queries to see which router has been queried, has no outstanding queries itself, and yet is taking a long time to answer.

Starting from *NewYork*, the next router to check for SIA routes would be 172.16.251.2 (line 28). Finding the culprit router in large networks is a difficult task, because queries fan out to a large number of routers. Checking the router logs would give a clue as to which router(s) had the SIA condition.

Increase active timer

Another option is to increase the active timer. The default value of the active timer is three minutes. If you think the SIA condition is occurring because the network diameter is too large, with several slow-speed links (such as Frame Relay PVCs), it is possible that increasing the active timer will allow enough time for responses to return. The following command shows how to increase the active timer:

```
router eigrp 10
timers active-time minutes
```

For the change to be effective, the active timer must be modified on every router in the path of the query.

EIGRP Bandwidth on Low-Speed Links

EIGRP limits itself to using no more than 50% of the configured bandwidth on router interfaces. There are two reasons for this:

1. Generating more traffic than the interface can handle would cause drops, thereby impairing EIGRP performance.

2. Generating a lot of EIGRP traffic would result in little bandwidth remaining for user data.

EIGRP uses the bandwidth that is configured on an interface to decide how much EIGRP traffic to generate. If the bandwidth configured on an interface does not match the physical bandwidth (the network architect may have put in an artificially low or high bandwidth value to influence routing decisions), EIGRP may be generating too little or too much traffic. In either case, EIGRP can encounter problems as a result of this. If it is difficult to change the *bandwidth* command on an interface because of such constraints, allocate a higher or lower percentage to EIGRP with the following command in interface configuration mode:

```
ip bandwidth percent eigrp AS-number percentage
```

Network Logs

Check the output of the *show logging* command for EIGRP/DUAL messages. For example, the following message:

```
%DUAL-3-SIA: Route XXX stuck-in-active state in IP-EIGRP
```

indicates that the route *XXX* was SIA.

IOS Version Check, Bug Lists

The EIGRP implementation was enhanced in IOS Releases 10.3(11), 11.0(8), and 11.1(3) with respect to its performance on Frame Relay and other low-speed networks. In the event of chronic network problems, check the IOS versions in use in your network. Also use the bug navigation tools available on the Cisco web site.

Debug Commands

As always, use *debug* commands in a production network only after careful thought. Having to resort to rebooting the router can be very unappetizing. The following is a list of EIGRP *debug* commands:

- *debug eigrp neighbors* (for neighbor-relationship activity)
- *debug eigrp packet* (all EIGRP packets)
- *debug eigrp ip neighbor* (if the previous two commands are used together, only EIGRP packets for the specified neighbor are shown)

Summing Up

EIGRP offers the following radical improvements over RIP and IGRP:

- Fast convergence—convergence is almost instantaneous when a feasible successor is available.
- Variable Length Subnet Masks are supported—subnet mask information is exchanged in EIGRP updates. This allows for efficient use of the address space, as well as support for discontiguous networks.
- Route summarization at arbitrary bit boundaries, reducing routing-table size.
- No regular routing updates—network bandwidth and router CPU resources are not tied up in periodic routing updates, leading to improved network manageability.
- Ease of configuration—EIGRP can be configured with almost the same ease as IGRP. However, troubleshooting DUAL can be difficult.

These EIGRP benefits come at the price of higher memory requirements (in addition to the routing table, EIGRP requires memory for the topology table and the neighbor table). DUAL is complex and can be very CPU-intensive, especially during periods of network instability when CPU resources are already scarce. Also, don't forget that the EIGRP is a Cisco proprietary protocol.

EIGRP is in use today in several mid-sized networks.

CHAPTER 5

Routing Information Protocol Version 2 (RIP-2)

In this chapter:

- Getting RIP-2 Running
- RIP-2 Packet Format
- RIP-1/RIP-2 Compatibility
- Classful Versus Classless Routing Protocols
- Classful Versus Classless Route Lookup
- Authentication
- Route Summarization
- Summing Up

RIP Version 2 is not a new protocol—it is RIP Version 1 with some additional fields in the route update packet, key among them being subnet mask information in each route entry. The underlying DV algorithms in RIP-2 are identical to those in RIP-1, implying that RIP-2 still suffers from convergence problems and the maximum hop-count limit of 16 hops. Hence, RIP-2 may not be your choice as the routing protocol for a large or mid-sized network with multiple paths between segments. However, the new features in RIP-2 may be compelling enough for you to consider migrating an existing RIP-1 network to RIP-2. The new features in RIP-2 are summarized here:

Subnet mask

> RIP-2 updates carry the subnet mask in each route entry, making RIP-2 a classless routing protocol that supports Variable Length Subnet Masks (VLSM), discontiguous address spaces, and CIDR blocks.

Next hop IP address

> RIP-2 updates carry the next hop IP address in each route entry. As we will see later, the next hop IP address is useful when routes are being redistributed between RIP-2 and another routing protocol.

Authentication data

> Every RIP-2 packet can carry authentication data to validate the source of the RIP-2 update. Remember that RIP-1 has no security features—any host transmitting on UDP port 520 will be believed by neighbors running RIP-1.

Route tag

> RIP-2 updates carry a tag in each route entry that is not used by RIP but could be used to represent information such as the source of the route when the route is imported from another AS (for example, BGP).

These additions to the RIP-1 update take the place of the unused or "must be zero" octets in the RIP-1 packet. This strategic placement has a major goal—backward compatibility. Most versions of RIP-1 can process RIP-2 updates by ignoring the new fields.

Configuring and using RIP-2 is similar to RIP-1 and just as easy. A major reason for the long life of RIP may be the simplicity of the protocol and the ease of its use.

The next section gets RIP-2 running on TraderMary's network.

Getting RIP-2 Running

RIP-1—a *classful* routing protocol—does not support VLSM. We'll configure TraderMary's network using RIP-2—a *classless* routing protocol—much like we did using RIP-1, but we will use VLSM. The distinction between classful and classless protocols and the support of VLSM are discussed in detail in the section "Classful Versus Classless Routing Protocols."

TraderMary's network is an ideal candidate for VLSM because of the mix of user segments and serial links in the 172.16.0.0 address space. Using a 24-bit mask (255.255.255.0) on Ethernet segments yields 254 addresses per segment for hosts. However, serial links require only 2 IP addresses—using a 24-bit mask on a serial link wastes 252 addresses. A 30-bit mask (255.255.255.252) is more appropriate for a serial link, as it yields 2 usable IP addresses. How should 172.16.0.0 be segmented into 24-bit subnets for users on Ethernet segments and 30-bit subnets for serial links?

Using 24-bit masks (255.255.255.0) on Ethernet segments will give us 254 host addresses per user segment. Let's first use this mask to subnet 172.16.0.0. The resulting subnets can be listed as follows:

1. 172.16.1.0/24

2. 172.16.2.0/24

3. 172.16.3.0/24

4. ...

253. 172.16.253.0/24

254. 172.16.254.0/24

Let's now take one of these subnets (say, 172.15.250.0) and segment it further into 30-bit subnets for serial links. The resulting subnets can be listed as follows:

1. 172.16.250.0/30

2. 172.16.250.4/30

3. 172.16.250.8/30

4. 172.16.250.12/30

5. ...

63. `172.16.250.248/30`

64. `172.16.250.252/30`

In these two lists we have carved the `172.16.0.0` address space using two subnet masks: `255.255.255.0` for users on Ethernet segments and `255.255.255.252` for serial links. Let's recap the steps we took. First, we used the shorter mask (`255.255.255.0`) and listed the resulting subnets. Next, we used one subnet from the first step and subnetted it using the longer mask (`255.255.255.252`). The second step is sometimes referred to as *sub-subnetting*. If we were creating a nightmare of a network and had a third mask to work with as well, we would apply the third mask (the longest mask) on one or more subnets from either of the earlier steps. Following these steps ensures that we do not create overlapping subnets.

If TraderMary's network ran out of all 64 30-bit subnets, another 24-bit subnet (say, `172.16.251.0`) could be carved further to yield another 64 subnets.

See Figure 5-1 for the new addresses on TraderMary's network.

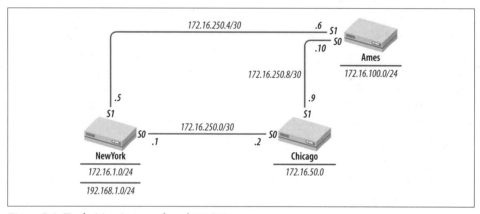

Figure 5-1. TraderMary's network with VLSM

The configuration for this network is as follows:

```
hostname NewYork
...
interface Ethernet0
ip address 172.16.1.1 255.255.255.0
!
interface Ethernet1
ip address 192.168.1.1 255.255.255.0
!
interface Serial0
description New York to Chicago link
ip address 172.16.250.1 255.255.255.252
!
interface Serial1
description New York to Ames link
bandwidth 56
```

```
ip address 172.16.250.5 255.255.255.252
...
router rip
version 2
network 172.16.0.0


hostname Chicago
...
interface Ethernet0
ip address 172.16.50.1 255.255.255.0
!
interface Serial0
description Chicago to New York link
ip address 172.16.250.2 255.255.255.252
!
interface Serial1
description Chicago to Ames link
ip address 172.16.250.9 255.255.255.0
...

router rip
version 2
network 172.16.0.0


hostname Ames
...
interface Ethernet0
ip address 172.16.100.1 255.255.255.0
!
interface Serial0
description Ames to Chicago link
ip address 172.16.250.10 255.255.255.0
!
interface Serial1
description Ames to New York link
bandwidth 56
ip address 172.16.250.6 255.255.255.0
...

router rip
version 2
network 172.16.0.0
```

Next, let's verify that all the routers are seeing all the 172.16.0.0 subnets:

```
NewYork#sh ip route
Codes: C - connected, S - static, I - IGRP, R - RIP, M - mobile, B - BGP
       D - EIGRP, EX - EIGRP external, O - OSPF, IA - OSPF inter area
       N1 - OSPF NSSA external type 1, N2 - OSPF NSSA external type 2
       E1 - OSPF external type 1, E2 - OSPF external type 2, E - EGP
       i - IS-IS, L1 - IS-IS level-1, L2 - IS-IS level-2, * - candidate default

Gateway of last resort is not set
```

```
C       192.168.1.0 is directly connected, Ethernet1
        172.16.0.0/16 is variably subnetted, 6 subnets, 2 masks
C       172.16.1.0/24 is directly connected, Ethernet0
C       172.16.250.0/30 is directly connected, Serial0
C       172.16.250.4/30 is directly connected, Serial1
R       172.16.50.0/24 [120/1] via 172.16.250.2, 0:00:11, Serial0
R       172.16.100.0/24 [120/1] via 172.16.250.6, 0:00:19, Serial1
R       172.16.250.8 [120/1] via 172.16.250.2, 0:00:11, Serial0
                     [120/1] via 172.16.250.6, 0:00:19, Serial1
```

Note that this routing table shows the mask associated with each subnet: /24 or /30.

RIP-2 is supported in Cisco IOS Versions 11.1 and later.

RIP-2 Packet Format

The additions in the RIP-2 update occupy the "must be zero" or unused fields in the RIP-1 update. This careful selection of fields allows older (pre-RIP-2) implementations of RIP to interpret a RIP-2 update by just ignoring the new fields. Let's look closely at the fields in the RIP-2 update shown in Figure 5-2.

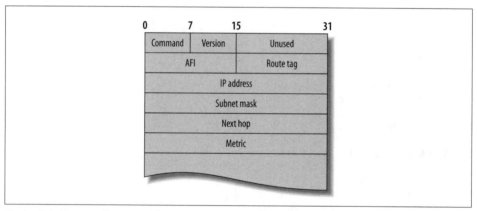

Figure 5-2. Format of RIP-2 update packet

RIP-2 updates are encapsulated in UDP port 520, like RIP-1 updates. However, the destination IP address for a RIP update can be the all-ones broadcast address of 255.255.255.255 or the reserved multicast address of 224.0.0.9. The use of the reserved multicast address frees devices not listening to RIP-2 from the task of unwrapping RIP-2 updates.

The fields *AFI*, *IP address*, and *metric* have the same semantics as in a RIP-1 update packet. See Chapter 2 for details on these fields. The *version* field in RIP-2 updates is 2.

The *route tag* field is not used by RIP but can be used to carry an attribute assigned to the route, such as the AS number of the EGP (for example, BGP) from which the route was imported. The use of route tags is discussed further in Chapter 8.

The *subnet mask* field in each route entry classifies RIP-2 as a *classless* routing protocol and permits the use of VLSM and the support of discontiguous networks.

The *next hop* IP address is usually identical to the IP address of the source of the RIP update. For example, in TraderMary's network, *NewYork* sends an update to *Ames* for 172.16.1.0. The source IP address of the RIP update will be 172.16.250.5, which is identical to the next hop IP address. In such situations, the next hop field will contain no useful information and is set to 0.0.0.0. However, consider the network shown in Figure 5-3.

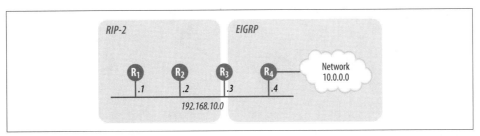

Figure 5-3. Next hop IP address

Routers *R1* and *R2* are running RIP-2. *R4* is running EIGRP, and *R3* is redistributing routes between EIGRP and RIP-2. *R4* learns 10.0.0.0 via EIGRP on interface *Serial0*. *R3* redistributes EIGRP into RIP-2. The next hop field can be used by *R3* to indicate to *R1* and *R2* that the next hop for 10.0.0.0 is 192.168.10.4. If the next hop field were not available, *R1* and *R2* would have sent traffic for 10.0.0.0 to *R3* (192.168.10.3), which would then have to forward the traffic to *R4*.

If authentication is in use, the *authentication fields* take the place of the first route entry in the RIP update packet. An AFI value of 0xFFFF indicates that the route entry contains authentication data (not another route entry). RFC 1723 describes only simple (unencrypted) password authentication. This is indicated by setting the authentication type to 2, which leaves 16 octets for the password. In addition to simple password authentication, Cisco also supports MD5 authentication. When using MD5, Cisco takes the first and last route entries in each update packet to carry cryptographic checksums.

RIP-1/RIP-2 Compatibility

In Chapter 2, we configured RIP as follows on *NewYork* in TraderMary's network:

```
hostname NewYork
...
router rip
network 172.16.0.0
```

This configuration of RIP on a router running IOS 11.1 or later allows the *receipt* of both RIP-1 and RIP-2 updates but the *sending* of only RIP-1 updates.

To modify this configuration to allow the receipt of only RIP-1 updates, specify Version 1 under RIP. In the new configuration, the router will discard any RIP-2 updates it receives and will send only RIP-1 updates:

```
hostname NewYork
...
router rip
version 1
network 172.16.0.0
```

By extension, the following modification allows the receipt of only RIP-2 updates. In this configuration, the router will discard any RIP-1 updates it receives and will send only RIP-2 updates:

```
hostname NewYork
...
router rip
version 2
network 172.16.0.0
```

RIP-1/RIP-2 Interworking

The behavior of RIP can be modified further in interface configuration mode to allow for interworking between RIP-1 and RIP-2 routers.

To send only Version 1 updates out of an interface (for example, when only RIP-1 listeners exist on a network), enter the following command in interface configuration mode:

```
ip rip send version 1
```

To send only Version 2 updates out of an interface (e.g., when only RIP-2 listeners exist on a network), enter the following command in interface configuration mode:

```
ip rip send version 2
```

To send Version 1 and 2 updates out of an interface (e.g., when RIP-1 listeners and RIP-2 listeners coexist on a network), enter the following command in interface configuration mode:

```
ip rip send version 1 2
```

To receive only Version 1 updates on an interface (and to discard any RIP-2 updates), enter the following command in interface configuration mode:

```
ip rip receive version 1
```

To receive only Version 2 updates on an interface (and to discard any RIP-1 updates), enter the following command in interface configuration mode:

```
ip rip receive version 2
```

To receive Version 1 and 2 updates from an interface, enter the following command in interface configuration mode:

```
ip rip receive version 1 2
```

As an example, router *Perth*, configured as follows:

```
hostname Perth
...
router rip
version 2
network 172.22.0.0
```

has RIP-2 routers on all interfaces except *Serial2*, which has a legacy router running RIP-1. To interwork with this RIP-1 router, configure the following on *Serial2*:

```
interface Serial2
ip rip receive version 1
ip rip send version 1
```

When interworking between RIP-1 and RIP-2 and using VLSM, remember that RIP-1 updates do not carry subnet mask information. The RIP-1 portion of your network may end up with improper masks. You may have to resort to static routes or a default route in the event of a discontiguity in the RIP-1 portion of the network.

Classful Versus Classless Routing Protocols

Classful routing protocols do not carry subnet masks; classless routing protocols do. Older routing protocols, including RIP and IGRP, are classful. Newer protocols, including RIP-2, EIGRP, and OSPF, are classless. What are the implications of using classful versus classless routing protocols in your networks?

Let's say that a router *R* received a RIP-1 update with the IP address 172.0.0.0. *R* would assume that the route being advertised was for the Class B network 172.0.0.0/16. In other words, since the subnet mask is lacking in the routing update, *R* assumes a natural mask of /8, /16, and /24 for Class A, B, and C addresses, respectively. The only time a classful routing protocol can associate a mask other than the natural mask with an update is if *R* has a directly connected network with an IP address belonging to the same class as the IP address received in the update. For example, when *Ames* receives an update of 172.16.1.0 from *NewYork*, *Ames* associates a mask of /24 with the update because *Ames* is able to deduce the mask from its own interface.

RIP-2 updates carry a subnet mask in each route entry. A routing protocol that carries subnet masks in its updates earns the label "classless routing protocol." The term "classless" implies that routing decisions are not tied to the class of the IP address—A, B, or C—but may be based on any portion of the 32-bit IP address as specified by the mask. Router *R* could receive an update with the address and mask 192.168.0.0 and 255.255.0.0. This would imply that traffic for all IP addresses with "192.168" in the first two octets should be routed as per the routing advertisement. RIP-2 is thus a classless routing protocol.

Since RIP-2 updates carry subnet masks, it is possible to associate different subnet masks within a single classful network—in other words, RIP-2 supports VLSM. VLSM, a feature of classless routing protocols, is discussed further in the next section.

VLSM

RIP-1 updates do not carry subnet mask information. A router receiving a RIP-1 route deduces the subnet mask from one of its own interfaces, if the router has the same network number. So, for example, when *NewYork* receives the update 172.16. 100.0 from *Ames* it assumes that the mask for this network number is 255.255.255.0 because *NewYork* has an interface (*Ethernet0*) with the same mask. When using RIP-1, there is no room for the support of VLSM.

RIP-2 updates carry subnet masks, so a router receiving the update does not have to guess the mask. RIP-2 updates can carry masks of any length. This permits the network engineer to assign subnet masks that match the true size of the host population. The RIP-2 configuration of TraderMary's network used 24-bit masks for user segments and 30-bit masks for serial links.

When carving a network number into subnets of varying length, it is key that the two subnet populations not overlap. One way to tackle this is to first carve the address space using the shorter mask and then use one or more of the resulting subnets and carve it further using the longer mask, as we did for TraderMary's network.

Use of Subnet Zero

A zero subnet has all zeros in the subnet portion of the IP address. For example, 172. 16.0.0/24 (with host addresses in the range 172.16.0.1 through 172.16.0.254) is a zero subnet. 192.168.100.0/26 is also a zero subnet: the subnet bits are bits 25 and 26 in the IP address, and both are zero.

Zero subnets cannot be used with classful routing protocols. This is because an update for the subnet (without the mask) is indistinguishable from an update for the entire network number. If router *R* received an update for 172.16.0.0, it could not tell if the update was for the entire Class B or just a zero subnet, such as 172.16.0.0/24. Similarly, an update for 192.168.100.0 could mean a path to the entire Class C or just to a zero subnet, such as 192.168.100.0/28. Because of this ambiguity, zero subnets are not permitted to be configured by Cisco IOS. However, a classless routing protocol clearly distinguishes between a zero subnet and the entire network. So, 172.16.0.0 255.255.255.0 would represent a zero subnet, whereas 172.16.0.0 255.255.0.0 would represent the entire network. To configure subnet zero on a router interface, a special command has to be turned on in global configuration mode:

```
ip subnet zero
```

This command relaxes the IOS restriction on configuring zero subnets.

Classless Inter-Domain Routing (CIDR)

Another feature of classless routing protocols is the support of CIDR. The primary use of CIDR is to reduce the size of routing tables by aggregating several classful

---

addresses in a single route entry. All Class C addresses in the range 192.168.0.0 through 192.168.255.0 can be represented by the single route 192.168.0.0/16.

The use of CIDR is most relevant in the Internet, where Class C addresses have been allocated to various service providers in blocks. We will thus reserve further discussion of CIDR to Chapter 7, where we discuss BGP and Internet routing.

Classful Versus Classless Route Lookup

To route a packet, all routers must extract the destination IP address in the packet header. Older (or "classful") routers take this address and compute its major Class A, B, or C network number (for example, the address 172.16.1.1 belongs to the major network 172.16.0.0). This major network number is matched in the routing table. If there is no matching major network number (and there is no default route in the routing table), the packet is dropped. If there is a match against the major network number, the router proceeds to match the subnet field. If there is no matching subnet field in the routing table, the packet is dropped. If there is a matching subnet field, the packet is routed as specified in the route entry. This "classful" routing behavior is described in more detail in Chapter 3.

Classless route lookups also refer to the destination IP address in the packet header. However, classless route lookups do not compute the major Class A, B, or C network number for the destination IP address. Instead, classless routing protocols use a rule called *longest prefix match*. By this rule, the destination IP address from the packet header is matched bit-by-bit against every destination IP address in the routing table. The route entry that has the longest bitwise match with the destination IP address is chosen for routing the packet.

To turn on classless route lookups, enter the following command in global configuration mode:

```
ip classless
```

To turn on classful route lookups, enter the following command in global configuration mode:

```
no ip classless
```

Authentication

There are two reasons to authenticate a routing update. First, for security. After all, if an intruder gains access to a network and begins announcing RIP routes, she will at least disrupt traffic and, in a worse scenario, may maliciously reroute traffic to steal critical data. The second reason for authenticating routing updates is to guard against misconfiguration. For example, using a password on a network backbone will ensure that if a router is attached to the backbone by mistake, it won't begin participating in the backbone routing protocol.

Cisco's implementation of RIP-2 supports two authentication modes: plain-text and MD5. Plain-text authentication works well to guard against misconfigurations but is not a great security solution, since plain-text passwords can be gleaned with a network sniffer.

Passwords must first be defined on each router in global configuration mode. Cisco uses the construct of a "key chain" to define passwords. Let's define a key chain with the name *EmpireStateBldg* on router *NewYork*. The passwords on this key chain are *2000feet* and *1782 feet*.

```
key chain EmpireStateBldg
  key 1
  key-string 2000feet
  key 2
  key-string 1782 feet
```

Routers *Chicago* and *Ames* in TraderMary's network must also be configured with the passwords *2000feet* and *1782 feet*. *Chicago* may be configured as follows:

```
key chain SearsTower
  key 1
  key-string 2000feet
  key 2
  key-string 1782 feet
```

Note that the names of the key chains are not significant: the names of the key chains can be different on each router. The passwords—*2000feet* and *1782 feet*—are significant and must match.

To configure these passwords on an interface, apply the key chain to the interface:

```
hostname NewYork
...
interface Ethernet0
ip address 172.16.1.1 255.255.255.0
!
interface Ethernet1
ip address 192.168.1.1 255.255.255.0
!
interface Serial0
description Link to Chicago
ip address 172.16.250.1 255.255.255.0
ip rip authentication key-chain EmpireStateBldg
!
interface Serial1
description Link to Ames
ip address 172.16.251.1 255.255.255.0
ip rip authentication key-chain EmpireStateBldg
ip rip authentication mode md5
...
router rip
version 2
network 172.16.0.0
```

In this configuration, *Serial1* (to *Ames*) is configured for encryption using MD5, whereas *Serial0* (to *Chicago*) is configured for plain-text authentication, which is the default. *Ames* and *Chicago* would have to be configured for MD5 and plain-text authentication, respectively.

A password encrypted using MD5 cannot be read in plain text, but someone could still copy the encrypted string and play it back. Hence, Cisco introduced the concept of key management, which allows you to define several passwords. The password used at any given time can be defined as follows:

```
key chain EmpireStateBldg
  key 1
  key-string 2000feet
  accept-lifetime 13:00:00 Dec 19 1999 13:00:00 Jan 14 2000
  send-lifetime 13:00:00 Dec 19 1999 13:00:00 Jan 14 2000
  key 2
  key-string 1782 feet
  accept-lifetime 12:00:00 Jan 14 2000 infinite
  send-lifetime 12:00:00 Dec 19 2000 infinite
```

In this example, *2000feet* is a valid password from 1:00 P.M., December 19, 1999 until 1:00 P.M., January 14, 2000. Note that there is an overlap of 1 hour on January 14 (12:00:00 to 13:00:00) during which both *2000feet* and *1782 feet* are valid passwords. This overlap is important to allow for differences in the clocks on the routers, although a time-synchronization protocol such as the Network Time Protocol can also be used to address this issue.

If the lifetime of a key is not specified, the password is always valid.

To check which passwords are active on a router at any given time, use the following command:

```
Chicago#sh key chain
Key-chain SearsTower:
    key 1 -- text "1782feet"
        accept lifetime (13:00:00 Dec 19 1999) - (13:00:00 Jan 14 2000) [valid now]
        send lifetime (13:00:00 Dec 19 1999) - (13:00:00 Jan 14 2000) [valid now]
```

Remember that authentication is available only in RIP Version 2; authentication is not an option when interworking between RIP-1 and RIP-2 routers.

Route Summarization

RIP-2 summarizes on route boundaries just like RIP-1. However, given that RIP-2 is a classless protocol and carries subnet mask information in its updates, it makes sense to allow the network engineer to turn off route summarization to support discontiguous networks. The following command in global configuration mode turns off route summarization:

```
router rip
no auto-summary
```

Summing Up

Why bother with RIP-2? RIP-2, after all, is still RIP. There are still the issues of convergence times and a maximum diameter of 15 hops. Routing updates are sent every 30 seconds and consume network resources. The metric does not account for link bandwidth or delay. These issues with RIP may loom large in your mind if you are building a network from scratch. You have the choice of other, newer routing protocols that do not present these headaches (although they do present other headaches). However, if you are building a small, homogenous network and are not too concerned about occasional convergence problems, RIP-2 may be ideal for you.

RIP-2 may also be a good choice if you are currently running RIP-1 and are happy with it. Maybe your network is small and likely to remain that way. Maybe the link types and speeds in your network are homogenous, so the issue of RIP metrics hasn't bothered you. And maybe there aren't so many paths between any pair of nodes that RIP gets lost during convergence. If you are happy with RIP-1, migrating to RIP-2 may be an excellent solution if you need VLSM, discontiguous address spaces, or authentication. You would still be dealing with RIP—familiar, easy to configure, and reliable—but would have the added benefits of Version 2.

Open Shortest Path First (OSPF)

Last year I flew from New York to Osaka for a conference. My journey began when I hailed a cab on Broadway in downtown New York. "JFK," I told the cabbie, telling her my destination was John F. Kennedy Airport. I was still pushing my luggage down the seat so I could pull my door shut when the cab started to move. The cabbie changed lanes twice before I got it shut. I did make it to JFK in one piece, where I presented my ticket and boarded a flight to Osaka. At Osaka Airport, the taxi driver bowed to me as he took my luggage from my hand. Once the luggage was properly stowed, he asked for my destination. "New Otani Hotel," I told him, and he bowed again and closed my side door.

This everyday story of a passenger in transit illustrates how a traveler is able to complete a journey in spite of the fact that the whereabouts of his destination are not known to every element in the system. The cabbie in New York knows only local destinations and so knows how to get to JFK but not to the New Otani Hotel. The airline routes passengers between major airports. The taxi driver in Osaka also knows only local destinations, so, when returning to New York, I tell the driver that my destination is "Osaka Airport," not "New York." Any single element of the transportation system knows only the *local* geography. This leads to obvious efficiencies: the cabbie in New York needs to know only the New York metropolitan area, and the taxi driver in Osaka needs to know only the area in and around Osaka; the airline is the backbone linking JFK to Osaka.

Much like the transportation system just described, Open Shortest Path First (OSPF) is a *hierarchical* routing protocol, implying that the IP network has a geography with each *area* possessing only local routing information. In contrast, RIP and IGRP are *flat,* implying that there is no hierarchy in the network—every router possesses routes to every destination in the network. Right away, you can see that a flat routing protocol has inherent inefficiencies—in our analogy, if the architecture of the transportation system was flat, the cabbie in New York would have to learn directions to the New Otani Hotel.

A hierarchical architecture, whether that of a transportation system or that of OSPF, allows the support of large systems because each area is responsible only for its local routes. RIP and IGRP cannot support very large networks because the routing overhead increases linearly with the size of the network.

Another radical difference from RIP and IGRP is that OSPF is not a DV protocol— OSPF is based on a Link State algorithm, Dijkstra. What is a Link State algorithm? *Link* refers to a router interface; in other words, the attached network. *State* refers to characteristics of the link such as its IP address, subnet mask, cost (or metric), and operational status (up or down). Routers executing OSPF describe the state of their directly connected links in *link state advertisement* (LSA) packets that are then flooded to all other routers. Using all the LSAs it receives, each router builds a topology of the network. The network topology is described mathematically in the form of a graph.

This topological database is the input to Dijkstra's Shortest Path First (SPF) algorithm. With itself as the root, each router runs the SPF algorithm to compute the shortest path to each network in the graph. Each router then uses its shortest-path tree to build its routing table. Compare this with DV protocols: DV protocols propagate routes from router to router (this is sometimes called routing by rumor) and each router chooses the best route (to each destination) from all the routes (to that destination) that it hears.

DV protocols have to set up special mechanisms to guard against bad routing information that could propagate from router to router. In contrast, routers running the SPF algorithm need to ensure the accuracy of their LS databases; as long as each router has the correct topology information, it can use the SPF algorithm to find the shortest path.

Dijkstra's algorithm is a wonderful tool but, as we shall see in more detail later, the SPF algorithm is expensive in terms of CPU utilization. The cost of running the algorithm increases quickly as the network topology grows. This would be a problem but, given OSPF's hierarchical structure, the network is divided into "small" areas, and the SPF algorithm is executed by each router only on its intra-area topology. So how do routers in two different areas communicate with each other? All areas summarize their routes to a special area called the *backbone area* or *area 0*. The backbone area in turn summarizes routes to all attached areas. Hence, traffic between any two areas must pass through the backbone area (see Figure 6-1).

OSPF derives its name from Dijkstra's SPF algorithm; the prefix "O" signifies that it's an "open" protocol and so is described in an "open" book that everyone can access. That open book is RFC 2328, thanks to John Moy. In contrast, IGRP and EIGRP are Cisco *proprietary* protocols. Multiple vendors support OSPF.

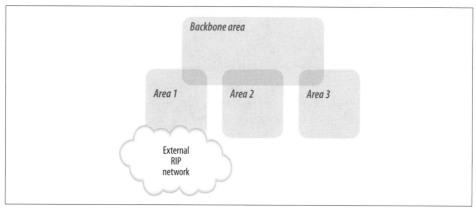

Figure 6-1. Overview of OSPF areas

Getting OSPF Running

Getting RIP, IGRP, and EIGRP running is easy, as we saw in earlier chapters. When TraderMary's network grew to London, Shannon, Ottawa, etc., the DV routing protocols adapted easily to the additions. Getting OSPF running on a small network is also easy, as we will see in this chapter. However, unlike RIP, IGRP, and EIGRP, OSPF is a hierarchical protocol. OSPF does not work well if the network topology grows as a haphazard mesh.

In this section, we will configure OSPF on a small network. In later sections, we will learn how to build hierarchical OSPF networks.

TraderMary's network, shown in Figure 6-2, can be configured to run OSPF as follows.

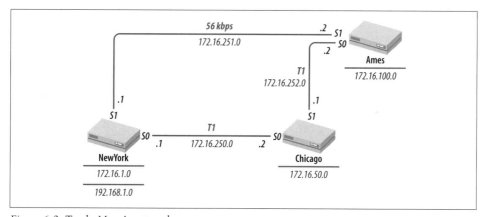

Figure 6-2. TraderMary's network

Like RIP and IGRP, OSPF is a distributed protocol that needs to be configured on every router in the network:

```
    hostname NewYork
    ...
    interface Ethernet0
    ip address 172.16.1.1 255.255.255.0
    !
    interface Serial0
    description New York to Chicago link
    ip address 172.16.250.1 255.255.255.0
    !
    interface Serial1
    description New York to Ames link
1   bandwidth 56
    ip address 172.16.251.1 255.255.255.0
    ...
    router ospf 10
    network 172.16.0.0 0.0.255.255 area 0
```

The *router ospf* command starts the OSPF process on the router. The syntax of this command is:

```
    router ospf process-id
```

The *process-id*, which should be between 1 and 65,535, is used to identify the instance of the OSPF process. The *process-id* configured in the previous example is 10. Router *Chicago* is similarly configured with the same *process-id*:

```
    hostname Chicago
    ...
    interface Ethernet0
    ip address 172.16.50.1 255.255.255.0
    !
    interface Serial0
    description Chicago to New York link
    ip address 172.16.250.2 255.255.255.0
    !
    interface Serial1
    description Chicago to Ames link
    ip address 172.16.252.1 255.255.255.0
    ...

    router ospf 10
    network 172.16.0.0 0.0.255.255 area 0
```

Router *Ames* is also configured with OSPF:

```
    hostname Ames
    ...
    interface Ethernet0
    ip address 172.16.100.1 255.255.255.0
    !
    interface Serial0
```

```
     description Ames to Chicago link
     ip address 172.16.252.2 255.255.255.0
     !
     interface Serial1
     description Ames to New York link
  2  bandwidth 56
     ip address 172.16.251.2 255.255.255.0
     ...

     router ospf 10
     network 172.16.0.0 0.0.255.255 area 0
```

We next identify the networks that will be participating in the OSPF process and associate an area ID with each network. The syntax of this command is:

```
network address wildcard-mask area area-id
```

The *address* and *wildcard-mask* fields identify a network by its IP address. Networks that match the *address* and *wildcard-mask* fields are associated with the area *area-id*. How is a network's IP address matched against *address* and *wildcard-mask*?

wildcard-mask is a string of zeros and ones. An occurrence of a zero in *wildcard-mask* implies that the IP address being checked must exactly match the corresponding bit in *address*. An occurrence of a one in *wildcard-mask* implies that the corresponding bit in the IP address field is a "don't care bit"—the match is already successful.

Thus, the following clause can be read as stating that the first 16 bits of an IP address must be exactly "172.16" for the address to match the clause and be associated with area 0 and that the next 16 bits of the IP address are "don't care bits":

```
network 172.16.0.0 0.0.255.255 area 0
```

Any IP address, such as 172.16.x.y, will match this *address/wildcard-mask* and be assigned the area ID of 0. Any other address, such as 10.9.x.y, will not match this *address/wildcard-mask*.

If an interface IP address does not match the *address/wildcard-mask* on a network statement, OSPF will check for a match against the next network statement, if there is another statement. Hence, the order of network statements is important. If an interface IP address does not match the *address/wildcard-mask* on any network statement, that interface will not participate in OSPF.

There is more than one method of assigning area IDs to networks. The most rigorous method specifically lists every network when making a match. The wildcard mask contains only zeros:

```
     hostname NewYork
     ...
     router ospf 10
     network 172.16.1.1 0.0.0.0 area 0
     network 172.16.250.1 0.0.0.0 area 0
     network 172.16.251.1 0.0.0.0 area 0
```

The most loose method is an all-ones wildcard mask:

```
hostname NewYork
...
router ospf 10
network 0.0.0.0 255.255.255.255 area 0
```

Note that in the second (loose) method, network 192.168.1.1 also belongs to area 0.

If an IP address does not match an area-ID specification, the match continues to the next statement. So, for example, a router may be configured as follows:

```
network 172.16.0.0 0.0.255.255 area 0
network 192.0.0.0 0.255.255.255 area 1
```

An IP address of 192.168.1.1 will not match the first statement. The match will then continue to the next statement. All IP addresses with "192" in the first 8 bits will match the second clause and hence will fall into area 1. A network with the address 10.9.1.1 will not match either statement and hence will not participate in OSPF.

The *area-id* field is 32 bits in length. You can specify the area ID in the decimal number system, as we did earlier, or in the dotted-decimal notation that we use for expressing IP addresses. Thus, the area ID 0.0.0.0 (in dotted decimal) is identical to the area ID 0 (in decimal); the area ID 0.0.0.100 (in dotted decimal) is identical to 100 (in decimal); and the area ID 0.0.1.0 (in dotted decimal) is identical to 256 (in decimal). The area ID of 0 is reserved for the backbone area. The area ID for nonbackbone areas can be in the range 1 to 4,294,967,295 (or, equivalently, 0.0.0.1 to 255.255.255.255).

The *show ip ospf interface* command shows the assignment of area IDs to network interfaces:

```
NewYork#sh ip ospf interface
...
Ethernet0 is up, line protocol is up
  Internet Address 172.16.1.1/24, Area 0
  Process ID 10, Router ID 172.16.251.1, Network Type BROADCAST, Cost: 10
  ...
Serial0 is up, line protocol is up
  Internet Address 172.16.250.1/24, Area 0
  Process ID 10, Router ID 172.16.251.1, Network Type POINT_TO_POINT, Cost: 64
...
Serial1 is up, line protocol is up
  Internet Address 172.16.251.1/24, Area 0

  Process ID 10, Router ID 172.16.251.1, Network Type POINT_TO_POINT, Cost: 1785
...
```

The routing tables for *NewYork*, *Chicago*, and *Ames* will show all 172.16.0.0 subnets. Here is *NewYork*'s table:

```
NewYork#sh ip route
Codes: C - connected, S - static, I - IGRP, R - RIP, M - mobile, B - BGP
       D - EIGRP, EX - EIGRP external, O - OSPF, IA - OSPF inter area
       N1 - OSPF NSSA external type 1, N2 - OSPF NSSA external type 2
```

```
               E1 - OSPF external type 1, E2 - OSPF external type 2, E - EGP
               i - IS-IS, L1 - IS-IS level-1, L2 - IS-IS level-2, * - candidate default

   Gateway of last resort is not set

5          172.16.0.0/16 is variably subnetted, 6 subnets, 2 masks
6  O           172.16.252.0/24 [110/128] via 172.16.250.2, 01:50:18, Serial0
   C           172.16.250.0/24 is directly connected, Serial0
   C           172.16.251.0/24 is directly connected, Serial1
7  O           172.16.50.1/32 [110/74] via 172.16.250.2, 01:50:18, Serial0
   C           172.16.1.0/24 is directly connected, Ethernet0
8  O           172.16.100.1/32 [110/138] via 172.16.250.2, 01:50:18, Serial0
```

The OSPF-derived routes in this table are labeled with an "O" in the left margin. Note that the routing table provides summary information (as in line 5). This line contains subnet mask information (24 bits, or 255.255.255.0) and the number of subnets in 172.16.0.0 (6).

OSPF Metric

Each OSPF router executes Dijkstra's SPF algorithm to compute the shortest-path tree from itself to every subnetwork in its area. However, RFC 2328 does not specify how a router should compute the cost of an attached network—this is left to the vendor. Cisco computes the cost of an attached network as follows:

Cost = 10^8/bandwidth of interface in bits per second

Using this definition, the OSPF cost for some common media types is shown in Table 6-1. Table 6-1 assumes default interface bandwidth. Note that the cost is rounded down to the nearest integer.

Table 6-1. Default OSPF costs

Media type	Default bandwidth	Default OSPF cost
Ethernet	10 Mbps	10
Fast Ethernet	100 Mbps	1
FDDI	100 Mbps	1
T-1 (serial interface)[a]	1,544 kbps	64
56 kbps (serial interface)	1,544 kbps	64
HSSI	45,045 kbps	2

[a] All serial interfaces on Cisco routers are configured with the same default bandwidth (1,544 kbits/s) and delay (20,000 ms) parameters.

The OSPF cost computed by a router can be checked with the command *show ip ospf interface*, as in line 4 in the code block in the previous section, where the cost of the Ethernet segment is 10. The composite cost of reaching a destination is the sum of the individual costs of all networks in the path to the destination and can be seen as output of the *show ip route* command in lines 6, 7, and 8.

The default value of the OSPF metric may not be adequate in some situations. For example, in TraderMary's configuration, the *NewYork → Ames* link runs at 56 kbps, but the default metric makes it appear to be a T-1. This was fixed by modifying the interface bandwidth, as in lines 3 and 4 in the previous section. The command to modify a bandwidth is:

    bandwidth kilobits

Keep in mind that modifying the interface bandwidth impacts other protocols that utilize the bandwidth parameter, such as IGRP. Modifying bandwidth may not always be viable. In such situations, the OSPF cost of an interface may be directly specified:

    ip ospf cost value

where *value* is an integer in the range 1 to 65,535 (OSPF sets aside two octets to represent interface cost, as we will see later in the section "How OSPF Works").

This approach to calculating OSPF costs does not work well for network speeds greater than 100 Mbps. The OSPF cost for all speeds greater than the reference bandwidth is rounded up to 1, and there is no way to distinguish between one network and another. The network engineer has two approaches to choose from here. First, manually configure the OSPF cost for all interfaces equal to or faster than 100 Mbps. For example, all FE interfaces may be configured with a cost of 8, OC-3 interfaces with a cost of 6, and GE interfaces with a cost of 4. Second, redefine the reference bandwidth with the following command:

    ospf auto-cost reference-bandwidth reference-bandwidth

where *reference-bandwidth* is in Mbps. When this command is used, the cost of an interface is calculated as:

Cost = reference-bandwidth-in-bps/bandwidth of interface in bits per second

This command is available in Cisco IOS Releases 11.2 and later. If the reference bandwidth is modified, it must be modified on all routers in the OSPF domain. The default value of *reference-bandwidth* is 10^8.

The developers of OSPF envisaged (as an optional feature) multiple *types of service* (TOS) with differing metrics for each TOS. Using this concept, bulk data may be routed, say, over a satellite link, whereas interactive data may be routed under the sea. However, the TOS concept has not been carried into any major implementations—Cisco supports only one TOS.

Definitions and Concepts

Dijkstra's algorithm solves the problem of discovering the shortest path from a single source to all vertices in a graph where the edges are each represented with a cost. For example, a car driver could use Dijkstra's algorithm to find the shortest paths from New York to major cities in the northeastern U.S. and Canada. The input to Dijkstra would be a graph that could be represented by a matrix like that shown in Table 6-2.

Table 6-2. Driving distances

Town name	Town name	Driving distance (miles)
New York	Washington	236
New York	Boston	194
Boston	Chicago	996
Washington	Chicago	701
New York	Toronto	496
Detroit	Chicago	288
Washington	Detroit	527
Boston	Toronto	555
Toronto	Detroit	292

The output would be the shortest paths from New York to all other cities in the graph. A geographical view of Table 6-2 is contained in Figure 6-3.

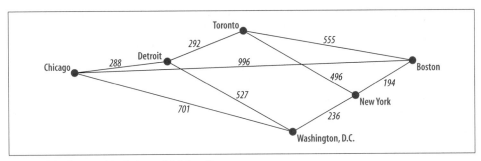

Figure 6-3. Geographical view of driving distances

There are six nodes in this graph: New York, Chicago, Boston, Toronto, Detroit, and Washington. There are nine edges in the graph, each represented by the distance between a pair of vertices. The SPF algorithm works as follows:

1. Starting at the source node—New York—build a list of one-segment paths originating at the source node. This list will be New York → Washington, New York → Boston, and New York → Toronto.

2. Sort this list in increasing order. The sorted list will be New York → Boston (194), New York → Washington (236), and New York → Toronto (496).

3. Pick the shortest path from this list—New York → Boston—and move Boston to the list of vertices for which the shortest path has been identified.

4. Next, append a new list of paths to the list that was defined in step 1. The list to be appended consists of one-segment paths starting from Boston. This list will be Boston → Chicago and Boston → Toronto. The composite list will be New York → Washington, New York → Toronto, Boston → Chicago, and Boston → Toronto.

The algorithm continues, as in step 2, and the composite list is sorted in increasing order with distances from the source node: New York → Washington (236), New York → Toronto (496), New York → Boston → Toronto (194 + 555 = 749), and New York → Boston → Chicago (194 + 996 = 1,190). In step 3, the shortest path is again picked from the top of the list and Washington is added to the list of vertices for which the shortest path has been identified. The algorithm continues until the shortest paths to all cities have been identified.

OSPF employs Dijkstra's SPF algorithm to compute the shortest path from a router to every network in the graph. In OSPF terminology, this graph of the network topology (similar to Table 6-2) is referred to as the topological database or the *link state database*. Each router executes the SPF algorithm with itself as the source node. The results of the SPF algorithm are the shortest paths to each IP network from the source node; hence, this constitutes the IP routing table for the router.

Although the database of Table 6-2 is relatively static—driving distances change only when new roads are built or old roads are closed—the LS database for a network is quite dynamic because of changes in the state of subnetworks. A link may go down or come up. A network administrator may make changes to the status of a link, such as shutting it down or changing its cost. Every time there is any change in a router's LS database, Dijkstra's SPF algorithm needs to be run again. It can be shown that the SPF algorithm takes ElogE time to run, where E is the number of edges in the graph.

As the size of a network grows, Dijkstra will consume more and more memory and CPU resources at each router. In other words, Dijkstra does not scale for large topologies. Fortunately, OSPF has a clever solution to this problem: break the network into *areas* and execute Dijkstra only on each *intra-area* topology.

An area is a collection of *contiguous* networks and routers that share a unique area ID. Each area maintains its own topological database: other areas do not see this topological information. The SPF algorithm is executed on each intra-area topology by the intra-area routers.

Containing the number of routers and networks in an area allows OSPF to scale to support large networks. The network can grow almost without bounds with the addition of new areas. If a single area becomes too large, it can be split into two or more areas.

Before a router can execute the SPF algorithm, it must have the most recent topological database for its area(s). Note the plural: a router may have interfaces in multiple areas. A topological change in an area will cause SPF to recompute on all routers with interfaces in that area. Routers in other areas will not be affected by the change. Breaking a network into areas is thus akin to breaking a network into smaller, independent networks.

Unlike flat networks such as RIP and IGRP in which each router has the same responsibilities and tasks, OSPF's hierarchy imposes a structure in which routers and even areas are differentiated with respect to their roles.

Backbone Area

The *backbone area* is of special significance in OSPF because all other areas must connect to it. The area ID of 0 (or 0.0.0.0) is reserved for the backbone. Figure 6-4 shows an OSPF network comprised of a backbone area and three other areas—areas 1, 2, and 3. Note that all inter-area traffic must pass through the backbone area, which implies that backbone routers must possess the complete topological database for the network.

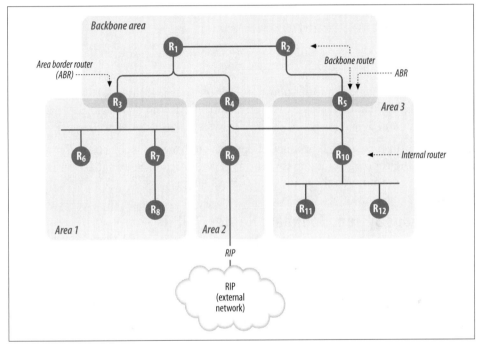

Figure 6-4. OSPF architecture: a high-level view

Backbone Router

A router with an interface in area 0 is referred to as a *backbone router*. A backbone router may also have interfaces in other areas. Routers *R1*, *R2*, *R3*, *R4*, and *R5* in Figure 6-4 are backbone routers.

The backbone routers hold a topological database that describes the state of all backbone links, summary links describing IP networks in areas 1, 2, and 3, and external links that describe the IP network in the RIP network.

Area or Regular Area

A *regular area* has a unique area ID in the range 1 (or 0.0.0.1) to 4,294,967,295 (255.255.255.255).

A router in, say, area 1 will hold topological information for the state of all area 1 links, summary links that describe IP networks in areas 0, 2, and 3, and external links that describe IP networks in those networks.

Internal Router

An *internal router* has interfaces in one area only. Routers R6, R7, and R8 in Figure 6-4 are internal routers in area 1.

Area Border Router (ABR)

An *area border router* has interfaces in more than one area. Routers R3, R4, and R5 in Figure 6-4 are ABRs.

An ABR has topological information for multiple areas. Router R3 is an ABR that holds topological databases for areas 0 and 1. Router R4 holds topological databases for areas 0, 2, and 3. Router R5 holds topological databases for areas 0 and 3.

An ABR can summarize the topological database for one of its areas. Router R3 may summarize the topological database for area 1 into area 0. Summarization is key in reducing the computational complexity of the OSPF process.

Autonomous System Boundary Router (ASBR)

An *autonomous system boundary router* imports routing information from another AS into OSPF. The routes imported into OSPF from the other AS are referred to as *external routes*.

Router R9 in Figure 6-4 is an ASBR. R9 imports RIP routes from an external network into OSPF. An ASBR may be configured to summarize external routes into OSPF.

Stub Area

Consider an area with no direct connections to any external networks. Importing external records into this area may be unnecessary because all traffic to external networks must be routed to the ABRs. Such an area can use a default route (in place of external routes) to send all external IP traffic to its ABRs.

Configuring an area as a *stub area* blocks the advertisement of external IP records at the ABRs and instead causes the ABRs to generate default routes into the stub area.

Routers in a stub area hold a topological database that describes the state of all local links, summary links describing IP networks in other areas, but no external networks. This reduction in the size of the topological database saves on processor and memory resources. A stub area may use routers with less memory/CPU power or use the spare memory/CPU resources to build a *large* stub area.

There is a potential disadvantage to configuring an area as a stub area. For example, if area 3 in Figure 6-4 is configured as a stub area, R4 and R5 will each advertise a default route into the stub area. An external route may be closer to R4, but routers in the stub area will lose that information and route all external traffic to R4 or R5, depending on which one is closer. Stub areas cannot support external connections since stub routers do not carry external LSAs. Stub areas cannot support virtual links, which I'll discuss later in this chapter, for similar reasons.

Totally Stubby Area

A *totally stubby area* carries the concept of a stub area further by blocking summary records for IP networks in other areas at the ABRs. All inter-area and external traffic is matched to the default route announced by the ABR(s).

In terms of LSA types, routers in totally stubby areas hold a topological database that describes the state of all local links only.

Just like a stub area, a totally stubby area cannot support connections to external networks.

Not So Stubby Area (NSSA)

Not so stubby areas are stub areas with one less restriction: NSSAs can support external connections. In all other respects, NSSAs are just like stub areas—routers in NSSAs do not carry external LSAs, nor do they support virtual links.

Any area that can be configured as a stub area but needs to support an external network can be changed into an NSSA.

OSPF Topological Database

The OSPF topological database is composed of link state advertisements (LSAs). OSPF routers originate LSAs describing a piece of the network topology; these LSAs are flooded to other routers that then compose a database of LSAs. There are several types of LSAs, each originating at a different router and describing a different component of the network topology. The various types of LSAs are:

Router LSA (type 1)
> A router LSA describes a router's links (or interfaces). All routers originate router LSAs. A router LSA is flooded to all intra-area routers.

Network LSA (type 2)
> A network LSA describes a broadcast network (such as an Ethernet segment) or a non-broadcast multi-access (NBMA) network (such as Frame Relay). All routers attached to the broadcast/NBMA network are described in the LSA. A network LSA is flooded to all intra-area routers.

Summary LSA (type 3)

A summary LSA describes IP networks in another area. The summary LSA is originated by an ABR and flooded outside the area. Summary LSAs are flooded to routers in all OSPF areas except totally stubby areas.

ASBR summary LSA (type 4)

ASBR summary LSAs describe the route to an ASBR. The mask associated with these LSAs is 32 bits long because the route they advertise is to a host—the IP address of the ASBR. ASBR summary LSAs originate at ASBRs. ASBR summary LSAs are flooded to routers in all OSPF areas except stub areas.

External LSA (type 5)

External LSAs describe routes external to the OSPF process (in another autonomous system). An external route can be a default route. External LSAs originate at the ASBR. External LSAs are flooded throughout the OSPF network, except to stub areas.

NSSA external LSA (type 7)

NSSA external LSAs describe routes to external networks (in another autonomous system) connected to the NSSA. Unlike type 5 external LSAs, NSSA external LSAs are flooded only within the NSSA. Optionally, type 7 LSAs may be translated to type 5 LSAs at the ABR and flooded as type 5 LSAs.

OSPF Route Types

Every router in OSPF uses its local topological database as input to the SPF algorithm. The SPF algorithm yields the shortest path to every known destination, which is then used to populate the IP routing table as one of four route types:

Intra-area route

An intra-area route describes the route to a destination within the area.

Inter-area route

An inter-area route describes the route to a destination in another area. The path to the destination comprises an intra-area path, a path through the backbone area and an intra-area path in the destination network's area. An inter-area route is sometimes referred to as a summary route.

External route (type 1)

An external route describes the route to a destination outside the AS. The cost of a type 1 external route is the sum of the costs of reaching the destination in the external network and the cost of reaching the ASBR advertising the route.

External route (type 2)

An external route describes the route to a destination outside the AS. The cost of a type 2 external route is the cost of reaching the destination in the external network only; it does not include the cost of reaching the ASBR advertising the route.

When routing a packet, the routing table is scanned for the most specific match. For example, say that the destination IP address in the packet is 10.1.1.254 and the routing table contains entries for 10.1.1.0/24 and 10.1.1.192/26. The most specific match will be the route 10.1.1.192/26. Now, what if 10.1.1.192/26 was known as an intra-area route and an inter-area route? OSPF prefers routes in the following order: intra-area routes (most preferred), inter-area routes, type 1 external routes, and type 2 external routes (least preferred).

Note the order in which the rules were applied: first the route with the most specific match was identified and then the OSPF preferences were applied. Thus, when routing the packet with the destination address 10.1.1.254, if the routing table shows 10.1.1.0/24 as an intra-area route and 10.1.1.192/26 as a type 2 external route, the most specific match (10.1.1.192/26) will win. If OSPF has multiple equal-cost routes to a destination, it will load-balance traffic over those routes.

How OSPF Works

OSPF routers must first discover each other before they can exchange their topological databases. Once each router has the complete topological database, it can use the SPF algorithm to compute the shortest path to every network. This section focuses on neighbor discovery and the exchange of topological databases.

Let's begin at the beginning. OSPF packets are encapsulated directly in IP with the protocol field set to 89. The destination IP address in OSPF depends on the network type. OSPF uses two IP multicast addresses on broadcast and point-to-point networks: 225.0.0.5 for all OSPF routers and 224.0.0.6 for all DR/BDR (designated router/backup designated router) routers. Using IP multicast addresses is more efficient than using broadcast addresses. If broadcast addresses are used, all attached devices must receive the broadcast packet, unwrap it, and then discard the contents if they are not running OSPF. NBMA networks and virtual links use unicast addresses because they do not support multicast addresses.

Following the IP header is the OSPF header (see Figure 6-5). The OSPF header is common to all types of OSPF packets. The following list defines the format of the OSPF header and the five types of OSPF packets:

Version
  The OSPF version in use. The current version number is 2.

Type
  There are five types of OSPF packets:

  Type 1
    Hello packets, described in the next section.

  Type 2
    Database description packets, described later under "Database Exchange."

Type 3
> Link state requests, described in "Database Exchange."

Type 4
> Link state updates, described in "Database Exchange."

Type 5
> Link state acknowledgments, described in "Database Exchange."

Packet length
> The length of the OSPF packet, including the header.

Router ID
> The router ID of the router originating the OSPF packet.

Area ID
> The area ID of the network on which this packet is being sent.

Checksum
> The checksum for the entire packet, including the header.

Au type
> The type of authentication scheme in use. The possible values for this field are:

0   No authentication

1   Clear-text password authentication

2   MD5 checksum

Authentication data
> The authentication data.

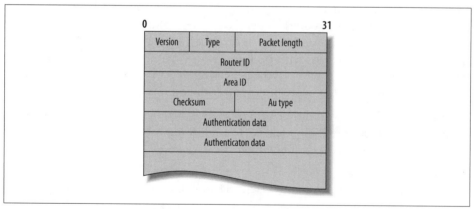

Figure 6-5. Format of an OSPF header

Neighbor Discovery: The Hello Protocol

Every router generates OSPF hello packets on every OSPF-enabled interface. Hello packets are sent every 10 seconds on broadcast media and every 30 seconds on non-broadcast media. Routers discover their neighbors by listening to hellos. The output of the command *show ip ospf neighbor* lists the neighbors that have been discovered.

Each hello packet contains the fields described in the following sections. The format of a hello packet is shown in Figure 6-6.

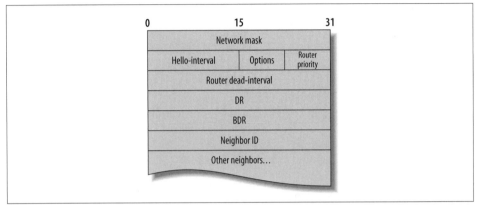

Figure 6-6. Format of hello packet

Router ID

When the OSPF process first starts on a router (e.g., when the router is powered up) it attempts to establish a *router ID*. The router ID is the name or label that will be attached to the node representing the router in the SPF topology graph. If OSPF cannot establish a router ID, the OSPF process aborts.

How does a router choose its router ID? There are two situations to consider here:

- If a router has one or more loopback interfaces, it chooses the highest IP address from the pool of loopback interfaces as its router ID. Loopback interfaces are always active.

- If a router has no loopback interfaces, it chooses the highest IP address from any of its active interfaces as its router ID. If a router has no active interface with an IP address, it will not start the OSPF process.

The router ID is chosen when the OSPF process first starts: the addition or deletion of interfaces or addresses on a router after the router ID has been selected does not change the router ID. A new router ID is picked only when the router is restarted (or when the OSPF process is restarted).

So, for example, the router ID of *NewYork* can be checked as follows:

```
NewYork#sh ip ospf
 Routing Process "ospf 10" with ID 172.16.251.1
 Supports only single TOS(TOS0) routes
 SPF schedule delay 5 secs, Hold time between two SPFs 10 secs
 ......
```

In this example, the router ID was derived using the router's highest IP address. It is usually preferable to configure loopback interfaces to assign predictable router IDs to OSPF routers (since a loopback interface is a virtual interface and will not go down, as a physical interface would). The router ID must be unique within the topology database.

The configuration on *NewYork* may be modified as follows:

```
hostname NewYork
!
interface Loopback0
 ip address 192.168.1.1 255.255.255.255
...
```

After *NewYork* is rebooted, its router ID will change as follows:

```
NewYork#sh ip ospf
 Routing Process "ospf 10" with ID 192.168.1.1
...
```

Since the router ID is critical to the OSPF process, it is important for the network engineer to maintain a table of all router IDs.

Note the following points:

1. Since the router ID is needed only to represent the router in the SPF graph, it is not required that OSPF advertise the router ID. However, if the router ID is advertised, it will be represented as a stub link in a router LSA.

2. A mask of `255.255.255.255` may be chosen for the loopback interface to conserve on network addresses, as in the earlier example.

3. If the router ID is not advertised, any unique address can be used to represent the router ID—the use of nonreserved IP addresses will not cause any routing-table conflicts.

Area ID

The area ID of the interface on which the OSPF packet is being sent.

Checksum

The checksum pertaining to the hello packet.

Authentication

The authentication method and authentication data.

Network mask

The network mask of the interface on which the hello packet is being sent.

Hello-interval

The duration between hello packets. The default value of hello-interval is 10 seconds on most interfaces.

The hello-interval can be modified with the following command in interface configuration mode:

```
ip ospf hello-interval seconds
```

Options

OSPF defines several optional capabilities that a router may or may not support. The options field is one octet long, as shown in Figure 6-7.

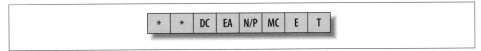

Figure 6-7. Format of the options field

Routers that support demand circuits set the DC bit; NSSA support is signified using the N bit. The E bit signifies that the router accepts external LSAs—stub routers turn off this bit. The T bit signifies the support of multiple types of service.

Router priority

A router with a higher priority takes precedence in the DR election algorithm. A value of 0 makes the router ineligible for DR/BDR election. The default value of this field is 1.

Router dead-interval

If no hello packets are received for the duration of the dead-interval, the neighbor is declared dead. This value can be altered with the following command in interface configuration mode:

```
ip ospf dead-interval value
```

Designated router (DR)

The designated router for multi-access networks. This field is set to 0.0.0.0 if no DR has been elected on the network.

Backup designated router

The IP address of the backup designated router's interface on this network. This field is set to 0.0.0.0 if no BDR has been elected on the network.

Neighbor router ID list

The neighbor router ID list is the list of neighboring routers from which this router has received hellos within the last dead-interval seconds. Before a router lists its neighbor in its hello packet, the two routers must agree on the following: area ID, authentication mechanism, network mask, hello-interval, router dead-interval, and options fields. If these values match, the routers become neighbors and start listing each other in their hello packets.

The following output shows *NewYork*'s neighbors:

```
NewYork#show ip ospf neighbor

Neighbor ID    Pri   State         Dead Time   Address        Interface
192.168.1.2     1    FULL/   -     00:00:31    172.16.250.2    Serial0
192.168.1.3     1    FULL/   -     00:00:32    172.16.251.2    Serial1
```

Note that the state of *NewYork*'s relationship with both neighbors is "Full," implying that the neighbors have exchanged LS databases to become adjacent. Under normal, stable conditions, the state of each neighbor relationship should be "2-way" or "Full." "2-way" implies that the neighbors have seen each other's hello packets but have not exchanged LSAs. In the process of maturing into a "Full" relationship, neighbors transition through the states "Exstart," "Exchange," and "Loading," indicating that neighbors have seen each other's hello packets and are attempting to exchange their LS databases. These are transitory states, all being well.

Then there are the problem states. "Down" indicates that a hello packet has not been received from the neighbor in the last router dead-interval. "Attempt" applies to NBMA networks and indicates that a hello has not yet been received from the neighbor. "Init" implies that a hello was received from the neighbor but its neighbor router ID list did not include the router ID of this router.

DR/BDR Election

Consider *n* routers on a broadcast network (such as Ethernet). If a router exchanged its topological database with every other router on the network, $(n \times (n - 1)) / 2$ adjacencies would be formed on the segment. This would create a lot of OSPF overhead traffic. OSPF solves this problem by electing a *designated router* (DR) and a *backup designated router* (BDR) on each broadcast network. Each router on a broadcast network establishes an adjacency with only the DR and the BDR. The DR and the BDR flood this topology information to all other routers on the segment.

DR/BDR election can be described in the following steps. Remember that the DR/BDR election process occurs on every multi-access network (not router). A router may be the DR on one interface but not another.

The following description assumes that a router *R* has just been turned up on a multi-access network:

1. On becoming active on a multi-access network, the OSPF process on router *R* begins receiving hellos from neighbors on its interface to the multi-access network. If the hellos indicate that there already are a DR and a BDR, the DR/BDR election process is terminated (even if *R*'s OSPF priority is higher than the current DR/BDR priority).

2. If hellos from neighbors indicate that there is no active BDR on the network, the router with the highest priority is elected the BDR. If the highest priority is shared by more than one router, the router with the highest router ID wins.

3. If there is no active DR on the network, the BDR is promoted to DR.

The following can be stated as corollaries of the above rules:

1. If a DR and BDR have already been elected, bringing up a new router (even with a higher priority) will not alter the identities of the DR/BDR.

2. If there is only one DR-eligible router on a multi-access network, that router will become the DR.

3. If there are only two DR-elegible routers on a multi-access network, one will be the DR and the other, the BDR.

A router with a higher priority takes precedence during DR election. A priority value of 0 indicates that the router is ineligible for DR election. The default priority value is 1. Routers with low memory and CPU resources should be made ineligible for DR election.

The router interface priority may be modified with the following command in interface configuration mode:

```
ip ospf priority number
```

where *number* is between 0 and 255.

The state of an OSPF interface (including the result of the DR/BDR election process) can be seen as output of the *show ip ospf interface* command:

```
     NewYork#sh ip ospf interface
     Ethernet0 is up, line protocol is up
       Internet Address 172.16.1.1/24, Area 0
       Process ID 10, Router ID 172.16.251.1, Network Type BROADCAST, Cost: 10
  9    Transmit Delay is 1 sec, State DR, Priority 1
       Designated Router (ID) 172.16.251.1, Interface address 172.16.1.1
 10    No backup designated router on this network
       Timer intervals configured, Hello 10, Dead 40, Wait 40, Retransmit 5
         Hello due in 00:00:02
 11    Neighbor Count is 0, Adjacent neighbor count is 0
       Suppress hello for 0 neighbor(s)
     ...
```

Note that *NewYork* is the DR on *Ethernet0*. Since there is no other router on this network, there is no BDR (line 10) and the router has not established any adjacencies (line 11).

Interface State

The state of an interface can have one of the following values:

Down
> The interface state is down as indicated by lower-level protocols, and no OSPF traffic has been sent or received yet.

Loopback
> The interface is looped and will be advertised in LSAs as a host route.

Point-to-point
> The interface is up and is recognized as a serial interface or a virtual link. After entering the point-to-point state, the neighbors will attempt to establish adjacency.

Waiting
> This state applies only to broadcast/NBMA networks on which the router is attempting to identify the DR/BDR.

DR
> This router is the DR on the attached network.

Backup
> This router is the BDR on the attached network.

DRother
> This router is neither the DR nor the BDR on the attached network. The router will form adjacencies with the DR and BDR (if they exist).

As an example, the state of *NewYork*'s interface to *Chicago* is point-to-point (line 12) and *NewYork* and *Chicago* have established adjacency (lines 13 and 14):

```
NewYork#sh ip ospf interface
...
Serial0 is up, line protocol is up
  Internet Address 172.16.250.1/24, Area 0
  Process ID 10, Router ID 172.16.251.1, Network Type POINT_TO_POINT, Cost: 64
12  Transmit Delay is 1 sec, State POINT_TO_POINT,
  Timer intervals configured, Hello 10, Dead 40, Wait 40, Retransmit 5
    Hello due in 00:00:01
13  Neighbor Count is 1, Adjacent neighbor count is 1
14    Adjacent with neighbor 69.1.1.1
  Suppress hello for 0 neighbor(s)
```

Neighbor Relationship

Not all neighbors establish adjacency. Neighbors may stay at "2-way" or enter into a "Full" relationship, depending on the type of network, as follows:

Point-to-point networks
> Routers on point-to-point networks always establish adjacency.

Broadcast networks
Routers on broadcast networks establish adjacency only with the DR and the BDR, maintaining a 2-way relationship with the other routers on the network.

Non-broadcast multi-access (NBMA) networks
Routers on NBMA networks establish adjacency only with the DR and the BDR.

Virtual links
Routers on virtual links always establish adjacency.

Database Exchange

The *database description (DD) packet* is used to describe the contents of the LS database to a peer OSPF router. Only LSA headers are sent in DD packets; the peer router responds by sending its own LSA headers in DD packets.

The LSA header (Figure 6-8) uniquely identifies a piece of the OSPF network topology. The key fields in the LSA header are the *advertising router*, *LS type*, and *link state ID*. The advertising router is the router ID of the originator of the LSA. The LS type identifies the type of the LSA that follows. The link state ID depends on the LS type, as shown in Table 6-3.

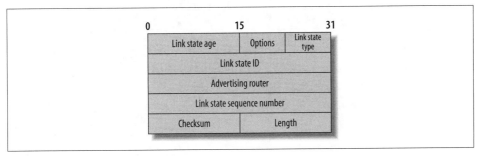

Figure 6-8. Format of an LSA header

Table 6-3. LS type and link state ID

LS type	Link state ID
1 (router LSA)	Router ID of the originator of the LSA
2 (network LSA)	IP address of the DR's interface to the multi-access network
3 (summary LSA)	IP address of the destination network
4 (ASBR summary LSA)	Router ID of the ASBR
5 (external LSA)	IP address of the destination network

Several copies of an LSA may be circulating in a network. The *LS sequence number*, a signed 32-bit integer, helps identify the most recent LSA. The first instance of an LSA record contains a sequence number field of 0x80000001. Each new instance of the LSA contains a sequence number that is one higher. The maximum sequence number is 0x7fffffff, after which the sequence numbers are recycled. The sequence number helps identify the most recent instance of an LSA.

Upon receiving LSA headers in DD packets, both routers check to see if this piece of the OSPF topology is already contained in their LS databases. In this process, the advertising router, LS type, and link state ID fields (from the LSA header) are compared against the router's LS database. If no matching records are found or if a matching record is found with a lower sequence number, the complete LSA is requested using the *link state request packet*. The LS request packet contains the LSA header to help identify the record being sought.

In response to a link state request, a router issues a link state update containing the LSA. The LSA completely describes the piece of OSPF topology in question. LS updates are issued (a) in response to an LS request, as just described; (b) because of a change in the state of the link; and (c) every 30 minutes, with a new sequence number and the age field set to 0.

All LS updates are acknowledged in *link state acknowledgment packets* (see Figure 6-9).

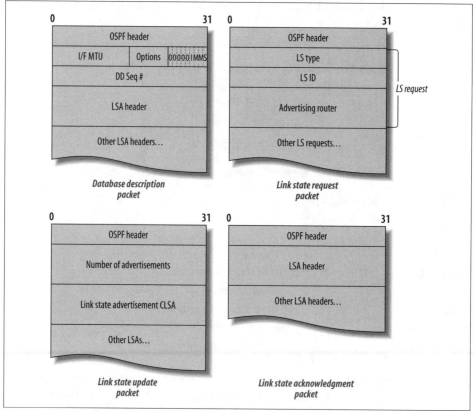

Figure 6-9. Database description, link state request, link state update, and link state acknowledgment packets

There are six types of LSA records, each representing a different piece of the network topology. We'll use TraderMary's network with a French extension (Figure 6-10) to take a closer look at the various LSA types.

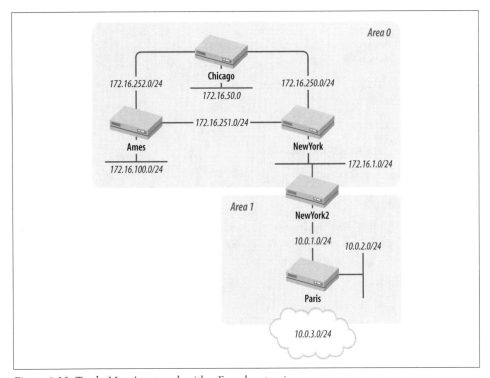

Figure 6-10. TraderMary's network with a French extension

TraderMary's network in New York is configured as follows. *NewYork2* is an ABR with a serial link in area 1 to router *Paris* (line 15).

```
   hostname NewYork2
   !
   interface Loopback0
    ip address 192.168.1.4 255.255.255.0
   !
   interface Ethernet0
    ip address 172.16.1.2 255.255.255.0
    ip pim sparse-mode
   !
   interface Serial1
    description Paris link
    ip address 10.0.1.2 255.255.255.0
    bandwidth 56
   !
   router ospf 10
    network 172.16.0.0 0.0.255.255 area 0
15  network 10.0.0.0 0.255.255.255 area 1
```

Paris is an ASBR redistributing RIP routes from a legacy network into OSPF (line 16):

```
hostname Paris
!
interface Loopback0
 ip address 192.168.1.5 255.255.255.255
!
interface Ethernet0
 ip address 10.0.2.1 255.255.255.0
!
interface Serial1
 description link to NewYork2
 ip address 10.0.1.1 255.255.255.0
!
router ospf 10
16   redistribute rip metric 100 subnets
 network 10.0.0.0 0.255.255.255 area 1
!
router rip
 network 10.0.0.0
```

The 10.0.0.0 subnets—10.0.1.0, 10.0.2.0, and 10.0.3.0—are known to both the OSPF and RIP processes on router *Paris*. Let's see how *NewYork* learns these subnets. Here is *NewYork*'s routing table:

```
NewYork#sh ip route
...
     10.0.0.0/24 is subnetted, 3 subnets
17   O IA    10.0.2.0 [110/1805] via 172.16.1.2, 00:07:45, Ethernet0
18   O E2    10.0.3.0 [110/100] via 172.16.1.2, 00:07:46, Ethernet0
19   O IA    10.0.1.0 [110/1795] via 172.16.1.2, 00:07:46, Ethernet0
     192.168.1.0/32 is subnetted, 1 subnets
   C     192.168.1.1 is directly connected, Loopback0
     172.16.0.0/24 is subnetted, 6 subnets
   O     172.16.252.0 [110/128] via 172.16.250.2, 00:07:46, Serial0
   C     172.16.250.0 is directly connected, Serial0
   C     172.16.251.0 is directly connected, Serial1
   O     172.16.50.0 [110/74] via 172.16.250.2, 00:07:46, Serial0
   C     172.16.1.0 is directly connected, Ethernet0
   O     172.16.100.0 [110/192] via 172.16.250.2, 00:07:46, Serial0
```

Note that the routing table shows that *NewYork* learns 10.0.3.0 as an external route whereas 10.0.1.0 and 10.0.2.0 are learned as inter-area routes (lines 17–19)—this is because inter-area routes are preferred over external routes. The OSPF order of route preference, from most preferred to least preferred, is as follows: intra-area, inter-area, type 1 external, type 2 external.

Router LSA (type 1)

A router LSA describes the advertising router's directly connected links. Routers *Chicago*, *Ames*, *NewYork*, and *NewYork2* advertise router LSAs that are flooded throughout area 0. *NewYork*'s LS database holds router LSAs from all these routers, but for the sake of brevity I'll show only the contents of the LSA from *NewYork2*.

The number of links (as in line 20 in the upcoming code block) described in the LSA is 1. Although *NewYork2* has two directly connected links—an Ethernet segment and a serial link—only the Ethernet segment is described in the LSA to *NewYork*. This is because the serial link is in area 1 and router LSAs do not cross OSPF area boundaries.

The link described is a *transit network* (line 21), implying that there are multiple routers on the link. Other link types are point-to-point (for serial links), stub network (for a network with only one router), and virtual link (for OSPF virtual links).

The value of the link ID field depends on the type of link being described, as shown in Table 6-4.

Table 6-4. Link type and link ID

Link type	Link ID
Point-to-point	Neighbor's router ID
Transit network	DR's IP address on network
Stub network	IP network number or subnet number
Virtual link	Neighbor's router ID

In our example, the DR is *NewYork*, so the link ID (in line 22) contains *NewYork*'s IP address.

The contents of the link data field also depend on the link type, as shown in Table 6-5.

Table 6-5. Link type and link data

Link type	Link data
Point-to-point	IP address of network interface
Transit network	IP address of network interface
Stub network	IP network number or subnet number
Virtual link	MIB II ifIndex for the router's interface

In our example, the link data field (in line 23) specifies the IP address of *NewYork2*:

```
NewYork#sh ip ospf database router

        OSPF Router with ID (192.168.1.1) (Process ID 10)

Routing Bit Set on this LSA

  LS age: 209

  Options: (No TOS-capability, DC)
  LS Type: Router Links
  Link State ID: 192.168.1.4

  Advertising Router: 192.168.1.4
```

```
        LS Seq Number: 800000FF
        Checksum: 0x2BA1
        Length: 36
        Area Border Router
        AS Boundary Router
20      Number of Links: 1

21        Link connected to: a Transit Network
22        (Link ID) Designated Router address: 172.16.1.1
23        (Link Data) Router Interface address: 172.16.1.2
            Number of TOS metrics: 0
              TOS 0 Metrics: 10
```

Network LSA (type 2)

A network LSA describes broadcast/NBMA networks. The network LSA is originated by the DR and describes all attached routers.

The LSA in the following example is self-originated, as seen in the advertising router
field (line 24), which shows *NewYork*'s own router ID. The network LSA describes
the mask on the multi-access network (line 25) and the IP addresses of the routers on
the multi-access network (lines 26 and 27).

```
        NewYork#sh ip ospf database network

              OSPF Router with ID (192.168.1.1) (Process ID 10)


                Net Link States (Area 0)

        Routing Bit Set on this LSA
        LS age: 1728
        Options: (No TOS-capability, DC)
        LS Type: Network Links
        Link State ID: 172.16.1.1 (address of Designated Router)
24      Advertising Router: 192.168.1.1
        LS Seq Number: 800000F4
        Checksum: 0x172B
        Length: 32
25      Network Mask: /24
26       Attached Router: 192.168.1.1
27       Attached Router: 192.168.1.4
```

Summary LSA (type 3)

A summary LSA is advertised by an ABR and describes inter-area routes.

The summary LSAs in the following example are originated by *NewYork2* (192.168.
1.4) and describe routes to 10.0.1.0 and 10.0.2.0, respectively. The link state ID
describes the summary network number (lines 28 and 31). Note that each LSA
describes just one summary network number.

```
NewYork#sh ip ospf database summary

        OSPF Router with ID (192.168.1.1) (Process ID 10)


            Summary Net Link States (Area 0)

    Routing Bit Set on this LSA
    LS age: 214
    Options: (No TOS-capability, DC)
    LS Type: Summary Links(Network)
28  Link State ID: 10.0.1.0 (summary Network Number)
29  Advertising Router: 192.168.1.4
    LS Seq Number: 80000062
    Checksum: 0x85A
    Length: 28
30  Network Mask: /24
      TOS: 0     Metric: 1785

    Routing Bit Set on this LSA
    LS age: 214
    Options: (No TOS-capability, DC)
    LS Type: Summary Links(Network)
31  Link State ID: 10.0.2.0 (summary Network Number)
32  Advertising Router: 192.168.1.4
    LS Seq Number: 80000061
    Checksum: 0x62F5
    Length: 28
33  Network Mask: /24
      TOS: 0     Metric: 1795
```

ASBR summary LSA (type 4)

An ASBR summary LSA describes the route to the ASBR. The mask associated with a type 4 LSA is 32 bits long because the route advertised is to a host—the host being the ASBR. ASBR summary LSAs are originated by ABRs.

The link state ID (line 34) in this example describes the router ID of *Paris*, which is the ASBR redistributing RIP into OSPF. The advertising router is the ABR—*NewYork2* (line 35).

```
NewYork#sh ip ospf database asbr-summary

        OSPF Router with ID (192.168.1.1) (Process ID 10)


            Summary ASB Link States (Area 0)

    Routing Bit Set on this LSA
    LS age: 115
    Options: (No TOS-capability, DC)
    LS Type: Summary Links(AS Boundary Router)
```

```
34    Link State ID: 192.168.1.5 (AS Boundary Router address)
35    Advertising Router: 192.168.1.4
      LS Seq Number: 80000061
      Checksum: 0x9A63
      Length: 28
      Network Mask: /0
         TOS: 0      Metric: 1785
```

External LSA (type 5)

External LSAs originate at ASBRs and describe routes external to the OSPF process. External LSAs are flooded throughout the OSPF network, with the exception of stub areas.

Network 10.0.1.0 is learned via RIP from *NewYork2*, which floods an external LSA with a link state ID of 10.0.1.0. Interestingly, 10.0.1.0 is also known as an inter-area route (see the section "Summary LSA (type 3)"). Router *NewYork* prefers the IA route (see line 19) but will keep the external LSA in its topological database. The advertising router (line 37) is *Paris*, the ASBR, which redistributes RIP into OSPF. The forwarding address (in line 39) is 0.0.0.0, indicating that the destination for 10.0.1.0 is the ASBR. The LSA (in line 40) specifies an external route tag of 0, which indicates a type 1 external route; a value of 1 would indicate a type 2 external route.

```
NewYork#sh ip ospf database external

       OSPF Router with ID (192.168.1.1) (Process ID 10)


          Type-5 AS External Link States

      LS age: 875
      Options: (No TOS-capability, No DC)
      LS Type: AS External Link
36    Link State ID: 10.0.1.0 (External Network Number )
37    Advertising Router: 192.168.1.5
      LS Seq Number: 80000060
      Checksum: 0x6F27
      Length: 36
38    Network Mask: /24
       Metric Type: 2 (Larger than any link state path)
       TOS: 0
       Metric: 100
39    Forward Address: 0.0.0.0
40    External Route Tag: 0
    ...
```

Note that *NewYork*'s external database contains two other LSAs—with link state IDs of 10.0.2.0 and 10.0.3.0—which were not shown here.

NSSA external LSA (type 7)

NSSA external LSAs describe routes external to the OSPF process. However, unlike type 5 external LSAs, NSSA external LSAs are flooded only within the NSSA.

There are no type 7 LSAs in this network. In fact, there aren't even any NSSAs in this network:

```
NewYork#sh ip  ospf database nssa-external

        OSPF Router with ID (192.168.1.1) (Process ID 10)
```

The format of the NSSA external LSA is identical to that of the AS external LSA, except for the forwarding address field. The forwarding address field in an NSSA external LSA always indicates the address to which traffic should be forwarded.

Flooding of LSAs

LSAs are generated every 30 minutes, or sooner if there is a change in the state of a link. LSAs are exchanged between routers that have established *adjacency*, as was described earlier.

The rules for the flooding of LSAs are governed by the hierarchical structure of OSPF, as given in Table 6-6.

Table 6-6. Rules for the flooding of LSAs

LSA type	Originating router	Area in which flooded
Router LSA (type 1)	Every router	Router's local area.
Network LSA (type 2)	DR	Router's local area.
Summary LSA (type 3)	ABR	Nonlocal area.
ASBR summary LSA (type 4)	ASBR	All areas except stub area, totally stubby area, or NSSA.
External LSA (type 5)	ASBR	All areas except stub area, totally stubby area, or NSSA.
NSSA external LSA (type 7)	ASBR	Router's local area. NSSA external LSA may be forwarded by ABR as a type 5 LSA.

Route Summarization

RIP-1 and IGRP automatically summarize subnets into a major network number when crossing a network-number boundary. OSPF does not automatically summarize routes. Route summarization in OSPF must be manually configured on an ABR or an ASBR. Further, OSPF allows route summarization on any bit boundary (unlike RIP and IGRP, which summarize only classful network numbers).

Summarizing routes keeps the routing tables smaller and easier to troubleshoot. However, route summarization in OSPF is not just a nice thing to do—it is necessary to reduce the size of the OSPF topology database, especially in a large network. A large topology database requires a large amount of router memory, which slows down all processes, including SPF calculations.

To allow summarization at ABRs and ASBRs, IP addresses must be carefully assigned. First, allocate enough addresses to each area to allow for expansion. Then set a bit boundary on which to summarize routes. This is easier said than done. Most network engineers inherit a network with a haphazard mess of addresses and changing requirements.

Summarizing at the ABR (Inter-Area Summarization)

Consider TraderMary's network in Figure 6-10. Network 10.0.0.0 exists in area 1, and network 172.16.0.0 exists in area 0. Let's see how we can summarize on these area boundaries.

The command to summarize at an ABR is:

```
area area-id range address mask
```

where *area-id* is the area whose routes are to be summarized, *address* is a network number, and *mask* specifies the number of bits in *address* to summarize.

The OSPF configuration on *NewYork2* can now be modified to summarize 172.16.0.0 routes into area 1 (line 41) and 10.0.0.0 routes into area 0 (line 42).

```
   hostname NewYork2
   ...
   router ospf 10
    redistribute static metric 10
    network 172.16.0.0 0.0.255.255 area 0
    network 10.0.0.0 0.255.255.255 area 1
41  area 0 range 172.16.0.0 255.255.0.0
42  area 1 range 10.0.0.0 255.0.0.0
```

The routing table in *Paris* is now as follows. Note that *Paris* has only one summary route for 172.16.0.0/16 (line 43).

```
   Paris#show ip route
   ...
   10.0.0.0/24 is subnetted, 2 subnets
   C       10.0.2.0 is directly connected, Ethernet0
   C       10.0.1.0 is directly connected, Serial1
           192.168.1.0/32 is subnetted, 1 subnets
   C       192.168.1.5 is directly connected, Loopback0
43 O IA 172.16.0.0/16 [110/74] via 10.0.1.2, 1d23h, Serial1
```

The routing table for *NewYork* is now as follows. Note that *NewYork* has only one summarized route for 10.0.0.0/8 (line 44).

```
   NewYork#sh ip route
   ...
```

```
O IA 10.0.0.0/8 [110/1795] via 172.16.1.2, 1d23h, Ethernet0
       192.168.1.0/32 is subnetted, 1 subnets
C         192.168.1.1 is directly connected, Loopback0
       172.16.0.0/24 is subnetted, 6 subnets
O         172.16.252.0 [110/128] via 172.16.250.2, 1d23h, Serial0
C         172.16.250.0 is directly connected, Serial0
C         172.16.251.0 is directly connected, Serial1
O         172.16.50.0 [110/74] via 172.16.250.2, 1d23h, Serial0
C         172.16.1.0 is directly connected, Ethernet0
44  O     172.16.100.0 [110/192] via 172.16.250.2, 1d23h, Serial0
```

When an EIGRP router summarizes, it automatically builds a route to *null0* for the summarized route. (This is explained in detail in the section "Route Summarization" in Chapter 4). The router to *null0* prevents packets that do not match a specific entry in the routing table from following a default route. (The route to *null0* causes the packet to be dropped). However, as you saw earlier, OSPF does not build a null route. You may want to manually add a static route to *null0* on the ABR.

Summarizing at the ASBR (or External Route Summarization)

In the configuration in Figure 6-10, *Paris* is the ASBR redistributing RIP into OSPF. Note from the figure that the RIP network contains routes in the network 10.3.0.0/24 (the RIP subnets may be 10.3.1.0/24, 10.3.2.0/24, 10.3.3.0/24, … 10.3.255.0/24). It is desirable to summarize 10.3.0.0/16 into the OSPF network rather than carrying the individual subnets.

The routes being redistributed into OSPF can be summarized at the ASBR (which is *Paris* in the previous example) using the following command:

```
summary-address address mask
```

where *address* defines a summary IP address and *mask* describes the range of addresses.

Router *Paris* may thus be configured as follows to summarize 10.3.0.0/16 into the OSPF network:

```
hostname Paris
!
interface Loopback0
 ip address 192.168.1.5 255.255.255.255
!
interface Ethernet0
 ip address 10.0.2.1 255.255.255.0
!
interface Serial1
 ip address 10.0.1.1 255.255.255.0
!
router ospf 10
 summary-address 10.3.0.0 255.255.252.0
```

```
    redistribute rip metric 100 subnets
    network 10.0.0.0 0.255.255.255 area 1
    !
 router rip
    network 10.0.0.0
```

The LS database will now contain a single external LSA with a link state ID of 10.3.
0.0 advertised by *Paris*.

Default Routes

Earlier chapters showed how a default route could be used for branch office connectivity. A default route can also be used when connecting to the Internet to represent
all the routes in the Internet. Let's say that TraderMary established a connection
from *NewYork2*, *Serial2* (line 45) to an Internet service provider (ISP). A static
default route is also installed on *NewYork2* (line 47), pointing to the ISP.

NewYork2 is configured as in line 46 to source a default route. The keyword *always*
implies that the default route must be originated whether or not the default route is
up. *metric-value* is the metric to associate with the default route (the default for this
field is 10). Note that this redistribution of a default route into OSPF makes
NewYork2 an ASBR. The keyword *metric-type* can be set to 1 or 2 to specify whether
the default route is external type 1 or 2 (the default is 2).

```
    hostname NewYork2
    !
45  interface Serial2
    description Connection to the ISP
    ip address 146.146.1.1 255.255.255.0
    !
 router ospf 10
    network 172.16.0.0 0.0.255.255 area 0
46  default-information originate always metric-value 20 metric-type 1
    !
47  ip route 0.0.0.0 0.0.0.0 interface serial2
```

Since the keyword *always* was specified, the default route will not disappear from the
OSPF routing table if *Serial2* (the link to the ISP) is down. If TraderMary has two (or
more) routers connecting to ISPs and each router announced a default route into
OSPF, do not use the *always* keyword—if one ISP connection is lost, traffic will find
its way to the other ISP connection.

To ensure that the default route is always announced (even if *Serial2* goes down)
choose the *always* option.

A default route of type 1 includes the internal cost of reaching the ASBR. If Trader-
Mary has multiple Internet connections, announcing a default route from each with a
metric type of 1 would have the advantage that any router in the network would find
the closest ASBR.

Virtual Links

TraderMary is planning to establish a new office in Paris with an area ID of 2. The first router in area 2 will be called *Paris2*. A direct circuit needs to be established from *NewYork2* (the ABR) to *Paris2*, since all OSPF areas must connect directly to the backbone (area 0). This international circuit has a long installation time. And, since a physical path is already available to area 2 via area 1, you may ask if OSPF provides some mechanism to activate area 2 before the *NewYork2* → *Paris2* circuit can be installed. The answer is yes. OSPF defines virtual links (VLs) which can extend the backbone area. Area 2 will directly attach to the backbone via the VL. A VL may be viewed as a point-to-point link belonging to area 0. The endpoints of a VL must be ABRs.

In our example in Figure 6-11, a virtual link may be defined from *NewYork2* to *Paris2* through area 1.

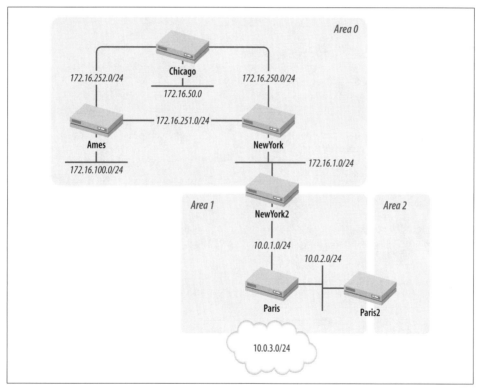

Figure 6-11. Virtual link to area 2

The syntax for configuring a virtual link is as follows:

```
area area-id virtual-link router-id [hello-interval seconds] [retransmit-interval
seconds] [transmit-delay seconds] [dead-interval seconds] [[authentication-key key] |
[message-digest-key keyid md5 key]]
```

where *area-id* specifies the transit area and *router-id* specifies the ABR with which the neighbor relationship is to be established. The four timers refer to the time between hello packets (default is 10 s), the time between LSA retransmissions (default is 5 s), the time by which LSAs are aged when they transmit this interface (default is 1 s), and the router dead-interval (default is four times the hello-interval). The parameter *key* is a string of characters up to 8 bytes long, *keyid* is in the range 1– 255, and *key* is an alphanumeric string up to 16 characters in length.

Remember that a virtual link can be created only between ABRs and can traverse only one area. *Paris2* is an ABR because it has connectivity to areas 1 and 2. *NewYork2* is an ABR with connectivity to areas 0 and 1. Thus, a virtual link may be configured between *Paris2* and *NewYork2* traversing area 1:

```
hostname Paris2
!
interface Loopback1
 ip address 192.168.1.6 255.255.255.255
!
interface Loopback2
 ip address 192.168.2.1 255.255.255.0
!
interface Ethernet0
 ip address 10.0.2.2 255.255.255.0
!
router ospf 10
 network 10.0.0.0 0.255.255.255 area 1
 network 192.168.2.0 0.0.0.255 area 2
 area 1 virtual-link 192.168.1.4
```

```
hostname NewYork2
!
interface Loopback0
 ip address 192.168.1.4 255.255.255.255
!
interface Ethernet0
 ip address 172.16.1.2 255.255.255.0
!
interface Serial1
 ip address 10.0.1.2 255.255.255.0
 bandwidth 56
!
router ospf 10
 redistribute static metric 10
 network 172.16.0.0 0.0.255.255 area 0
 network 10.0.0.0 0.255.255.255 area 1
 area 1 virtual-link 192.168.1.6
```

The status of the virtual link can be verified as follows:

```
Paris2#sh ip ospf virtual-link
Virtual Link to router 192.168.1.4 is up
```

```
    Transit area 1, via interface Ethernet0, Cost of using 74
    Transmit Delay is 1 sec, State POINT_TO_POINT,
    Timer intervals configured, Hello 10, Dead 40, Wait 40, Retransmit 5
      Hello due in 0:00:00
    Adjacency State FULL


NewYork2#show ip ospf virtual-link
Virtual Link OSPF_VL0 to router 192.168.1.6 is up
  Run as demand circuit
  DoNotAge LSA not allowed (Number of DCbitless LSA is 8).
  Transit area 1, via interface Serial1, Cost of using 1795
  Transmit Delay is 1 sec, State POINT_TO_POINT,
  Timer intervals configured, Hello 10, Dead 40, Wait 40, Retransmit 5
    Hello due in 00:00:05
  Adjacency State FULL
```

VLs cannot traverse stub areas (or totally stubby areas or NSSAs). This is because VLs belong to area 0, and in order for area 0 to route correctly it must have the complete topology database. Stub areas do not contain the complete topology database.

VLs find one other use in OSPF—they may be used to repair the network in the event that an area loses its link to the backbone. For example, in Figure 6-4, the loss of the link *R1 → R4* will isolate area 2 from the rest of the network. Until the *R1 → R4* link is repaired, a VL may be defined between *R4* and *R5* to join area 2 to the backbone.

Demand Circuits

The cost of a demand circuit, such as an ISDN link or a dial-up line, is dependent on its usage. It is desirable to use a demand circuit only for user traffic and not for overhead such as OSPF hellos or periodic LSAs. RFC 1793 describes modifications to OSPF that allow the support of demand circuits. This is an optional capability in OSPF; a router will set the DC bit in the options field if it supports the capability. Routers that support the capability will also set the high bit of the LS age field to 1 to indicate that the LSA should not be aged. This bit is also referred to as the do-not-age bit. OSPF demand circuits suppress periodic hellos and LSAs, but a topology change will still activate the demand circuit since LSA updates are required to keep the LS database accurate. Since any large network is likely to experience frequent topology changes, it may be prudent to define demand circuits in stub areas. Stub areas have a limited topology database and hence are shielded from frequent topology changes.

If a demand circuit is created in a stub area, all routers in the stub area must support the DC option—routers that do not support demand circuits will misinterpret the age field (as the high bit is set). An LSA with the DC bit set to 1 is flooded into an area only if all LSAs in the database have their DC bits set to 1.

To configure an interface as a demand circuit, enter the following command in inter-face configuration mode on one end of the demand circuit:

```
ip ospf demand-circuit
```

LSA updates will bring up the demand circuit only if there is a change in topology.

Stub, Totally Stubby, and Not So Stubby Areas

External LSAs are flooded through the OSPF backbone as well as through all regular areas. Let's test this using TraderMary's network of Figure 6-10. A static route for 192.168.3.0 is defined (pointing to *null0*) on *Chicago* and redistributed into OSPF. Router *Chicago* then advertises an external LSA with a link state ID of 192.168.3.0:

```
hostname Chicago
!
router ospf 10
 redistribute static metric 100 metric-type 1 subnets
 network 172.16.0.0 0.0.255.255 area 0
!
ip route 192.168.3.0 255.255.255.0 Null0
```

The LSA is flooded to all routers in the network. Let's check *Paris* as an instance:

```
Paris#sh ip ospf database external

        OSPF Router with ID (192.168.1.5) (Process ID 10)


                AS External Link States

    Routing Bit Set on this LSA
    LS age: 158
    Options: (No TOS-capability)
    LS Type: AS External Link
    Link State ID: 192.168.3.0 (External Network Number )
    Advertising Router: 192.168.1.3
    LS Seq Number: 80000001
    Checksum: 0x8F67
    Length: 36
    Network Mask: /24
      Metric Type: 1 (Comparable directly to link state metric)
      TOS: 0
      Metric: 100
      Forward Address: 0.0.0.0
      External Route Tag: 0
```

The route to 192.168.3.0 also appears in the routing table:

```
Paris#sh ip route
...
```

```
Gateway of last resort is not set
...
O E1 192.168.3.0/24 [110/302] via 10.0.1.2, 00:02:08, Serial1
...
```

Flooding external LSAs throughout an OSPF network may be a waste of resources. Stub areas block the flooding of external LSAs, as we will see in the next section.

Stub Areas

Referring to Figure 6-1, the router in area 1 that connects to the RIP network floods external LSAs into the network. It appears that nothing is gained by importing external LSAs into areas 2 and 3, which can point all external routes to their ABRs using default routes. Representing every external LSA in areas 2 and 3 would be a waste of resources. With this in mind, OSPF defines *stub areas*. When an area is defined as a stub area, all external LSAs are blocked at the ABRs, and, in place, the ABRs source a single default route into the stub area.

All routers in a stub area must be configured as stub routers. Stub routers form adjacencies only with other stub routers and do not propagate external LSAs. (How does a router know if its neighbor is a stub router? The E bit in the hello packet is turned to zero if the router is a stub router).

Area 1 in TraderMary's network can be made stubby via the following configuration changes:

```
hostname NewYork2
...
router ospf 10
network 172.16.0.0 0.0.255.255 area 0
network 10.0.0.0 0.255.255.255 area 1
area 1 stub


hostname Paris
...
router ospf 10
 redistribute rip
 network 10.0.0.0 0.255.255.255 area 1
area 1 stub
```

The routing table for *Paris* now shows a default route pointing to the ABR (*New-York2*) but does not show the external route to 192.168.3.0 (sourced by *Chicago*):

```
Paris#sh ip route
...
Gateway of last resort is 10.0.1.2 to network 0.0.0.0
...
O*IA 0.0.0.0/0 [110/65] via 10.0.1.2, 00:00:35, Serial1
O IA 172.16.0.0/16 [110/74] via 10.0.1.2, 1d23h, Serial1
...
```

After making this change, however, we will find that the network has lost connectivity to 10.0.3.0, which represents the RIP external network connecting to router *Paris*. The reason for this is rather obvious: stub areas do not propagate external LSAs. In other words, an ASBR cannot belong to a stub area.

The other major restriction with stub areas is that they cannot support virtual links, because they don't have the complete routing table. An area that needs to support a VL cannot be a stub area.

Any area that does not contain an ASBR (i.e., does not support a connection to an external network) and is not a candidate for supporting a virtual link should be made a stub area.

There is one major disadvantage to configuring an area as a stub area. When multiple ABRs source a default route, the routers in the stub area may fail to recognize the shortest path to the destination network. This may help determine whether you choose to implement an area as a regular area or as a stub area.

Totally Stubby Areas

Totally stubby areas carry the concept of stub areas further by blocking all summary LSAs in addition to external LSAs.

In the configuration in the previous section, where *Paris* is configured as a stub area, the LS database for *Paris* will not show external LSAs but will still show all summary LSAs, so *Paris*'s routing table still shows the summarized inter-area route to 172.16. 0.0/16. If *NewYork2* did not summarize the 172.16.0.0 subnets, *Paris* would show all six 172.16.0.0 subnets: 172.16.1.0/24, 172.16.50.0/24, 172.16.100.0/24, 172.16.250. 0/24, 172.16.251.0/24, and 172.16.252.0/24. Totally stubby areas, unlike stub areas, replace all inter-area routes (in addition to external routes) with a default route.

Area 1 can be configured as a totally stubby area by modifying the configuration of *NewYork2* as follows. No change is required to router *Paris*.

```
hostname NewYork2
!
router ospf 10
 redistribute static metric 10
 network 172.16.0.0 0.0.255.255 area 0
 network 10.0.0.0 0.255.255.255 area 1
 area 1 stub no-summary
```

Paris's routing table now does not contain any IA routes (other than the default sourced by *NewYork2*):

```
Paris#sh ip route
...
Gateway of last resort is 10.0.1.2 to network 0.0.0.0

     10.0.0.0/24 is subnetted, 2 subnets
```

```
C        10.0.2.0 is directly connected, Ethernet0
C        10.0.1.0 is directly connected, Serial1
      192.168.1.0/32 is subnetted, 1 subnets
C        192.168.1.5 is directly connected, Loopback0
0*IA 0.0.0.0/0 [110/65] via 10.0.1.2, 00:00:23, Serial1
```

Totally stubby areas have the same restrictions as stub areas—no ASBRs (no external LSAs) and no virtual links. Also, like stub areas, totally stubby areas see all ABRs as equidistant to all destinations that match the default route. When multiple ABRs source a default route, the routers in the totally stubby area may not recognize the shortest path to the destination network.

NSSAs

What if a stub area needs to learn routes from another routing protocol? For example, *Paris*—in area 1—may need to learn some RIP routes from a legacy network. NSSAs—as specified in RFC 1587—allow external routes to be imported into an area without losing the character of a stub area (i.e., without importing any external routes from the backbone area).

NSSAs import external routes through an ASBR in type 7 LSAs. Type 7 LSAs are flooded within the NSSA. Type 7 LSAs may optionally be flooded into the entire OSPF domain as a type 5 LSAs by the ABR(s) or be blocked at the ABR(s). As with any stub area, NSSAs do not import type 5 LSAs from the ABR.

The option (of whether or not to translate a type 7 LSA into a type 5 LSA at the NSSA ABR) is indicated in the P bit (in the options field) of the type 7 LSA. If this bit is set to 1, the LSA is translated by the ABR into a type 5 LSA to be flooded throughout the OSPF domain. If this bit is set to 0, the LSA is not advertised outside the NSSA area.

All routers in the NSSA must be configured with the *nssa* keyword (line 48):

```
    hostname NewYork2
    !
    router ospf 10
     redistribute static metric 10
     network 172.16.0.0 0.0.255.255 area 0
     network 10.0.0.0 0.255.255.255 area 1
48   area 1 nssa
```

There are three optional keywords for NSSA configuration:

```
    area 1 nssa ?
49   default-information-originate
50   no-redistribution
51   no-summary
```

When configured on the NSSA ABR, the *default-information-originate* keyword (line 49) causes the ABR to source a default route into the NSSA.

The *no-redistribution* keyword (line 50) is useful on NSSA ABRs that are also ASBRs. The *no-redistribution* keyword stops the redistribution of external LSAs (from the other AS) into the NSSA.

The *no-summary* keyword (line 51) gives you another oxymoron—it makes the NSSA a totally stubby NSSA, so no type 3 or 4 LSAs are sent into the area.

NSSAs are thus a variant of stub areas with one less restriction—external connections are allowed. In all other respects, NSSAs are just stub areas.

NBMA Networks

Remember how a DR is elected—basic to DR election is the broadcast or multicast capability of the underlying network. NBMA networks such as Frame Relay or X.25 have no inherent broadcast or multicast capability, but they can simulate a broadcast network if fully meshed. However, a fully meshed network with n nodes requires $n \times (n-1)/2$ virtual circuits. The cost of $n \times (n-1)/2$ virtual circuits may be unpalatable, and besides, the failure of a single virtual circuit would disrupt this full mesh.

One option around a fully meshed network is to (statically) configure the DR for the network. The DR will then advertise the NBMA network as a multi-access network using a single IP subnet in a network LSA.

Another option is to configure the network as a set of point-to-point networks. This is simpler to configure, manage, and understand. However, each point-to-point network wastes an IP subnet. So what? You can use VLSM in OSPF, with a two-bit subnet for each point-to-point network. That is a good argument. However, the trade-off is the processing overhead of an LSA for each point-to-point network.

Let's look at examples of each of these options.

NewYork2 is set up with a serial interface to support Frame Relay PVCs to offices in Miami and New Orleans, as shown in Figure 6-12.

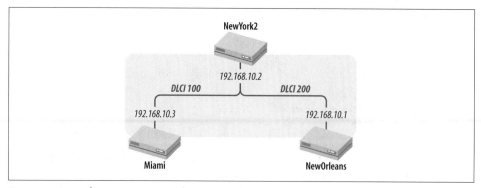

Figure 6-12. TraderMary's Frame Relay network

The command *ip ospf network broadcast* (lines 52, 53, and 55) makes OSPF believe that the attached network is multi-access, like an Ethernet segment. However, since the network has no true broadcast capability, the priorities on *NewYork2*, *Miami*, and *NewOrleans* must be specified to force *NewYork2* to be the DR on the NBMA network. *NewYork2* will become the DR while the state of the interface on *Miami* and *NewOrleans* will be DRother (implying that the interface has not been elected the DR). *NewYork2* uses the default priority of 1. *Miami* and *NewOrleans* are configured with a priority value of 0 (lines 54 and 56), which makes them ineligible for DR election.

```
      hostname NewYork2
      !
      interface Serial3
       ip address 192.168.10.2 255.255.255.0
       encapsulation frame-relay
52     ip ospf network broadcast
       ip ospf hello-interval 30
       keepalive 15
       frame-relay lmi-type ansi
      !
      router ospf 10
      network 192.168.10.0 0.0.0.255 area 0


      hostname Miami
      !
      interface Serial0
       no ip address
       encapsulation frame-relay
       keepalive 15
       frame-relay lmi-type ansi
      !
      interface Serial0.1 point-to-point
       ip address 192.168.10.3 255.255.255.0
53     ip ospf network broadcast
       ip ospf hello-interval 30
54     ip ospf priority 0
       frame-relay interface-dlci 100
      !
      router ospf 10
       network 192.168.10.0 0.0.0.255 area 0


      hostname NewOrleans
      !
      interface Serial0
       no ip address
       encapsulation frame-relay
       bandwidth 1544
       keepalive 15
       lat enabled
       frame-relay lmi-type ansi
```

```
 !
 interface Serial0.1 point-to-point
  ip address 192.168.10.1 255.255.255.0
55 ip ospf network broadcast
  ip ospf hello-interval 30
56 ip ospf priority 0
  frame-relay interface-dlci 200
 !
 router ospf 10
 network 192.168.10.0 0.0.0.255 area 0
```

IOS releases prior to 10.0 did not support the command *ip ospf network broadcast* and required the static configuration of neighbors and their priorities:

```
neighbor ip-address [priority number] [poll-interval seconds]
```

where *ip-address* is the IP address of the neighbor, *number* is the neighbor's priority (0–255), and *seconds* is the dead router poll interval.

The NBMA network may be modeled as a collection of point-to-point networks. Configure the routers the same way, but configure the interfaces as point-to-multipoint instead of broadcast and do not specify the OSPF priority, since a point-to-multipoint network does not elect a DR (the hello protocol is used to find neighbors):

```
ip ospf network point-to-multipoint
```

The point-to-multipoint network consumes only one IP subnet but creates multiple host routes.

You can also use subinterfaces to model the NBMA network as a collection of point-to-point networks. Routers at the ends of a point-to-point subinterface always form adjacency, much like routers at the ends of a serial interface. No DR election takes place. Since OSPF supports VLSM, one cannot argue that this will waste IP address space. However, using point-to-point subinterfaces in lieu of a single broadcast network generates LSAs for every subinterface, which adds to the processing overhead.

OSPF Design Heuristics

The following sections provide a partial and ad hoc checklist to use when executing an OSPF design. As with any other discipline, the engineer will do best if he spends time understanding the details of OSPF and then designs his network as simply as possible.

OSPF Hierarchy

Building a large, unstructured OSPF network is courting disaster. The design of the OSPF network must be clearly defined: all changes in the OSPF environment must bear the imprint of the OSPF architecture. For example, when adding a new router, the network engineer must answer the following questions:

- Will the router be an area router, a stub router, or an ABR?
- If the router is an ABR or an ASBR, what routes should the router summarize?
- What impact would the failure of the router have on OSPF routing?
- Will this router be a DR/BDR?
- How will this router affect the performance of other OSPF routers?

IP Addressing

IP addresses must be allocated in blocks that allow route summarization at ABRs. The address blocks must take into account the number of users in the area, leaving room for growth. VLSM should be considered when planning IP address allocation.

Router ID

Use loopback addresses to assign router IDs. Choose the router IDs carefully—the router ID will impact DR/BDR election on all attached multi-access networks. Keep handy a list of router IDs and router names. This will make it easier to troubleshoot the network.

DR/BDR

Routers with low processor/memory/bandwidth resources should be made DR-ineligible. A router that becomes the DR/BDR on multiple networks may see high memory/CPU utilization.

Backbone Area

Since all inter-area traffic will traverse the backbone, ensure that there is adequate bandwidth on the backbone links. The backbone area will typically be composed of the highest-bandwidth links in the network, with multiple paths between routers.

The backbone should have multiple paths between any pair of nonbackbone areas. A partitioned backbone will disrupt inter-area traffic—ensure that there is adequate redundancy in the backbone.

Use the backbone solely for inter-area traffic—do not place users or servers on the backbone.

Number of Routers in an Area

The maximum number of routers in an area depends on a number of factors—number of networks, router CPU, router memory, etc.—but Cisco documentation suggests that between 40 and 50 is a reasonable number. However, it is not uncommon to have a couple of hundred routers in an area, although problems such as flaky links may overload the CPU of the routers in the area. As a corollary of the previous argument, if you think that the total number of routers in your network will not exceed 50, all the routers can be in area 0.

Number of Neighbors

If the number of routers on a multi-access network exceeds 12 to 15 and the DR/BDR is having performance problems, look into a higher-horsepower router for the DR/BDR. Note that having up to 50 routers on a broadcast network is not uncommon. The total number of neighbors on all networks should not exceed 50 or so.

Route Summarization

To summarize the routes:

- Allocate address blocks for each area based on bit boundaries. As areas grow, keep in mind that the area may ultimately need to be split into two. If possible, allocate addresses within an area in contiguous blocks to allow summarization at the time of the split.

- Summarize into the backbone at the ABR (as opposed to summarizing into the nonbackbone area). This reduces the sizes of the LS database in the backbone area and the LS databases in the nonbackbone areas.

- Route summarization has the advantage that a route-flap in a subnet (that has been summarized) does not trigger an LSA to be flooded, reducing the OSPF processing overhead.

- If an area has multiple ABRs and one ABR announces more specific routes, all the traffic will flow to that router. This is good if this is the desired effect. Otherwise, if you intend to use all ABRs equally, all ABRs must have identical summary statements.

- Summarize external routes at the ASBR.

- Golden rule: summarize, summarize, summarize.

VLSM

OSPF LSA records carry subnet masks; the use of VLSM is encouraged to conserve the available IP address space.

Stub Areas

An area with only one ABR is an ideal candidate for a stub area. Changing the area into a stub area will reduce the size of the LS database without the loss of any useful routing information. Remember that stub areas cannot support VLs or type 5 LSAs.

Virtual Links

Design the network so that virtual links are not required. VLs should be used only as emergency fixes, not as a part of the design.

OSPF Timers

In an all-Cisco network environment, the OSPF timers (hello-interval, dead-interval, etc.) can be left to their default values; in a multivendor environment, however, the network engineer may need to adjust the timers to make sure they match.

Troubleshooting OSPF

OSPF is a complex organism and hence can be difficult to troubleshoot. However, since the operation of OSPF has been described in great detail by the standards bodies, the network engineer would do well to become familiar with its internal workings. The following sections describe some of the more common OSPF troubles.

OSPF Area IDs

When you're using multiple network area statements under the OSPF configuration, the order of the statements is critical. Check that the networks have been assigned the desired area IDs by checking the output of the *show ip ospf interface* command.

OSPF Does Not Start

The OSPF process cannot start on a router if a router ID cannot be established. Check the output of *show ip ospf* to see if a router ID has been established. If a router ID has not been established, check to see if the router has an active interface (preferably a loopback interface) with an IP address.

Verifying Neighbor Relationships

Once a router has been able to start OSPF, it will establish an interface data structure for each interface configured to run OSPF. Check the output of *show ip ospf interface* to ensure that OSPF is active on the intended interfaces. If OSPF is active, check for the parameters described in the section "How OSPF Works." Many OSPF problems may be traced to an incorrectly configured interface.

```
NewYork#sh ip ospf interface
...
Ethernet0 is up, line protocol is up
   Internet Address 172.16.1.1/24, Area 0
   Process ID 10, Router ID 172.16.251.1, Network Type BROADCAST, Cost: 10
   Transmit Delay is 1 sec, State DR, Priority 1
```

```
         Designated Router (ID) 172.16.251.1, Interface address 172.16.1.1
         No backup designated router on this network
         Timer intervals configured, Hello 10, Dead 40, Wait 40, Retransmit 5
           Hello due in 00:00:02
         Neighbor Count is 0, Adjacent neighbor count is 0
         Suppress hello for 0 neighbor(s)
       Serial0 is up, line protocol is up
59       Internet Address 172.16.250.1/24, Area 0
60       Process ID 10, Router ID 172.16.251.1, Network Type POINT_TO_POINT, Cost: 64
         Transmit Delay is 1 sec, State POINT_TO_POINT,
         Timer intervals configured, Hello 10, Dead 40, Wait 40, Retransmit 5
           Hello due in 00:00:01
         Neighbor Count is 1, Adjacent neighbor count is 1
           Adjacent with neighbor 69.1.1.1
         Suppress hello for 0 neighbor(s)
```

Remember that two routers will not form a neighbor relationship unless the parameters specified in the hello protocol match.

```
    NewYork#show ip ospf neighbor

    Neighbor ID    Pri   State         Dead Time   Address       Interface
    192.168.1.2     1    FULL/  -      00:00:31    172.16.250.2  Serial0
    192.168.1.3     1    FULL/  -      00:00:32    172.16.251.2  Serial1
```

If two routers have not been able to establish a neighbor relationship and both are active on the multi-access network (i.e., they are able to ping each other), it is likely that their hello parameters do not match. Use the *debug ip ospf adjacency* command to get details on hello parameter mismatches.

Route Summarization

If an area has multiple ABRs and one ABR announces more specific routes than the others, all the traffic will flow to that router. This is good if this is the desired effect. Otherwise, if you intend to use all ABRs equally, all ABRs must have identical summary statements.

Overloaded Routers

The design engineer should be familiar with OSPF—ABRs do more work than internal routers, and DRs/BDRs do more work than other routers. A router that becomes the DR/BDR on multiple networks does even more work. Routers in stub areas and NSSA areas do less work.

SPF Overrun

To check the number of times the SPF algorithm has executed, use the command *show ip ospf*. A flapping interface may result in frequent executions of the SPF algorithm that, in turn, may take CPU time away from other critical router processes.

```
        NewYork#sh ip ospf
61      Routing Process "ospf 10" with ID 172.16.251.1
        Supports only single TOS(TOS0) routes
62      SPF schedule delay 5 secs, Hold time between two SPFs 10 secs
        Number of DoNotAge external LSA 0
        Number of areas in this router is 1. 1 normal 0 stub 0 nssa
           Area BACKBONE(0)
           Number of interfaces in this area is 3
           Area has no authentication
63         SPF algorithm executed 24 times
           Area ranges are
           Link State Update Interval is 00:30:00 and due in 00:11:48
           Link State Age Interval is 00:20:00 and due in 00:11:48
           Number of DCbitless LSA 1
           Number of indication LSA 0
           Number of DoNotAge LSA 0
```

In this example, the SPF algorithm has been executed 24 times since the router was rebooted (line 63). Note that SPF is scheduled to delay its execution for 5 seconds after the receipt of an LSA update and the minimum time between SPF executions is set to 10 seconds (line 61). This keeps SPF from using up all the processor resources in the event that an interface is flapping.

To change these timers, use the following command under the OSPF configuration:

```
timers spf <schedule delay in seconds> <hold-time in seconds>
```

Using the LS Database

Since the LS database is the input to the SPF algorithm, you can analyze it to troubleshoot missing routes. Analyzing the LS database can be particularly useful when you're working with stub areas, totally stubby areas, or NSSAs, since these areas block certain LSAs.

The output of *show ip ospf database database-summary* is a useful indicator of the size of the LS database and its components. The command *show ip ospf database* shows the header information from each LSA.

Network Logs

The output of the command *show log* contains useful historical data and may be used to analyze a network outage.

Debug Commands

The most useful *debug* commands are *debug ip ospf adjacency* and *debug ip ospf events*. These commands are useful in troubleshooting neighbor relationships. Other *debug* commands available are *debug ip ospf flood, debug ip ospf lsa-generation, debug ip ospf packet, debug ip ospf retransmission, debug ip ospf spf,* and *debug ip ospf tree.*

Summing Up

OSPF can support very large networks—the OSPF hierarchy allows almost unlimited growth because new areas can be added to the network without impacting other areas. Dijkstra's SPF algorithm leads to radical improvements in convergence time, and OSPF does not suffer from the routing loop issues that DV protocols manifest.

OSPF exhibits all the advantages of a classless routing protocol. Variable Length Subnet Masks permit efficient use of IP addresses. Discontiguous networks can be supported since LSAs carry subnet mask information, and routes can be summarized at arbitrary bit boundaries. Summarization reduces routing protocol overhead and simplifies network management.

Furthermore, OSPF does not tie up network bandwidth and CPU resources in periodic routing updates. Only small hello packets are transmitted on a regular basis.

These OSPF benefits come at a price:

- OSPF is a complex protocol requiring a structured topology. A haphazard environment, without a plan for network addresses, route summarization, LS database sizes, and router performance, will yield a real mess.

- A highly trained staff is required to engineer and operate a large OSPF network.

- OSPF maintains an LS database that requires sizeable memory, and the SPF algorithm can hog CPU resources if the size of the topology database has grown out of bounds. Splitting an area to reduce the size of the LS database may not be straightforward, depending on the topology of the area.

- OSPF assumes a hierarchical network topology—migrating a network from another protocol to OSPF requires extensive planning.

CHAPTER 7

Border Gateway
Protocol 4 (BGP-4)

My first passport, issued by the Government of India in 1981, bore a curious stamp in bold red ink on one of its first pages: "NOT VALID FOR TRAVEL IN THE REPUBLIC OF SOUTH AFRICA."

Toward the end of the 1990s, I was traveling through Europe with a U.S. passport. Upon landing at Schiphol Airport in Amsterdam, I was stopped by an officer and led to a small room off to the side. There, I was made to remove my left shoe and sock. The officer checked my sock carefully before letting me go. Once I had cleared Dutch customs, I freely roamed up and down that beautiful country, walking barefoot over grass and flowers, past windmills.

Nations have policies concerning who can pass through their borders. So, India did not permit its citizens to grace the Republic of South Africa during its reign of apartheid. And the Dutch bar entry into their country if your left sock is not fresh and clean.

What does all this have to do with internetworking, or BGP-4, for that matter? Each network is an autonomous system (AS) managed by a single technical entity and under one political administration. ASs are akin to nation states. Much as nation states apply their immigration policies at international airports, seaports, and land border points, the Internet is composed of ASs that use Border Gateway Protocol 4 (BGP-4) to implement inter-AS IP routing policies.

What is a routing policy? Consider the topology in Figure 7-1. TraderMary has two links to the Internet: to ISP-A and ISP-B. TraderMary may implement a policy that all traffic should exit and enter their network via ISP-A and that the link to ISP-B should be used only for backup. ISP-Global connects to both ISP-US and ISP-Finland. ISP-US and ISP-Finland may enter into an arrangement with ISP-Global to carry transit traffic for them across the Atlantic. All three ISPs would need to reflect this arrangement in their routing policies.

The interior gateway protocols (IGPs) we discussed in earlier chapters—RIP, IGRP, EIGRP, and OSPF—relied on a single composite metric to choose the best route to a destination. BGP-4 implements routing policies based on a new paradigm—a set of *attributes* accompanying each route are used to pick the "shortest" path across multiple ASs, while also satisfying one or more routing policies.

RIP, IGRP, and OSPF are examples of IGPs. IGPs are designed for intra-AS routing. BGP-4 is an exterior gateway protocol (EGP), designed for inter-AS routing.

BGP-4 may be used to set up routing between any two ASs. However, the most interesting and complex use of BGP-4 is in the Internet: to connect client networks (such as TraderMary) to their ISPs and ISPs to other ISPs. This chapter will focus on the use of BGP-4 in connecting clients, such as TraderMary, to their ISPs.

BGP was first defined in RFC 1105 (1989) and was updated to BGP-2 in RFC 1163 (1990), to BGP-3 in RFC 1267 (1991), and then to BGP-4 in RFC 1771 (1995). BGP-4 is the first version that handles aggregation of prefixes along Classless Inter-Domain Routing (CIDR) lines, as described in the next section. BGP-4 may live longer than its forerunners because it is capable of supporting new attributes to keep up with an evolving Internet.

Background

An AS in the Internet must be identifiable via a unique, registered AS number and one or more unique, registered IP addresses. IP addresses in the Internet are not carved along the classful A, B, and C boundaries, but instead use the concepts of Classless Inter-Domain Routing (CIDR).

This section describes how an AS number and an IP block may be acquired and the concepts behind CIDR. I begin with a discussion of the various types of ASs.

AS Types

An AS is a network managed by a single technical entity and under one political administration. Figure 7-1 shows nine different ASs connected to each other in a small mesh that may be seen as a microcosm of the Internet. Architecturally, these ASs may be quite similar. Functionally, however, all ASs are not equal. TraderMary, BrotherX, and SisterY are clients of the ISPs to which they connect. These ASs do not carry *transit* traffic, implying that if you pick any IP packet from these networks, its source *or* destination IP address will be internal to the AS. These ASs are referred to as *stub* ASs.

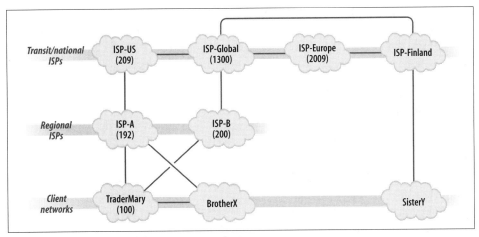

Figure 7-1. An attempt to define structure in the Internet

Local ISPs or regional ISPs provide transit service to stub ASs, implying that local/regional ISPs carry transit traffic for the stub AS to other networks. The local and regional ISPs, in turn, are clients of national ISPs and transit ISPs, which provide transit service over wider geographies.

The moment I describe these rules, I must admit that the rules are meant to be broken. For example, it is common for larger stub ASs to bypass local/regional ISPs and connect directly to national/transit ISPs.

Stub ASs may be further classified to describe their connectivity to the Internet, as follows. BrotherX's network has a single connection to ISP-A. BrotherX's network may be described as *singly-homed*. TraderMary may be described as *multi-homed*, since it connects to ISP-A and ISP-B.

Multi-homing to the same ISP guards against the failure of a single link but not against failures in the ISP's network. *Multi-homing to different ISPs* also guards against failures in an ISP's network.

Gluing AS to AS... Physical Connectivity in the Internet

At a physical level, stub ASs typically connect to an ISP via a serial link. TraderMary may lease a T-3 line to ISP-A and a T-1 line to ISP-B; BrotherX may lease a 56-kbps circuit to ISP-A.

ISPs establish connections with each other at higher speeds. The NSF originally helped establish *network access points* (NAPs) that provided the infrastructure over which various ASs could exchange routes and traffic. The original NAPs were run by Sprint (Pennauken, NJ), PacBell (San Francisco), Ameritech (Chicago), and MFS (Washington, D.C. and San Jose). Now, there are dozens of "Internet Exchanges" where ISPs and other ASs may connect. Several exchange points maintain excellent web sites with details on their services. For example, the Ameritech (Chicago) exchange (*http://www.aads.net/main.html*) uses ATM to provide high-speed connectivity. PAIX (*http://www.paix.net*) is located in Palo Alto, CA. The Commercial Internet Exchange (*http://www.cix.net*) is a not-for-profit organization that provides various interconnection options at different prices. In addition to the Exchanges, ISPs establish *private* peering arrangements in which two ASs set up a private network to exchange routes and traffic.

Internet Registries: IP Addresses and AS Numbers

Each device in the Internet must be identified by a unique IP address registered with one of the Internet Registries. ARIN (*http://www.arin.net*) registers IP addresses for the Americas, the Caribbean, and parts of Africa; RIPE NCC (*http://www.ripe.net*) takes care of the same tasks for Europe, the Middle East, and other parts of Africa; and APNIC (*http://www.apnic.net*) is responsible for Asia and the Pacific Region.

In the early to mid 1990s, it was recognized that the Internet was facing two critical issues. First, the available IP address space, especially that of Class B numbers, was rapidly depleting. The Class A address space was too big for most users and the Class C address space was too small. Second, just as more and more addresses were being allocated to users and organizations, the size of the Internet routing table was growing more rapidly than router processing power.

RFCs 1517, 1518, 1519, and 1520 proposed a solution to these twin problems: Classless Inter-Domain Routing (CIDR).

Classless Inter-Domain Routing (CIDR)

CIDR was revolutionary. To begin with, CIDR did away with fixed Class A, B, and C addresses. This takes a little retraining for us old-timers who grew up on classful addressing. We were taught that for a network of 1,000 hosts you would need a Class B address, Class A being too big and Class C being too small. However, since 1,000 hosts can be addressed with 10 bits, any network number with 10 bits in the host field and 32 − 10 = 22 bits in the network field would suffice. In CIDR parlance, such a network is described as "/22," implying that there are 22 bits in the network field. These 22 bits can be derived from any of the address ranges that were classically described as Class A, B, and C. Thus, 20.1.4.0/22, 150.100.252.0/22, and 192.168.68.0/22 are all valid CIDR blocks with 22 bits in the network field. The network administrator may then subnet the 10 bits in the host field as appropriate, just as she would if assigned a classful IP address. By allocating addresses in blocks that match user requirements, CIDR reduces the rate at which the available IP address pool is depleting.

CIDR goes a step further to reduce the size of IP routing tables. The CIDR schema proposes that clients derive IP addresses from their connected ISP rather than directly from an Internet Registry. In other words, ISPs derive address blocks from Internet Registries and carve them for their clients. This address-allocation schema is described as *topological* since clients derive IP addresses based on their physical connectivity. The advantage of this schema is that each ISP needs to advertise only one *aggregate* route for all its connected clients, rather than individual prefixes for each client.

All this deserves an example. Consider ISP-X. Let's say that ISP-X owns the IP address block 180.180.0.0/16. *Uncle-P* connects to ISP-X and requires 8 bits to address his hosts. In other words, the client requires a "/24". ISP-X will assign, say, 180.180.1.0/24 to *Uncle-P*. Then, the next day, *Uncle-Q* connects to ISP-X and also requires 8 bits to address his hosts. ISP-X will assign, say, 180.180.2.0/24 to *Uncle-Q*. ISP-X's own routing tables hold detailed routes for all subnets in the 180.180.0.0/16 block, but ISP-X advertises only one prefix—180.180.0.0/16—to all other ASs. In other words, ISP-X issues an aggregate 180.180.0.0/16 to other ISPs. This is illustrated in Figure 7-2.

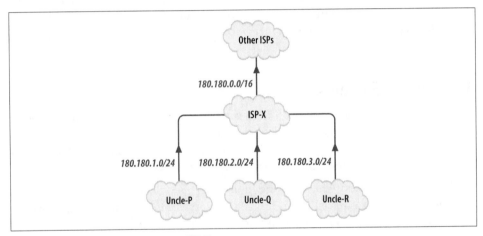

Figure 7-2. Route aggregation using CIDR

One problem with this method of address assignment is that when *Uncle-P* decides to use a different ISP—say, ISP-Y—*Uncle-P* has to return the 180.180.1.0 block to ISP-X and readdress all his devices from a new block of addresses procured from ISP-Y. This plan forces *Uncle-P* to renumber his IP addresses when he changes his ISP.

Multi-homing to different ISPs also creates problems with this schema. *Uncle-Q* has the address block 180.180.1.0/24 from ISP-X, but he also connects to ISP-Z. ISP-Z would have to carry BrotherX's specific route, 180.180.1.0/24. In other words, since ISP-Z advertises BrotherX's prefix, the routing tables in the attached ASs will see both the aggregate 180.180.0.0/16 from ISP-X and 180.180.1.0 from ISP-A. However, addresses may still be aggregated at a higher level in the network, based on address hierarchy.

Route aggregation using CIDR is hierarchical, since address blocks have been allocated by geography. Ideally, an ISP in Europe should see an aggregate for all CIDR-derived routes in Japan and another aggregate for all CIDR-derived routes in Australia.

Prior to IOS Release 12.0, a router assumed that all routing information it received was classful. This implies that the router assumed that all networks had IP addresses that were assigned along classful lines. The following command turns off classful behavior in IOS releases earlier than 12.0. Releases 12.0 and later assume classless behavior by default.

```
ip classless
```

Further, in classful behavior, the use of subnet zero creates confusion in the IP routing table. If 180.180.0.0 were to be subnetted with a 24-bit mask, the subnet zero would be 180.180.0.0/24. This subnet is easily confused with the entire address space 180.180.0.0/16 if there are no masks in routing updates. Hence, with classful routing protocols, it was common for the IOS to prevent the configuration of the subnet zero on any user interface. The following command in global configuration mode allows the configuration of subnet zero:

```
ip subnet-zero
```

Acquiring an IP Address

Every organization attached to the Internet must have a *unique* IP address in order for it to have an unambiguous path in the Internet. A stub AS may derive an IP address block from its ISP using the CIDR schema (as *Uncle-P* did from ISP-X) or it may apply for an IP address block directly from an Internet Registry.

CIDR-derived addresses reduce routing-table overhead in the Internet. Internet Registry–derived addresses have the advantage of being *portable*: if the stub AS moves to a different ISP, there is no need to renumber IP devices.

All devices in a network typically do not access the Internet directly. User workstations and servers employ a proxy device (such as a firewall) that has one interface on an internal network and another on the Internet. The proxy device originates a TCP session on behalf of the user. The proxy must have a registered IP address on its Internet interface. The internal addresses are not visible on the Internet and so do not need to be registered. The IP addresses we have seen thus far on TraderMary's network have come from the pool of private addresses reserved by the Internet Assigned Numbers Authority (IANA). This pool of private addresses is defined by the following ranges (see RFC 1918 for further details):

```
10.0.0.0    - 10.255.255.255  (10/8 prefix)
172.16.0.0  - 172.31.255.255  (172.16/12 prefix)
192.168.0.0 - 192.168.255.255 (192.168/16 prefix)
```

RFC 1918 sets these addresses aside for use by *any* organization for numbering its devices. These prefixes cannot be advertised into the (public) Internet.

In the example we'll look at later, TraderMary uses the registered Class C addresses 192.200.200.0/24 and 160.160.0.0/16 to connect to ISP-A.

Acquiring an AS Number

Each AS running BGP-4 is associated with an AS number. This AS number must be unique and unambiguous for BGP-4 to operate correctly.

Each AS in the Internet should be identified by an AS number that is registered with one of the Internet Registries. ARIN registers AS numbers for the Americas, the Caribbean, and parts of Africa; RIPE NCC takes care of the same tasks for Europe, the Middle East, and other parts of Africa; and APNIC does the same for Asia and the Pacific Region.

Every AS in the Internet must have a unique AS number. However, a stub AS that is singly-homed to an ISP may "borrow" its ISP's AS number or use one of the AS numbers reserved for private use by IANA. The range of private AS numbers is 64,512 through 65,535.

Getting BGP Running

Starting BGP on a router is similar to starting any other routing process, such as RIP or IGRP. The command to start BGP is:

    router bgp *AutonomousSystemNumber*

where *AutonomousSystemNumber* is the AS number of the local router.

This is where the similarity with other routing protocols stops. When configured under BGP, the following network statement:

    network *IPAddress* [mask A.B.C.D]

specifies the prefix to announce to BGP peers. Compare this with the configuration of IGPs, where the network-number statement has very different semantics: it specifies the attached networks on which to discover neighbors or peers.

Speaking of peers, there are no mechanisms in BGP-4 to automatically discover neighbors. BGP-4 requires that peers *must* be specified by IP address. The command to specify a peer is:

    neighbor *IPAddress* remote-as *AutonomousSystemNumber*

where *IPAddress* specifies the peer with an AS number of *AutonomousSystemNumber*.

Let's look at TraderMary's configuration for its connection to ISP-A, as shown in Figure 7-3. Line 1 in the following code block starts BGP with a local AS number of 100. Line 3 specifies that the prefix 192.200.200.0/26 be announced to *TrdrMary-1*'s BGP peers. Line 4 specifies that the network number 30.0.0.0 be announced as well, with an 8-bit mask (the natural classful mask is used when a mask is not specified).

Line 5 specifies that all static routes should also be announced. (There are two static routes known to *TrdrMary-1*, as shown in lines 7 and 8). Line 6 specifies that *TrdrMary-1*'s BGP peer (ISP-A) has an IP address of 192.100.100.254 and an AS number of 192. This is the only neighbor statement, so in this example *TrdrMary-1* has only one peer: ISP-A.

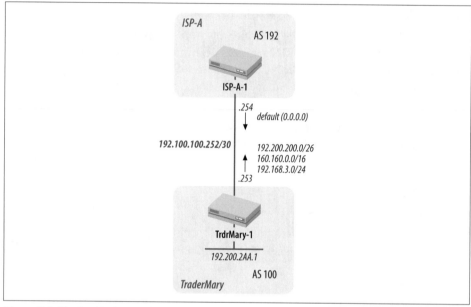

Figure 7-3. TraderMary's connection to ISP-A

Here's what the configuration looks like:

```
hostname TrdrMary-1
!
interface Loopback0
 ip address 192.168.1.10 255.255.255.255
!
interface Ethernet0
 description * External Network *
 ip address 192.200.200.1 255.255.255.192
!
interface Ethernet1
 ip address 172.16.1.3 255.255.255.0
!
interface Serial1
 description * to ISP-A *
 ip address 192.100.100.253 255.255.255.252
...
```
```
1  router bgp 100
2   no synchronization
3   network 192.200.200.0 mask 255.255.255.192
```

```
4    network 30.0.0.0
5    redistribute static
6    neighbor 192.100.100.254 remote-as 192
     !
     ip classless
7    ip route 160.160.1.0 255.255.255.0 Ethernet1
8    ip route 192.168.3.0 255.255.255.0 Ethernet1
```

The configuration on *ISP-A-1* is very similar. Line 9 starts BGP on *ISP-A-1* with the AS number 192. Line 10 specifies the default route being announced to TraderMary. Line 11 specifies that *ISP-A-1*'s BGP peer (*TrdrMary-1*) has an IP address of 192.100.100.253 and an AS number of 100:

```
     hostname ISP-A-1
     !
     interface Loopback9
      ip address 98.2.0.1 255.255.0.0
     !
     interface Serial0
      ip address 192.100.100.254 255.255.255.252
     !
9    router bgp 192
10     network 0.0.0.0
11     neighbor 192.100.100.253 remote-as 100
     !
     no ip classless
12   ip route 0.0.0.0 0.0.0.0 Null0
```

The first question to ask after both peers have been configured is whether the peers *see* each other. The following command checks the status of the neighbor relationship between *TrdrMary-1* and *ISP-A-1*:

```
     TrdrMary-1#sh ip bgp neighbor 192.100.100.254
13   BGP neighbor is 192.100.100.254,  remote AS 192, external link
       Index 1, Offset 0, Mask 0x2
14     BGP version 4, remote router ID 98.2.0.1
15     BGP state = Established, table version = 5, up for 00:00:42
       ...
```

Line 15 indicates that the BGP state is *Established*, which implies that the peers see each other.

The configuration in lines 3, 4, and 5 suggests that *TrdrMary-1* intends to announce the following prefixes to *ISP-A-1*:

```
     192.200.200.0/26
     30.0.0.0/8
     160.160.0.0/16
     192.168.3.0/24
```

and the configuration in line 10 suggests that *ISP-A-1* intends to announce the following prefix to *TrdrMary-1*:

```
     0.0.0.0/0
```

Let's check the routing tables for these prefixes:

```
TrdrMary-1#sh ip route
Codes: C - connected, S - static, I - IGRP, R - RIP, M - mobile, B - BGP
       D - EIGRP, EX - EIGRP external, O - OSPF, IA - OSPF inter area
       N1 - OSPF NSSA external type 1, N2 - OSPF NSSA external type 2
       E1 - OSPF external type 1, E2 - OSPF external type 2, E - EGP
       i - IS-IS, L1 - IS-IS level-1, L2 - IS-IS level-2, * - candidate default

Gateway of last resort is 192.100.100.254 to network 0.0.0.0

     192.200.200.0/26 is subnetted, 1 subnets
C       192.200.200.0 is directly connected, Ethernet0
     172.16.0.0/24 is subnetted, 1 subnets
C       172.16.1.0 is directly connected, Ethernet1
     192.168.1.0/32 is subnetted, 1 subnets
C       192.168.1.10 is directly connected, Loopback0
S    192.168.3.0/24 is directly connected, Null0
     192.100.100.0/30 is subnetted, 1 subnets
C       192.100.100.252 is directly connected, Serial1
     160.160.0.0/24 is subnetted, 1 subnets
S       160.160.1.0 is directly connected, Ethernet1
B*   0.0.0.0/0 [20/0] via 192.100.100.254, 00:00:46
```

TrdrMary-1 does receive the default route (as expected) and modifies its gateway of last resort to 192.100.100.254 (the IP address of *ISP-A-1*).

ISP-A-1 receives three routes from *TrdrMary-1*, as shown in lines 16, 17, and 18:

```
     ISP-A-1#sh ip route
     ...
     Gateway of last resort is 0.0.0.0 to network 0.0.0.0

          192.200.200.0/26 is subnetted, 1 subnets
16   B       192.200.200.0 [20/0] via 192.100.100.253, 00:00:23
17   B    160.160.0.0/16 [20/0] via 192.100.100.253, 00:00:23
     S*   0.0.0.0/0 is directly connected, Null0
18   B    192.168.3.0/24 [20/0] via 192.100.100.253, 00:20:51
     ...
```

However, if you look carefully at *ISP-A-1*'s routing table, you'll see that 30.0.0.0/8 (which *TrdrMary-1* attempted to announce on line 4) is missing. Why is 30.0.0.0/8 not in *ISP-A-1*'s routing table? Think on this. We will get back to this question in the next section.

How BGP Works

BGP's underlying algorithm is the simple DV protocol—when a BGP speaker hears a prefix via multiple paths, it selects the "best" path for insertion in the routing table and announces this "best" path to other peers.

We are already familiar with the DV protocol via RIP and IGRP. However, unlike RIP and IGRP, BGP's purpose is inter-AS routing, which is a different beast from intra-AS routing. The architects of BGP created several new structures to support inter-AS routing. This section gives an overview of these new structures.

Let's start at the beginning. A unique, registered AS number is required for the BGP process to connect to the Internet. Then, unlike IGPs, BGP does not contain any mechanism for automatic neighbor discovery. The network administrator must manually define BGP neighbors. This is appropriate given that the neighbor may be in another AS.

Protocols such as RIP and OSPF are generous in exchanging updates; the network statement permits all known subnets to be announced in updates. BGP operates under a different paradigm—updates should be tightly controlled. Cisco's implementation of BGP gives several methods to control not only the prefixes that are announced but also the associated attributes.

As the Internet routing protocol, BGP must support a very large routing table: the current size of the Internet routing table is roughly 70,000 prefixes. Given this size, periodic refreshing (such as every 30 s in a RIP network) of this table (with the associated attributes) would be very costly. Hence, the BGP protocol specification calls for the prefix table to be exchanged only once, when BGP neighbors first see each other. Thereafter, BGP updates only announce new prefixes or withdraw previously announced prefixes.

This incremental or *quiet* approach to announcing prefixes reduces the routing protocol overhead but creates a new twist. Suppose that a BGP router X lost a link to a neighbor Y. All paths known via Y would be deleted. Now, let's suppose that router X had a second-best route via another neighbor, Z. Since there are no periodic updates in BGP, X would never discover the new path via Z. BGP gets around this problem by storing all prefixes learned via all neighbors in a table called the *BGP table*. The second-best route can now be learned from the BGP table. The BGP table can be quite huge and can require a considerable chunk of router memory, especially when there are multiple neighbors.

Small, homogenous networks can get away with a single metric to describe the best path to a destination—for example, RIP uses hop count to choose the "shortest" path. Given the complexity of inter-AS routing, no single metric can describe the best path across various ASs running multiple IGPs on heterogeneous media. BGP defines a rich set of attributes that describe each path to a destination. These attributes describe the path in various ways, allowing network administrators to implement various routing policies. As an example, the AS-PATH attribute is a list of AS numbers that describe the path to the destination. Other attributes describe the origin of the prefix, the IP address of the border router that should be used as the next hop, the community to which the prefix belongs, a preference indication for the advertised route, etc.

The BGP route-selection algorithm uses the attribute list to select a single best path to each known destination. Understanding this route-selection algorithm is critical to manipulating BGP attributes to set routing policies.

The *route map* commands in Cisco IOS may be used to manipulate BGP attributes. The use of route maps is described later in this chapter.

Lastly, we must talk a little more about neighbor relationships. Neighbors come in two varieties: external and internal. If the neighbors are in different ASs, the BGP protocol between the neighbors is described as *External-BGP* (E-BGP). If the neighbors are in the same AS, the neighbor relationship is described as *Internal-BGP* (I-BGP).

Why do we need I-BGP? After all, isn't BGP's purpose inter-AS routing? Yes. Consider an AS with multiple E-BGP routers. In order for the AS to have a consistent routing policy, all BGP speakers in the AS must have identical BGP tables. I-BGP is used to propagate BGP tables through the AS to maintain a consistent routing policy.

Starting BGP

The command to start the BGP process on a Cisco router is:

```
router bgp AutonomousSystemNumber
```

where *AutonomousSystemNumber* is the local AS number. The AS number may be acquired as described earlier in the section "Acquiring an AS Number."

Neighbor Relationship

IGPs such as RIP broadcast or multicast updates, forming neighbor relationships with all directly connected routers. In contrast, neighbor relationships in BGP-4 are one-to-one between gateway and gateway.

After starting the BGP process, each gateway must specify its neighbor, or peer. The command to specify the peer is:

```
neighbor ip_address remote-as ASNumber
```

A gateway may have several neighbors, so multiple instances of the *neighbor* command may be listed under the BGP process. In the following example, TraderMary has added ISP-B (line 20) as a neighbor. The new topology is as shown in Figure 7-4.

```
hostname TraderMary-1
!
interface Loopback0
 ip address 192.168.1.10 255.255.255.255
!
interface Ethernet0
```

```
  ip address 192.200.200.1 255.255.255.192
 !
 interface Ethernet1
  ip address 172.16.1.3 255.255.255.0
 !
 interface Serial0
  description * to ISP-B *
  ip address 200.1.1.253 255.255.255.252
 !
 interface Serial1
  description * to ISP-A *
  ip address 192.100.100.253 255.255.255.252
 !
 router bgp 100
  no synchronization
  network 192.200.200.0 mask 255.255.255.192
  network 30.0.0.0
  redistribute static
```
19   **neighbor 192.100.100.254 remote-as 192**
20   **neighbor 200.1.1.254 remote-as 200**
```
 !
 ip classless
 ip route 160.160.1.0 255.255.255.0 Ethernet1
 ip route 192.168.3.0 255.255.255.0 Ethernet1
```

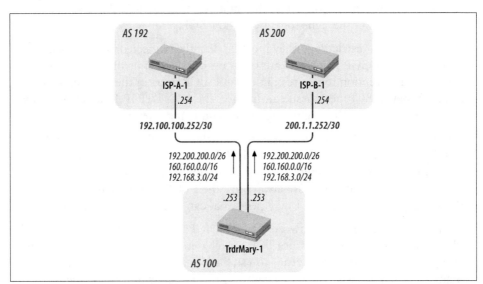

Figure 7-4. TraderMary's neighbors: ISP-A and ISP-B

ISP-A is configured with TraderMary as a neighbor:

```
hostname ISP-A-1
...
interface Serial0
 description * to TraderMary *
```

```
    ip address 192.100.100.254 255.255.255.252
    !
router bgp 192
 neighbor 192.100.100.253 remote-as 100
 neighbor 192.100.100.253 default-originate
 !
no ip classless
ip route 0.0.0.0 0.0.0.0 Null0
```

And ISP-B is also configured with TraderMary as a neighbor:

```
hostname ISP-B-1
...
interface Serial1
 description * to TraderMary *
 ip address 200.1.1.254 255.255.255.252
 !
router bgp 200
 network 0.0.0.0
 neighbor 200.1.1.253 remote-as 100
 !
no ip classless
ip route 0.0.0.0 0.0.0.0 Null0
```

Since ISP-A and ISP-B have different AS numbers than TraderMary, they are E-BGP peers; when the BGP neighbors are in the same AS, they are I-BGP peers. The neighbor-building process is the same for E-BGP and I-BGP.

E-BGP peers have a restriction—they must be directly connected. This is usually not an issue because E-BGP neighbors are often on opposite ends of a serial link. (We will explore an exception to this restriction on E-BGP peers in the section "Load Balancing.") When E-BGP peers issue an update, the NEXT-HOP IP address is modified to the IP address of the originating router's outgoing interface.

I-BGP peers need not be directly connected. Further, I-BGP peers do not modify the NEXT-HOP IP address. When running I-BGP, it is useful to configure loopback addresses on the peering routers and use these addresses to source the I-BGP session. Since loopback interfaces are always up, the I-BGP session will stay up as long as there is any path between the I-BGP peers that can be discovered via an IGP.

Since all BGP exchanges are between a pair of BGP speakers, TCP port 179 can be used for reliability. (IGPs do not use TCP for reliability. Can you think of the reason for this?) Bear in mind that in order to establish a TCP session for the purpose of exchanging BGP messages, the BGP neighbors must be able to route IP datagrams to each other. In other words, the BGP neighbors must be able to reach each other via an IGP.

The following command specifies the source of a BGP TCP session, where *interface* may be the loopback interface:

```
neighbor ip_address update-source interface
```

In the absence of this command, the source interface is the closest interface to the neighbor, as known via an IGP. We will see a use for this command in the section "Load Balancing."

The command *show ip bgp neighbor* shows the state of the neighbor relationship between BGP peers. Let's take the BGP peers *TrdrMary-1* and *ISP-A-1* as an example:

```
       TrdrMary-1#sh ip bgp neighbor 192.100.100.254
   21  BGP neighbor is 192.100.100.254,  remote AS 192, external link
         Index 1, Offset 0, Mask 0x2
   22    BGP version 4, remote router ID 98.2.0.1
   23    BGP state = Established, table version = 5, up for 00:00:42
   24    Last read 00:00:42, hold time is 180, keepalive interval is 60 seconds
         Minimum time between advertisement runs is 30 seconds
         Received 54821 messages, 0 notifications, 0 in queue
         Sent 54826 messages, 0 notifications, 0 in queue
         Connections established 12; dropped 11
         Last reset 00:01:05, due to : User reset request
   25    No. of prefix received 1
         Connection state is ESTAB, I/O status: 1, unread input bytes: 0
   26  Local host: 192.100.100.253, Local port: 11070
   27  Foreign host: 192.100.100.254, Foreign port: 179
       ...
```

Line 21 indicates the AS number of the remote BGP peer (ISP-A) and also shows that this is an *external link* (the local AS number is different from the remote AS number). If the BGP peers had the same AS numbers, line 21 would show *internal link*.

The BGP router ID (line 22) is the highest IP address configured on the router. However, if loopback interfaces are configured on the router, the router ID is the highest loopback address configured on the router.

Line 23 shows key information about the neighbor relationship. "BGP state = Established" indicates that the peers have successfully established a TCP connection. If the BGP peers had been unsuccessful in setting up a BGP session, line 23 would show a BGP state of *Idle*, *Active*, or *Connect*.

Initially, BGP peers exchange full BGP routing tables. After that exchange, only incremental updates are sent. A version number (line 23) tracks updates to the BGP routing table and can be used for troubleshooting. A rapidly increasing version number indicates that a route may be flapping.

After establishing a BGP session, the routers exchange *keepalives* every 60 seconds (line 24). The default hold-time is 180 seconds, following the standard rule in protocol design that if you miss them three times, you strike them off your list. Thus, if no keepalives are heard from a neighbor for 180 seconds, all routes learned from that neighbor are erased and the session is closed.

Line 25 shows the number of IP prefixes that have been received from the remote peer.

Lines 26 and 27 show the IP addresses of the BGP peers. Note that TCP port 179 was used on the foreign host; the local host used an ephemeral port number of 11070.

BGP Message Types

There are four message types in BGP. The *open message* allows BGP peers to identify their capabilities to each other, the *update message* is used to advertise/withdraw prefixes, the *notification message* is used to send errors/close the session, and the *keepalive message* serves to keep the BGP session up. These four message types are described in further detail in the following sections.

Open

The purpose of the open message is for BGP peers to identify their capabilities to each other. This is the first message to be sent after BGP peers have established a TCP session.

Each open message specifies the following parameters defining the capabilities of the sender of the message:

BGP version number
> Almost all implementations now use Version 4 (since it is the only version to support CIDR).

AS number
> If the AS number sent does not match the AS number configured in the neighbor statement of the peer receiving the open message, the recipient sends a notification message indicating an error condition.

Hold timer
> The duration of inactivity that will cause the sender of the open message to tear down the session. The hold timer is reset every time a keepalive or update message is received.

BGP identifier
> This is the highest loopback address configured on the router and serves to uniquely identify the sender of the open message.

Optional parameters length
> The length of the *optional parameters* field.

BGP peers may authenticate each other using the MD-5 algorithm, whose "message digest" may be placed in the open message as an optional parameter. A new optional parameter called *capability* permits BGP peers to evaluate each other's capabilities for the support of new network-layer protocols such as IP multicast and IP Version 6. This new parameter—capability—is backward compatible, allowing a peer that does not support the parameter to maintain a session with a peer that does support the parameter.

Update

The update message is at the heart of BGP. Update messages are used to announce one or more prefixes to a BGP peer. The sender of the prefix must have a route to the prefix advertised, following the next-hop routing paradigm.

Sooner or later a network failure or change will cause the sender of the prefix to lose its route to the prefix it advertised. Hence, the update message must also include the ability to withdraw previously advertised prefixes. The update message specifies the following parameters:

Withdrawn routes length
    The length of the *withdrawn routes* field.

Withdrawn routes
    A list of IP prefixes that the sender had announced but now wishes to withdraw. This could be a result of a change in the network topology or configuration.

Total path attributes length
    The length of the *attributes length* field.

Path attributes
    A list of BGP attributes that apply to the prefixes described in the *network layer reachability information* field.

Network layer reachability information (NLRI)
    A list of prefixes that the sender is advertising to its peer. Note that the path attributes listed earlier apply to all prefixes in the NLRI field.

Notification

Notification messages are used to indicate an error condition such as the expiry of the hold timer, the receipt of an unrecognized attribute type, an invalid AS number, etc. The underlying TCP session is closed after a notification message is sent.

An *error code* field in the notification message identifies the type of error.

Keepalive

The default interval between keepalive messages is 60 seconds (on Cisco routers). As per the specification, the hold timer is reset upon receipt of a keepalive or an update message.

Originating Routes

Now that we know how to start BGP and establish BGP neighbor relationships, we are ready to advertise prefixes between neighbors. There are three methods of transferring routes into the BGP table. Two of these methods were used by *TrdrMary-1* in the example in "Getting BGP Running."

```
      hostname TrdrMary-1
      ...
      router bgp 100
       no synchronization
28     network 192.200.200.0 mask 255.255.255.192
29     network 30.0.0.0
30     redistribute static
       neighbor 192.100.100.254 remote-as 192
```

In lines 28 and 29, the network statement was used to insert routes into the BGP table. The syntax of the network statement is as follows:

```
network IPAddress [mask mask]
```

In line 28, 192.200.200.0 was advertised with a 26-bit mask, as specified by the network statement. When a mask is not specified, the natural classful mask is used in the BGP update. Hence, we would expect to see the prefix 30.0.0.0/8 in *ISP-A-1*'s routing table. However, as we saw earlier, there is no entry for 30.0.0.0/8 in *ISP-A-1*'s routing table. Did you think about the reason for this? You may want to take a moment before reading on...

TrdrMary-1 did not advertise 30.0.0.0/8 to *ISP-A-1* because *TrdrMary-1* has no IGP route for 30.0.0.0/8. This could be verified by checking *TrdrMary-1*'s BGP table: there is no entry for 30.0.0.0/8 in that table. A router should not advertise a route for which it does not have a path. Hence, the network-number statement alone is not enough to advertise a prefix; the router must also have a route for the prefix via an IGP. When the network statement is used to advertise a prefix, the ORIGIN attribute for the route is set to IGP.

Line 30 illustrates another mechanism for inserting prefixes into BGP updates: the *redistribute static* command.

TrdrMary-1 has two static routes, defined as follows:

```
ip route 160.160.1.0 255.255.255.0 Ethernet1
ip route 192.168.3.0 255.255.255.0 Ethernet1
```

Both routes are carried into *TrdrMary-1*'s BGP table, and henceforth to *ISP-A-1*, but not quite as TraderMary may have wanted. The static route for 160.160.1.0/24 gets copied as 160.160.0.0/16! This is because the default behavior is to use natural classful network numbers. To carry network numbers exactly as specified in the static route entries, use the BGP subcommand:

```
no auto-summary
```

When the *redistribute static* statement is used to advertise a prefix, BGP sets the ORIGIN attribute to *Incomplete*.

The last method for carrying routes into BGP is to redistribute an IGP into BGP. So, for example, the following command redistributes all routes known to the OSPF process into BGP:

```
redistribute ospf 10
```

When redistributing a dynamic protocol into BGP, there is the risk of not knowing what information is getting injected into BGP. Further, a flap in the IGP table will send ripples through all BGP tables of all routers that receive the prefixes that changed. This can be a big ripple when dealing with the Internet. In fact, ISPs will penalize routes that are repeatedly flapping, by not advertising the routes to other peers. (This is referred to as *BGP dampening*). Needless to say, redistributing a dynamic protocol into BGP is not the preferred method of transferring routes into BGP.

When an IGP is redistributed into BGP, the ORIGIN attribute is set to "?".

In addition to these three methods of inserting prefixes into update packets, a BGP peer will also advertise any prefixes it hears from other BGP peers. This behavior is typical of DV routing protocols: pass the rumor along.

E-BGP Versus I-BGP

We have already seen a use of E-BGP in TraderMary's network. TraderMary's network has an E-BGP peer in ISP-A. The single default route received from ISP-A can be redistributed into TraderMary's IGP, so there is no need for I-BGP in Trader-Mary's network.

ISPs typically have multiple peers in other ASs. Each external router in the ISP receives routing information from all its E-BGP peers. For the AS to have a consistent routing policy, all external routers in the ISP's network must share their BGP tables with each other. I-BGP peering between these routers allows them to share their BGP tables.

E-BGP peers modify the content of the routing information that is exchanged. As an example, E-BGP peers modify the NEXT-HOP attribute to point to their own IP addresses. I-BGP peers do not modify the content of the routing information that is exchanged. This ensures that all I-BGP speakers in the AS have a consistent BGP table and hence a consistent routing policy. The architects of the AS can then set up policies (such as "border routers P and Q will serve as exit points for destinations X, Y, and Z") and propagate these policies throughout the AS via I-BGP.

When a BGP speaker receives an update from an E-BGP peer, it redistributes that update to all internal and external BGP peers. However, when a BGP speaker receives an update from an I-BGP peer, it redistributes that update to external, but not internal, peers. In Figure 7-5, R receives an update from an E-BGP neighbor. This update is redistributed to K, S, T, and U. But when S receives the update from R, it forwards it only to L, not to U or T.

In other words, when a BGP speaker receives an update from an I-BGP peer, it does not redistribute that update to other I-BGP peers. This restriction prevents routing updates from looping between I-BGP peers within the AS.

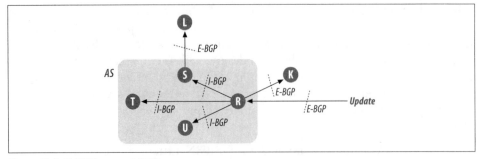

Figure 7-5. E-BGP versus I-BGP

Hence, in Figure 7-5, BGP speaker *R* must establish I-BGP relationships with *S*, *T*, and *U*. For the same reason, *S*, *T*, and *U* must establish I-BGP relationships with each other. In other words, a full I-BGP mesh is necessary for the AS to maintain a consistent BGP table.

A full I-BGP mesh ($n \times (n - 1)$) / 2 sessions, where *n* is the number of I-BGP peers) is prohibitive even for mid-sized ASs. There are two common methods to get around implementing a full I-BGP mesh: *route reflectors* (RRs) and *confederations*. Both methods are based on the divide-and-conquer paradigm that also finds use in several computer algorithms.

When using RRs, the backbone is divided into clusters. Each cluster has an RR and several clients. The RRs must maintain a full I-BGP mesh, but a client in a cluster needs to maintain a session only with its RR. The job of the RRs is to forward updates to clients.

Confederations divide the backbone into sub-ASs. Each sub-AS must have a full I-BGP mesh. E-BGP is run between the confederations.

Synchronization

Let's say that the IGP in use by ISP-A is slow compared to I-BGP (see Figure 7-7 later in this chapter). So, when *TrdrMary-1* advertises 192.200.200.0/24 to *ISP-A-1*, *ISP-A-3* may get possession of this route via I-BGP before *ISP-A-4* does via IGP. *ISP-A-3* modifies the NEXT-HOP attribute for 192.200.200.0/24 to its own IP address and begins to advertise the prefix to ISP-US. ISP-US begins forwarding traffic for 192.200.200.0/24 to *ISP-A-3*. *ISP-A-3*'s NEXT-HOP for 192.200.200.0/24 is 192.100.100.253, so it forwards the traffic to *ISP-A-4*. However, *ISP-A-4* promptly drops the traffic, since it has not yet learned this prefix via IGP. In other words, a "black hole" has occurred in the network due to the lack of synchronization between BGP and IGP. This black hole lasts until *ISP-A-4* learns the route to 192.200.200.0/24.

The moral of this story is that *ISP-A-3* should not advertise 192.200.200.0/24 to ISP-US until all the routers in the AS learn the prefix via IGP. In routing parlance, this is described as the *synchronization* of BGP with IGP.

Synchronization is on by default on Cisco routers, implying that a BGP speaker will not advertise a prefix to an E-BGP neighbor until it also learns that prefix via IGP. It is safe to turn off synchronization when the AS is not carrying any transit traffic. Nontransit ASs such as TraderMary should turn off synchronization to avoid the overhead of BGP/IGP interaction. The command to turn off synchronization is:

```
router bgp
no synchronization
```

The BGP Table

IGPs, such as RIP, maintain only the best route to any given destination. If the path to a destination becomes unavailable, RIP must wait for another update with a path to the same destination. However, BGP is a quiet protocol (a prefix is announced only once unless there is a change). If the best path is lost, how can BGP discover the second-best path?

The BGP process maintains a table that contains all known prefixes via all paths. The following output shows the BGP table for *TrdrMary-1* in the configuration described in Figure 7-4:

```
TrdrMary-1#sh ip bgp
BGP table version is 4, local router ID is 192.168.1.10
Status codes: s suppressed, d damped, h history, * valid, > best, i - internal
Origin codes: i - IGP, e - EGP, ? - incomplete

       Network          Next Hop         Metric LocPrf Weight Path
31  *  0.0.0.0          200.1.1.254          0             0 200 i
32  *>                  192.100.100.254                    0 192 i
    *> 160.160.0.0      0.0.0.0              0         32768 ?
    *> 192.168.3.0      0.0.0.0              0         32768 ?
    *> 192.200.200.0    0.0.0.0              0         32768 i
```

The following is a column-by-column description of the entries in the BGP table.

">" indicates the best route, which will be installed in the routing table. For example, network 0.0.0.0 is known via 200.1.1.254 (line 31) and 192.100.100.254 (line 32). The preferred path is via 192.100.100.254, as indicated by the ">" in line 32. Note that this table records the path via 200.1.1.254, even though that is not the preferred path.

Network describes the prefix in question. The BGP table lists locally generated prefixes as well as prefixes learned from other peers.

Next Hop describes the IP address to forward packets to for the prefix in the *Network* field. The next hop for prefixes learned from E-BGP peers is the IP address of the external router. The next hop for locally generated entries is 0.0.0.0.

Metric is the MED (Multi-Exit Discriminator) attribute associated with the prefix. The default value of this attribute is 0.

LocPrf is the value of the LOCAL-PREF attribute attached to the prefix. A higher LOCAL-PREF value indicates a more desirable route. The default value of the attribute is "?".

Weight is a Cisco proprietary attribute. The default values of the Weight attribute are 32,768 for locally originated prefixes and 0 for prefixes advertised to a neighbor.

Path is the AS-PATH attribute and is represented in the table just before the Origin code. Thus, 0.0.0.0 is known via AS path 192 (which is the AS number of ISP-A) and AS path 200 (which is the AS number of ISP-B). The AS path is empty for locally generated prefixes such as 192.168.3.0.

The last column in the BGP table describes the ORIGIN attribute. The Origin codes of "i", "e", and "?" refer to the ORIGIN attribute. 0.0.0.0 and 192.200.200.0/26 were inserted into BGP with network statements, so the Origin code is "i". 160.160. 0.0 and 192.168.3.0 were inserted into BGP with the *redistribute static* command, so the Origin code is "?".

Attributes

Akin to the description in my passport of my age, place of birth, and the border points I have crossed (there are stamps saying "Heathrow", "Amsterdam", "New Delhi", and "New York"), which helps immigration officers decide whether to check my left or right shoe or to send me back to New York, each prefix in a BGP update message is accompanied by a set of *attributes*. Just as the information in a passport allows an immigration officer to implement her nation's immigration policies, BGP's attributes allow ASs to implement their own routing policies.

The number of attributes in a BGP update is variable, because some attributes are *mandatory* whereas others are *discretionary*. Every route update must be accompanied by all mandatory attributes, while discretionary attributes may or may not be sent in the update.

All BGP attributes fall into one of another two categories: *well-known* or *optional*. A well-known attribute must be recognized by all BGP implementations. An optional attribute need not be supported by all BGP implementations.

Lastly, all BGP attributes fall into one of another two categories: *transitive* or *non-transitive*. A nontransitive attribute is of significance only to the AS that receives the update—the attribute is not advertised to other ASs. A transitive attribute is of global significance and is forwarded in updates to other ASs.

It is common to use *route maps* on Cisco routers to control or modify routing information entering or leaving a routing process. Route maps have an intimate hook into BGP's attributes. Each route map is a set of numbered clauses. Clauses are applied in order of their sequence number. Each clause contains a condition against which a route update is *matched*. If a route update matches the specified condition, the *set* option is used to specify an action.

Let's look at the syntax of a route map:

```
route-map map-tag [[permit | deny] | [sequence-number]]
match clauses
set actions
```

where *map-tag* is the name of the route map; the *permit/deny* keywords specify whether to accept or reject the prefixes that match the match clause; the *match clauses* can check for AS path, BGP community list, IP address, etc.; and the *set* command can modify one of several attributes associated with the route.

A route map may be applied on a peer using the *neighbor* command:

```
neighbor ip-address route-map route-map-name {in | out}
```

In the following example, route map *example1* (clause 10) sets the MED attribute to 200 for prefixes matching access list 1. The second clause (20) permits the advertisement of all other IP addresses with a MED attribute of 150:

```
route-map example1 permit 10
 match ip address 1
 set metric 200
!
route-map example1 permit 20
 match ip address 2
 set metric 150
!
access-list 1 permit 11.0.0.0 0.255.255.255
access-list 2 permit 0.0.0.0 255.255.255.255
```

This route map may be applied to neighbor 1.1.1.1 for all outgoing updates, as shown here:

```
router bgp 100
...
neighbor 1.1.1.1 route-map example1 out
```

Route map *example2* (clause 10) sets the MED to 200, the ORIGIN to IGP, and the Weight to 1,000 for prefixes matching access list 3. The second clause (20) permits the advertisement of all other IP addresses with a MED attribute of 150, ORIGIN of IGP, and Weight of 2,000.

```
route-map example2 permit 10
 match ip address 3
 set metric 200
 set origin igp
 set weight 1000
!
route-map example2 permit 20
 match ip address 4
 set metric 150
 set origin igp
 set weight 2000
!
access-list 3 permit 11.0.0.0 0.255.255.255
access-list 4 permit 0.0.0.0 255.255.255.255
```

This route map may be applied to all updates learned from RIP:

```
router bgp 100
...
redistribute rip route-map example2
```

The following sections review each BGP attribute with regard to its use in implementing routing policies.

ORIGIN (type code 1)

As we saw earlier, there are three methods for injecting a prefix into a BGP update message: the *network* statement, the *redistribute static* command, and the *redistribute dynamic routing protocol* command. The ORIGIN attribute describes which of these methods was used. The length of the attribute is 1 octet and is coded as follows:

0—IGP
> The prefix is interior to the originating AS. This value is set when the *network* command is used to inject routes into BGP.

1—EGP
> The prefix was learned via an EGP.

2—Incomplete
> This most often means that the prefix was learned via static routes.

The Origin code is represented in the BGP table (*show ip bgp*) with the letters "i" for IGP, "e" for EGP, and "?" for Incomplete. Although it is well known and mandatory, the Origin code is not terribly useful in making routing decisions in today's Internet.

AS-PATH (type code 2)

A prefix may travel from AS to AS in update messages. In the network in Figure 7-1, ISP-A receives the prefix 192.200.200.0 from AS 100. ISP-US sees 192.200.200.0 through ASs 192 and 100. ISP-Global sees the prefix through ASs 209, 192, and 100.

Each prefix in an update message is associated with the AS-PATH attribute. The AS-PATH attribute is the list of ASs that describes the path to the prefix.

BGP uses a rather straightforward algorithm to construct the AS-PATH attribute. The attribute is the *empty* list in the AS that originates the prefix. When sending the prefix to an E-BGP neighbor, the originating AS prepends its AS number to the AS-PATH list. The AS-PATH list is not modified between I-BGP peers.

The AS-PATH attribute finds two uses. First, given multiple paths to a destination, BGP-4 will prefer the path with the shortest AS-PATH length. Second, the AS-PATH attribute is effective against routing loops: when an AS receives an update, it discards any prefixes whose AS-PATH list includes its own AS number.

Sometimes an AS will aggregate prefixes it learns from multiple ASs. *Uncle-P* and *Uncle-Q* advertise 180.180.1.64/26 and 180.180.1.128/26, respectively. These prefixes are aggregated by ISP-B into 180.180.1.0/24. The AS-PATH attribute can indicate that a prefix originated in multiple ASs using AS-SETs. So, when ISP-B advertises 180.180.1.0/24, it can indicate that this aggregate prefix came from ASs 1001 and 1002 using the AS-SET {1001, 1002}. Thus, ISP-Europe would see 180.180.1.0/24 with an AS-PATH of 200, {1001, 1002}, as shown in Figure 7-6.

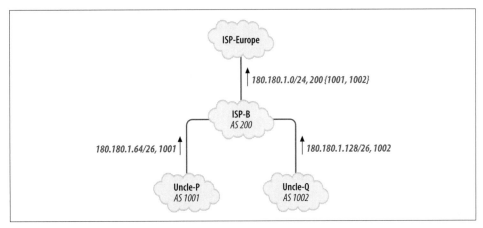

Figure 7-6. AS-PATH attribute

Since the AS-PATH attribute is used in making routing decisions, it is often manipulated to influence inbound routing policies. Say that TraderMary wants all inbound traffic to prefer its ISP-A link. The ISP-B link is to be used only when the ISP-A link is down. To implement its policy, *TrdrMary-1* can advertise 192.200.200.0/24 with a longer AS-PATH length out of ISP-B. We will see a detailed example of this later.

The AS-PATH attribute is often used to set policies such as "do not advertise any prefixes that originate in AS 556" or "prefer paths that traverse AS 905 over AS 111". A pattern matcher is required that will match AS-PATH attributes to such criteria. Regular expressions (which are also used in Unix for pattern matching, such as in the Unix command *grep*) are used to construct AS-PATH access lists. The following is a brief tutorial on regular expressions.

Most characters and digits in regular expressions match themselves. Thus, the regular expression 10p will match only the string "10p" (but this is not too interesting an example). The following symbols have special significance in regular expressions that will help us construct more interesting examples.

. *(period)*
 Matches any single character.

*

 Matches 0 or more occurrences of the previous regular expression.

+

 Matches 1 or more occurrences of the previous regular expression.

Combining the first two symbols in this list, the regular expression .* will match any string. The expression 100. will match any 4-character string beginning with 100, such as "100a", "1000", or "1009". The expression 1* will match the empty string, "1", "11", "111", etc.; the expression 1+ will match the same strings, with the exception of the empty string. Here are some other special symbols:

^ *(caret)*
> Matches the beginning of a string.

$ *(dollar)*
> Matches the end of a string.

_ *(underscore)*
> Matches a space character, comma character, left and right braces ({, }), and left and right parenthesis ((,)).

Combining the first two symbols, the regular expression ^$ will match the empty string. ^100_ will match any AS-PATH list that begins with 100, in other words, lists such as "100, 200, 130", "100, 130", or "100". Here are some other examples of the use of regular expressions in matching AS-PATH lists:

^100_
> Matches any sequence starting with 100.

_100_
> Matches any sequence with 100 somewhere in the path.

_100$
> Matches any sequence that ends with 100.

_100_200_
> Matches any sequence with 100 followed by 200 in the path.

.*
> Matches any sequence starting with the local AS.

^*
> Matches all ASs.

^$
> Matches this AS exactly.

More BGP path selections are made on the basis of the AS-PATH attribute than any other attribute. We'll use the AS-PATH attribute later, in the section "Connecting to the Internet."

The AS-PATH attribute is well known and mandatory.

NEXT-HOP (type code 3)

Each prefix in an update message is associated with a NEXT-HOP attribute, which describes the IP address of the interface that should receive traffic for the prefix in question. The NEXT-HOP attribute for E-BGP peers is usually the IP address of the

BGP peer advertising the prefix. So, when *ISP-A-1* advertises a default route to *TrdrMary-1*, NEXT-HOP is set to 192.100.100.254.

Consider the network shown in Figure 7-7. There are four routers in the network, joined in a star. *ISP-A-4* is at the center and is not running BGP; *ISP-A-4* learns routes via IGP. *ISP-A-1*, *ISP-A-2*, and *ISP-A-3* have E-BGP peers as shown, have I-BGP peering relationships with each other, and run IGP with *ISP-A-4*.

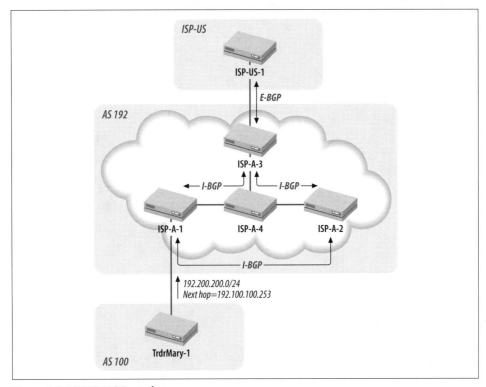

Figure 7-7. NEXT-HOP attribute

TrdrMary-1 advertises 192.200.200.0/24 to *ISP-A-1* via an E-BGP session and sets the NEXT-HOP attribute to itself (192.100.100.253).

ISP-A-1 advertises 192.200.200.0/24 to *ISP-A-2* and *ISP-A-3* via I-BGP sessions. *ISP-A-1* does not modify the NEXT-HOP attribute (which still reads 192.100.100.253). (We saw this in the section "E-BGP Versus I-BGP"—I-BGP neighbors carry the next hop unchanged, allowing the IGP to figure out the best route to the next hop).

ISP-A-4 is not running BGP, so *ISP-A-1* also redistributes the prefix into an IGP so that *ISP-A-4* can forward packets for this destination.

ISP-A-3 advertises the prefix to ISP-US, modifying the NEXT-HOP attribute to point to itself.

In other words, E-BGP peers modify the NEXT-HOP attribute to point to their own external IP addresses, whereas I-BGP peers do not modify the NEXT-HOP attribute.

Consider a more interesting use of the NEXT-HOP attribute, in the network shown in Figure 7-8. Routers A, B, and X are on a shared segment. A and B belong to AS 1 and X belongs to AS 2. A and X are E-BGP peers, but B is not a BGP speaker. When A advertises network 30.0.0.0, it would be most appropriate for X to send traffic for this prefix to B and not to A. This feature is referred to as *third-party next hop*.

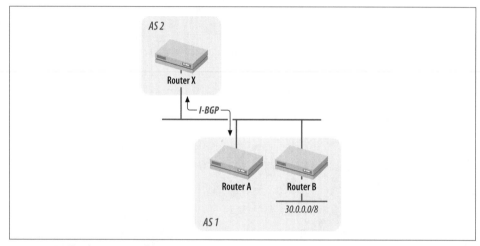

Figure 7-8. Third-party next hop

The NEXT-HOP attribute is well known and mandatory.

MED (type code 4)

Consider the network in Figure 7-9. There are two paths between AS 1 and AS 2. AS 1 prefers to receive traffic from AS 2 on link 1 (as opposed to link 2). AS 1 may use the Multi-Exit Discriminator (MED) attribute to signal its preference to AS 2. Router *A* advertises 11.0.0.0/8 to *X* with a MED value of 1; router *B* advertises 11.0.0.0/8 to *Y* with a MED value of 10. *X* and *Y* are I-BGP peers. A lower MED value indicates the preferred path. Both *X* and *Y* will prefer the *X* → *A* link to send traffic to AS 1.

The MED attribute is nontransitive, so it is of significance only between a pair of ASs. When AS 2 passes the prefix for network 11.0.0.0 to other ASs, it resets the MED value to 0. Since it is in the interest of ISPs to offload traffic at the closest exit point rather than at another gateway, ISPs usually ignore the MED attribute. The MED attribute may be of more use between two friendly ASs.

The MED attribute is optional and nontransitive. Remember that this attribute is significant only for inbound traffic.

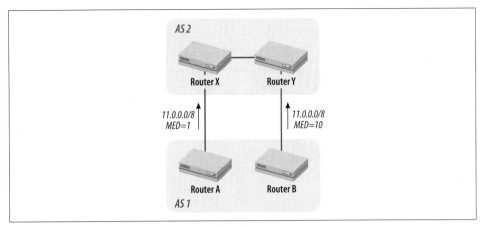

Figure 7-9. Multi-Exit Discriminator (MED) attribute

Weight

The Weight attribute is a Cisco proprietary attribute that is used locally by a router to select a path when multiple paths are available to a prefix. The Weight attribute is not exchanged in any BGP updates (I-BGP or E-BGP).

In the network in Figure 7-10, both P (AS 100) and Q (AS 300) announce 13.0.0.0/8 to R. Let's say that R prefers to route traffic for 13.0.0.0 via AS 100. R can use the Weight attribute to indicate this preference. The following configuration shows how this may be achieved.

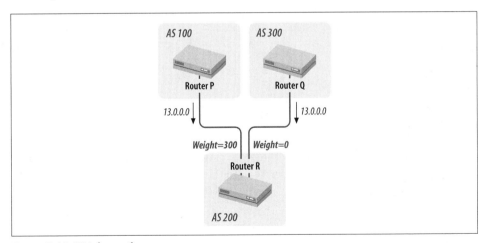

Figure 7-10. Weight attribute

The *route-map weight* is applied to prefixes received from P (line 33). Clause 10 of *route-map weight* matches any prefix that matches access list 101. Access list 101 (line 34) matches the prefix 13.0.0.0/8. Thus, the prefix 13.0.0.0/8 is assigned a Weight of 300 when received from *P*:

```
hostname R
!
interface Serial0
 description * to Q (AS 300) *
 ip address 3.1.1.7 255.255.255.0
!
interface Serial1
 description * to P (AS 100) *
 ip address 3.1.1.254 255.255.255.252
!
router bgp 200
 no synchronization
 neighbor 3.1.1.9 remote-as 300
 neighbor 3.1.1.253 remote-as 100
33   neighbor 3.1.1.253 route-map weight in
!
34   ip access-list 101 permit ip 13.0.0.0 0.255.255.255 255.0.0.0 0.0.0.0
!
route-map weight permit 10


35   match ip address 101
 set weight 300
!
route-map weight permit 20
```

The BGP table of *R* shows that 31.0.0.0/8 is received from both *P* (line 36) and *Q* (line 37). Line 36 shows a Weight of 300; line 37 shows a Weight of 0, which is the default value of the Weight attribute for prefixes received from other ASs. A higher value of the Weight attribute is preferable, so the next hop of *P* is installed in the routing table.

```
     R#sh ip bgp
     ...
        Network         Next Hop        Metric LocPrf Weight Path
36   *> 31.0.0.0        3.1.1.253          10         300 100 i
37   *                  3.1.1.9             0           0 300 i
```

The Weight attribute impacts only outgoing traffic. The default value of the Weight attribute is 32,768 for locally originated prefixes. This ensures that if a prefix is known via IGP as well E-BGP, the IGP route will be preferred.

LOCAL-PREF (type code 5)

The LOCAL-PREF attribute is similar to the Weight attribute, except LOCAL-PREF is exchanged between I-BGP peers. The LOCAL-PREF attribute is used to select an outgoing path when there are multiple exit points to another AS. A higher LOCAL-PREF value is preferred.

Consider the example of ISP-Europe in Figure 7-11. ISP-Europe may reach Trader-Mary via ISP-B or via ISP-Global and ISP-US. Let's say that ISP-Europe prefers the path via ISP-Global because it is more reliable.

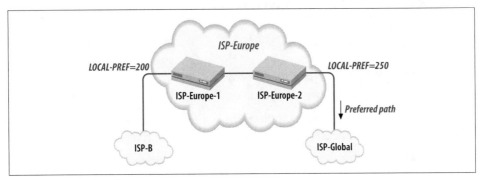

Figure 7-11. Local preference

In this example, *ISP-Europe-1* and *ISP-Europe-2* are I-BGP peers. *ISP-Europe-1* connects to ISP-B and assigns a LOCAL-PREF value of 200 to all prefixes (line 38):

```
     hostname ISP-Europe-1
     !
     interface Ethernet0
      ip address 10.1.1.4 255.255.255.0
     !
     interface Serial0
      description * to ISP-B *
      ip address 194.1.100.254 255.255.255.252
     !
     router bgp 2009
      no synchronization
      neighbor 10.1.1.1 remote-as 2009
      neighbor 194.1.100.253 remote-as 200
38    neighbor 194.1.100.253 route-map local-pref in
     !
     ip as-path access-list 1 permit _200_
     !
     route-map local-pref
      match as-path 1
      set local-preference 200
```

ISP-Europe-2 connects to ISP-Global and assigns a LOCAL-PREF value of 250 to all prefixes (line 39):

```
     hostname ISP-Europe-2
     !
     interface Ethernet0
      ip address 10.1.1.1 255.255.255.0
     !
     interface Serial0
      description * ISP-Global *
```

```
  ip address 2.1.1.7 255.255.255.0
  !
  router bgp 2009
   no synchronization
39  neighbor 2.1.1.9 remote-as 1300 route-map local-pref in
   neighbor 10.1.1.4 remote-as 2009
  !
  ip as-path access-list 1 permit _1300_
  !
  route-map local-pref
   match as-path 1
   set local-preference 250
```

The BGP tables of both routers reflect these preferences. So, for example, *ISP-Europe-1* installs both prefixes and indicates that the preferred path is via ISP-Global:

```
ISP-Europe-1#sh ip bgp
BGP table version is 9, local router ID is 98.2.0.1
Status codes: s suppressed, d damped, h history, * valid, > best, i - internal
Origin codes: i - IGP, e - EGP, ? - incomplete

     Network          Next Hop         Metric LocPrf Weight Path
*  192.200.200.0    194.1.100.253        10           0 200 100 i
*>i                  2.1.1.9              0     250     0 1300 209 192 100 i
...
```

ISP-Europe-2 shows the following BGP table:

```
ISP-Europe-2#sh ip bgp
...
*> 192.200.200.0    2.1.1.9              10    250     0 1300 209 192 100 i
```

Note that since I-BGP peers do not modify the NEXT-HOP attribute, *ISP-Europe-1* must have an IGP route to 2.1.1.9.

The LOCAL-PREF attribute is similar to the MED and Weight attributes because both affect outbound traffic. However, there are significant differences between the three attributes. The Weight attribute is significant only locally and impacts only outbound traffic. The MED attribute is significant only between two ASs and is used by one AS to control inbound traffic by dictating routing policy to another AS (which that AS may choose to ignore). The LOCAL-PREF attribute is used by the local AS to control its own outbound routing policies.

The LOCAL-PREF attribute is nontransitive and affects only outbound traffic.

Atomic Aggregate (type code 6)

An AS may propagate an aggregate route that causes loss of routing information. Let's say that AS 10 receives the prefixes 11.0.0.0/8 and 11.1.0.0/16 (from different neighbors) with different AS-PATH attributes. If AS 10 propagates only 11.0.0.0/8 to AS 11, AS 11 will have incomplete information about the prefix. In such situations, AS 10 is required to set the Atomic Aggregate attribute to indicate this loss of information. The Atomic Aggregate attribute should not be set if AS 10 uses the AS-SET attribute to indicate all of the originating ASs.

The Atomic Aggregate attribute is a well-known discretionary attribute.

Aggregator (type code 7)

ISP-X in Figure 7-2 aggregates prefixes received from *Uncle-P* and *Uncle-Q*. ISP-X may use the Aggregator attribute to specify the AS number and BGP router ID of the router performing the aggregation. The length of this attribute is always 6 octets: 4 for the AS number and 2 for the BGP router ID.

The Aggregator attribute is optional and transitive.

Community

Imagine the international flights descending upon London every few minutes from Nairobi, Naples, New Delhi, New York... The only way for an immigration officer to deal with this madness is to assign one or more categories to each arriving passenger—Political Refugee, Senior, Criminal, Musician-type, Brit, Au Pair, etc. Based on the assigned category, the immigration officer can make quick decisions regarding admission into the U.K.

Just like the immigration officer, an AS can assign a community to each prefix. Subsequent routing decisions can then be made based on the Community attribute.

In the following example, ISP-Finland attaches a Community attribute of 999 for prefixes learned from its clients (SisterY, in this example). ISP-Finland may attach a different Community attribute to prefixes learned from other ISPs.

```
hostname ISP-Finland-1
!
router bgp 1200
 neighbor 12.100.1.253 remote-as 108
 neighbor 12.100.1.253 route-map CLIENT in
!
ip as-path access-list 2 permit ^108$
!
route-map CLIENT permit 10
 match as-path 2
 set community 999
```

An examination of the details of the attributes attached to the received prefix will show the value of the Community attribute (line 40):

```
ISP-Finland-1#sh ip bgp 199.199.3.0
BGP routing table entry for 199.199.3.0/24, version 5
Paths: (1 available, best #1, advertised over I-BGP)
  108
    12.100.1.253 from 12.100.1.253 (192.168.1.10)
      Origin incomplete, metric 0, valid, external, best
40    Community: 999
```

Subsequent routing decisions may now be based on this Community attribute. So, all prefixes that match a Community attribute of 999 could be advertised to other ISPs, whereas prefixes learned from other ISPs may not be advertised to other ISPs. This will ensure that ISP-Finland is not misused as a transit ISP by other ISPs.

The Community attribute is optional and transitive.

Path Selection

Like RIP and IGRP, BGP is a DV protocol that uses the lowest metric to select the best path to a destination. Unlike RIP and IGRP, BGP's decision process is relatively complex. This complexity is due to the number of BGP attributes; each BGP attribute has a place in the decision process. Of course, if there is only one path to a prefix, the decision process described in this section is unnecessary: that single path wins. Unlike RIP and IGRP, BGP's decision process always yields a single best path: BGP does not install multiple paths to a destination (nor does it load-balance traffic over multiple paths).

Let's look at the BGP decision process. The input to this algorithm is a number of paths to the same prefix (with the same prefix length), known via BGP. Each path is accompanied by a set of attributes. The output of the algorithm is a single best path to the prefix. The best path is a candidate for advertisement to other BGP peers and to be placed into the routing table.

1. Choose the path with the highest Weight, a Cisco proprietary attribute. If the paths cannot be discriminated based on the Weight attribute, continue to the next criterion.

2. Choose the path with the highest LOCAL-PREF value. If the paths cannot be discriminated based on the LOCAL-PREF attribute, continue to the next criterion.

3. Choose the path that was locally originated via a *network* or *aggregate* command. If the paths cannot be discriminated based on this criterion, continue to the next criterion.

4. Choose the path with the shortest AS-PATH attribute. If the paths cannot be discriminated based on the AS-PATH attribute, continue to the next criterion. To disable the AS-PATH attribute as a factor in the selection of the best route, use the *bgp bestpath as-path ignore* command.

5. Choose the path with the lowest ORIGIN attribute. (IGP is lower than EGP, EGP is lower than Incomplete). If the paths cannot be discriminated based on the ORIGIN attribute, continue to the next criterion.

6. Choose the path with the lowest MED attribute. If the paths cannot be discriminated based on the MED attribute, continue to the next criterion. By default, the MED attribute is considered only when a prefix is received from neighbors in the same AS. To allow the comparison of the MED attribute when the prefix

is received from neighbors in different ASs, use the BGP *always-compare-med* command.

7. Choose an E-BGP path over an I-BGP path. If the paths cannot be discriminated based on this criterion, continue to the next criterion.

8. Choose the path with the lowest IGP metric to the next hop. If the paths cannot be discriminated based on IGP metric, continue to the next criterion.

9. Choose the path originated by the BGP router with the lowest router ID.

Load Balancing

As per RFC 1771, BGP installs only one best path to a destination network. This scenario leaves little room to load-balance over multiple paths. However, it is possible to use an IGP (such as IGRP) to achieve load balancing between ASs.

In the network in Figure 7-12, ISP-A and ISP-B set up two links between each other over which traffic is to be load-balanced.

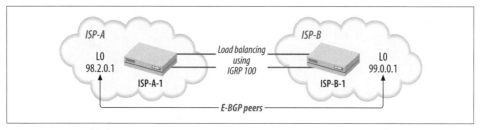

Figure 7-12. Load balancing

Both the peering routers set up loopback addresses (lines 41 and 46 in the following code blocks). BGP sessions between the peers are then established between the peers using these loopback addresses (lines 42 and 47 specify the loopback addresses of the neighbor; lines 43 and 48 say that the BGP TCP session should originate from the local loopback address). Since BGP normally expects its peers to be on a directly connected network, the *ebgp-multihop* command (lines 44 and 49) relaxes this restriction. None of this will work if each peer cannot route to the other's loopback IP address. Lines 45 and 50 set up IGRP between *ISP-A-1* and *ISP-B-1*, which permits the routers to share path information. Since IGRP will use both paths between the ASs to route to the peer's loopback address, all traffic between the ASs will use both paths.

```
     hostname ISP-A-1
     !
41   interface Loopback0
      ip address 98.2.0.1 255.255.0.0
     !
     interface Serial2
      description * to ISP-B *
```

```
   ip address 100.1.1.1 255.255.255.0
  !
  interface Serial3
   description * to ISP-B *
   ip address 100.1.2.1 255.255.255.0
  !
  router bgp 192
```

```
42 neighbor 99.0.0.1 remote-as 200
43 neighbor 99.0.0.1 update-source loopback0
44 neighbor 99.0.0.1 ebgp-multihop
   !
45 router igrp 100
   network 100.1.0.0
   network 98.0.0.0
```

The configuration of *ISP-B-1* mirrors that of *ISP-A-1*:

```
   hostname ISP-B-1
   !
46 interface Loopback0
   ip address 99.0.0.1 255.255.0.0
   !
   interface Serial2
   description * to ISP-A *
   ip address 100.1.1.2 255.255.255.0
   !
   interface Serial3
   description * to ISP-B *
   ip address 100.1.2.2 255.255.255.252
   !
   router bgp 200
47 neighbor 98.2.0.1 remote-as 192
48 neighbor 99.0.0.1 update-source loopback0
49 neighbor 99.0.0.1 ebgp-multihop
   !
50 router igrp 100
   network 100.1.0.0
   network 99.0.0.0
```

Route Filtering

The filtering of routes between ASs is key to implementing routing policies. The following section shows several route-filtering techniques.

Filtering by Prefix (Address/Mask) Information

The following BGP sub-command may be used to filter updates from a neighbor based on the IP prefix in the update packet:

```
neighbor ip-address distribute-list {access-list-number | name/prefix-list
prefixlistname} {in | out}
```

ip-address is the address of the BGP peer. The IP prefixes to be filtered may be specified in an access list or a prefix list.

Consider TraderMary's network again. An access list would be appropriate to block *TrdrMary-1* from learning its own internal numbers from ISP-A:

```
hostname TrdrMary-1
!
interface Serial1
 description * to ISP-A *
 ip address 192.100.100.253 255.255.255.252
...
router bgp 100
neighbor 192.100.100.254 remote-as 192
neighbor 192.100.100.254 distribute-list 1 in
!
access-list 1 deny 160.160.0.0
access-list 1 deny 192.200.200.0
access-list 1 permit 0.0.0.0 255.255.255.255
```

Simple access lists do not allow control over the subnet mask field. So, ISP-X may advertise 192.156.0.0/16 to peer *a.b.c.d* as follows:

```
hostname ISP-X-1
!
router bgp 222
neighbor a.b.c.d
neighbor a.b.c.d distribute-list 10 out
access-list 10 permit 192.156.0.0
```

However, this access list will permit 192.156.0.0/16, 192.156.0.0/17, 192.156.0.0/18, and so on. To ensure that ISP-X advertises only 192.156.0.0/16, we need to configure an extended access list that has room to specify the mask portion of the update:

```
access-list 101 permit ip 192.156.0.0 0.0.255.255 255.255.0.0 0.0.0.0
```

The format of the extended access list is:

```
access-list <number> permit ip <ip-address> <don't care bits> <mask> <don't care bits>
```

ISPs may use extended access lists on inbound updates to filter out all advertisements with masks longer than a specific length. Here, access list 102 will filter out all updates with masks longer than 24 bits:

```
access-list 102 deny ip 0.0.0.0 255.255.255.255 255.255.255.0 0.0.0.255
```

You can also use an IP prefix list for this task. The format of the *ip prefix-list* command is:

```
ip prefix-list list-name [seq seq-value] deny | permit network/len [ge ge-value]
[le le-value]
```

Here, the prefix list *xyz* allows only 192.156.0.0/16:

```
ip prefix-list xyz permit 192.156.0.0/16.
```

Note that a modification to the filters on a BGP peer with an existing BGP session will not take effect until the connection is reset using the *clear ip bgp* command.

Filtering by AS-PATH Information

The *ip as-path access-list* command permits updates to be filtered based on the attached AS-PATH information:

```
ip as-path access-list access-list-number {permit | deny} as-regular-expression
```

The *access-list-number* should be in the range 1–199. The keyword *permit/deny* specifies the action to be taken if the AS-PATH information in the update matches the *as-regular-expression*.

Let's say that TraderMary wants only updates that transit AS 131. The following configuration creates a route map called *only131* that refers to the AS-PATH access list 1, which matches only AS-PATH strings that include 131:

```
hostname TrdrMary-1
...
ip as-path access-list 1 permit _131_
!
router bgp 100

 neighbor 192.100.100.254 remote-as 192
 neighbor 192.100.100.254 route-map only131 in
!
route-map only131 permit 10
 match as-path 1
```

Connecting to the Internet

Several key design issues should be considered when connecting to the Internet. These issues impact the reliability, performance and cost of Internet connectivity. I will examine several design alternatives in the following sections, then look at a case study.

Design Alternatives

There are three alternatives regarding physical connectivity between the client and the ISP(s):

Singly-homed
> A single circuit may be adequate for a small organization generating a trickle of traffic. The client organization must choose an ISP and decide on the speed of the access circuit. However, if that single circuit breaks, the entire organization will be without Internet service. Hence, if the organization's access to the Internet is critical, multi-homing is warranted (even when the traffic volume is small).

Multi-homed to the same ISP

An organization may decide to implement multiple circuits between itself and its ISP for reliability. An organization that decides to multi-home has a more complex task at hand. Should the links be of the same speed? What should the link speeds be? How should inbound traffic be distributed over the links? How should outbound traffic be distributed over the links?

Multi-homed to different ISPs

A multi-homed organization may consider using more than one ISP for additional reliability. This will guard against failures in a single ISP network.

There are several options regarding the routing of traffic between the client organization and the Internet. Note that these options apply only to multi-homed clients; singly-homed clients have only one path for inbound and outbound traffic.

In the following discussion, I will distinguish between *inbound* and *outbound* traffic. The traffic flow from the client's network to the Internet is referred to as outbound. The reverse flow from the Internet to the client's network is referred to as inbound. Inbound and outbound flows need not be symmetrical.

There are several options regarding outbound traffic:

Default route

The simplest method of defining routes to external destinations is by configuring a default route (0.0.0.0). The default route will match any destination for which a more specific route is not known via the client's IGP. The configuration for the singly-homed client using a default route is identical to TraderMary's configuration in "Getting BGP Running." The single default route works well in a singly-homed scenario.

Partial routing table along with default routes

When a client is multi-homed—say, to two different ISPs—the two outbound paths are not equal. Some networks in the Internet will be closer via one path while others will be closer via the second path. A single default route cannot address this asymmetry. The client has two options here. The first option is for the client routers to import a partial set of routes from each ISP and use a default route for the remaining routes. The second option is to import the full routing table.

Full routing table

The full routing table may be useful in multi-homed environments to allow the most informed decision to be made. However, at the time that this book is being written, there are around 75,000 prefixes in the Internet. This places high demands on router memory and CPU resources. You should have a very good reason to import the full routing table.

Inbound routing decisions are made in the routing tables in other, external ASs. The client may set one or more BGP attributes in an attempt to influence the flow of inbound traffic. However, ISPs have their own routing policies and may disregard or override these attributes. Hence, the inbound routing policies should be implemented in conjunction with the ISP. The methods described here use the AS-PATH attribute.

Identical AS-PATH length
> The option here is for the client organization to advertise all its routes on all paths with identical AS-PATH information.

AS-PATH prepend
> The client organization may consider the AS-PATH *prepend* option to influence the path that inbound traffic will take.

The following case study implements the AS-PATH *prepend* option to load-balance traffic over two links.

A Case Study

BollywoodFilms has offices in Bombay and Madras in India. The corporation desires Internet connectivity. Given the notoriously poor telecommunications infrastructure in the South Asian subcontinent, they decide to establish two connections to the local ISP, ISP-SouthAsia. One connection is out of router *Bombay* and the other is out of router *Madras*. BollywoodFilms thus multi-homes to the same ISP. Figure 7-13 shows a topology of BollywoodFilms's external network.

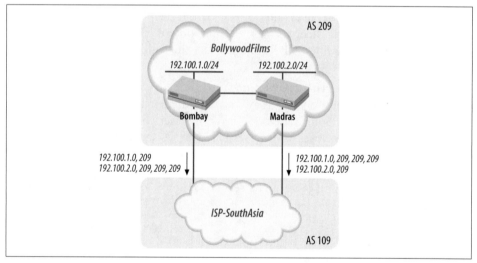

Figure 7-13. Internet connectivity for BollywoodFilms

BollywoodFilms owns networks 192.100.1.0/24 and 192.100.2.0/24. 192.100.1.0/24 connects to *Bombay* (line 51) and 192.100.2.0/24 connects to *Madras* (line 61). The configurations on the routers are as follows:

```
    hostname Bombay
    !
51  interface Ethernet0
     ip address 192.100.1.1 255.255.255.0
     !
52  interface Serial0
     ip address 146.100.100.254 255.255.255.252
     !
53  interface Serial1
     ip address 10.1.1.4 255.255.255.0
     !
    router bgp 209
54   network 192.100.1.0
55   network 192.100.2.0
56   neighbor 10.1.1.1 remote-as 209
57   neighbor 192.100.100.253 remote-as 109
58   neighbor 192.100.100.253 route-map metric-adj2 out
     !
    access-list 1 permit 192.100.2.0 0.0.0.255
    access-list 2 permit 192.100.1.0 0.0.0.255
    !
59  route-map metric-adj2 permit 10
     match ip address 1
     set as-path prepend 209 209
     !
60  route-map metric-adj2 permit 20
     match ip address 2


    hostname Madras
    !
61  interface Ethernet0
     ip address 192.100.2.1 255.255.255.0
     !
62  interface Serial0
     ip address 146.1.1.254 255.255.255.252
     !
63  interface Serial1
     ip address 10.1.1.1 255.255.255.0
     !
    router bgp 209
     no synchronization
64   network 192.100.1.0
65   network 192.100.2.0
66   neighbor 10.1.1.4 remote-as 209
67   neighbor 200.1.1.253 remote-as 109
68   neighbor 200.1.1.253 route-map metric-adj out
     !
    access-list 1 permit 192.100.1.0 0.0.0.255
    access-list 2 permit 192.100.2.0 0.0.0.255
    !
69  route-map metric-adj permit 10
     match ip address 1
```

```
    set as-path prepend 209 209
    !
70  route-map metric-adj permit 20
    match ip address 2
```

Note that both routers advertise 192.100.1.0 and 192.100.2.0 to the ISP (lines 54, 55, 64, and 65). This ensures that inbound traffic has an alternate path if one link fails. So, if *Bombay*'s link to the ISP fails, external users on 192.100.1.0 will receive inbound traffic via *Madras*, since *Madras* advertises 192.100.1.0 to the ISP. This configuration works because *Bombay* and *Madras* have a link between each other (lines 53 and 63) over which they have an I-BGP session (lines 56 and 66).

If you look a little deeper into the above configurations (lines 58, 59, 68, and 69), you'll see that *Bombay* and *Madras* do not advertise 192.100.1.0 and 192.100.2.0 equally. *Bombay* makes the AS-PATH attribute for 192.100.2.0 look unattractive to routers in the Internet by lengthening its AS-PATH attribute using the *as-path prepend* command. *Madras* uses the same technique to make 192.100.1.0 look unattractive to Internet routers. This ensures that when both ISP links are up, inbound traffic for 192.100.1.0 prefers to come directly into *Bombay* and inbound traffic for 192.100.2.0 prefers to come directly into *Madras*. Thus, a router in the ISP's network would have BGP table entries with two paths for each prefix:

```
    ISP-SAsia#sh ip bgp
    ...
       Network          Next Hop          Metric LocPrf Weight Path
71  *  192.100.1.0      146.1.1.254                        0 209 209 209 I
    *>                  146.100.100.254    0                0 209 i
72  *> 192.100.2.0      146.1.1.254        0                0 209 i
    *                   146.100.100.254    1                0 209 209 209 i
```

However, the ISP router would prefer the shorter AS-PATH:

```
    ISP-SAsia#sh ip route
    ...
73  B    192.100.1.0/24 [20/0] via 192.100.100.254, 00:05:58
74  B    192.100.2.0/24 [20/0] via 200.1.1.254, 00:01:44
```

ISP-SouthAsia thus sees a shorter path for 192.100.1.0 via *Bombay* (line 71) and a shorter path for 192.100.2.0 via *Madras* (line 72). If one of these lines goes down, all inbound traffic will reroute to the other link, since the BGP tables store both paths.

However, this completes only half the screenplay. The organization decides that outbound traffic from *Bombay* should exit via *Bombay* and outbound traffic from *Madras* should exit via *Madras*. To implement this policy, ISP-SouthAsia sends a default route to *Bombay* and *Madras*, respectively. So *Bombay* installs a default route that points out of its serial interface to ISP-SouthAsia (line 75) and *Madras* installs a default route that points out of its serial interface to ISP-SouthAsia (line 76):

```
    Bombay#sh ip route
    ...
    Gateway of last resort is 192.100.100.253 to network 0.0.0.0
```

```
75 B*   0.0.0.0/0 [20/0] via 192.100.100.253, 00:07:21
   ...


   Madras#sh ip route
   ...
   Gateway of last resort is 200.1.1.253 to network 0.0.0.0
76 B*   0.0.0.0/0 [20/0] via 200.1.1.253, 00:04:47
   ...
```

If *Bombay* loses its link to ISP-SouthAsia, it will use the default route it receives from *Madras* via the I-BGP peering relationship:

```
   Bombay#sh ip bgp
   BGP table version is 72, local router ID is 192.100.1.1
   Status codes: s suppressed, d damped, h history, * valid, > best, i - internal
   Origin codes: i - IGP, e - EGP, ? - incomplete

      Network        Next Hop        Metric LocPrf Weight Path
77 *> 0.0.0.0        192.100.100.253      0             0 109 ?
   * i               200.1.1.253          0    100      0 109 ?
```

And, likewise, *Madras* will use the default route it receives from *Bombay*:

```
   Madras#sh ip bgp
   BGP table version is 80, local router ID is 192.100.2.1
   Status codes: s suppressed, d damped, h history, * valid, > best, i - internal
   Origin codes: i - IGP, e - EGP, ? - incomplete

      Network        Next Hop        Metric LocPrf Weight Path
78 *> 0.0.0.0        200.1.1.253          0             0 109 ?
   * i               192.100.100.253      0    100      0 109 ?
```

Choosing an ISP

ISPs may be evaluated against several criteria that may be broadly classified under the headings Services, Architecture, Addressing/Routing, Operations Support, and Pricing. Some criteria will, of course, be more important to your organization than others.

Services

First and foremost is whether the ISP provides the services you need at your location. If you need T-3 access in Lisbon, Portugal, can the ISP meet your requirement?

Network Architecture

Is your application so critical that even a short outage would be intolerable? If so, you should look closely at the ISP's network architecture. Are there redundant routers at the points of presence (POPs)? Are there redundant links between POPs? What is the speed of the links between POPs?

What other ISPs and providers are peers of the ISP? If you are a wine merchant in Portugal and the majority of your distributors and customers are on ISP-Japan, you should find out how far your ISP is from ISP-Japan. Do they have direct peering? If not, how many intermediary networks are involved?

Addressing/Routing

Can the ISP carry the prefixes you want advertised? This may be an issue if you borrow a prefix from ISP-P but want to advertise the same prefix to ISP-Q.

Will the ISP support the routing policies you desire?

Operations

How is the ISP managed? What processes and resources does the ISP have in place for managing its resources? How does the ISP monitor traffic on its backbone? At what level of utilization is the network bandwidth upgraded? How is the network monitored for failures? What is the average downtime?

A client's first contact with the ISP will usually be with its Customer Service Department. The quality of response from the Customer Service Department can make a big difference when you are experiencing an outage and need "real"-time access to high-level engineering support. Readily available engineering design support and readily available, proficient engineers to help troubleshoot are important.

Price

Price, of course, is a concern. You may get a better price from a smaller, regional ISP than from one of the major ISPs. You may even get better service from a regional ISP. However, a larger ISP may score higher marks on its network architecture and performance.

Troubleshooting BGP

You might encounter your first problem with BGP when configuring a new peering relationship. The BGP session between the peers may not enter the Established state (the output of *show ip bgp neighbor* may show other states, such as *Idle*, *Connect*, or *Active*). Here are the first steps you should take when troubleshooting BGP:

1. Check the infrastructure between the peers: an ICMP ping test between the peers is a quick test of layer-3 reachability between the peers.

2. If layer 3 reachability exists between the peers, the configuration of the peers may be in error. Check the BGP configuration of neighbor IP addresses and AS numbers on each peer.

3. Check for IP filters (access lists) or firewalls between the peers that would prevent a BGP TCP session (on port 179) from being formed.

4. Is there a BGP version mismatch between the peers? Look for the BGP *neighbor ip-address version number* sub-command.

Once the neighbors have entered into the Established state, you may find that no prefixes or only some prefixes are being exchanged. Here are the steps you should take:

- If no prefixes are being exchanged, you may want to go back and make sure that the peers are indeed in an Established state.

- If some but not all prefixes are being exchanged, check to see if a filter (an access list, a prefix filter, or an attribute filter such as an AS-PATH filter) is blocking the update. The *show ip bgp neighbor ip-address* command will show the filters that are applied to the BGP session.

- Filter changes on established BGP sessions do not take effect until the BGP session is reset via a *clear* command. BGP connections need to be reset if any BGP policy (filter) changes are made. If the BGP table does not reflect the filters in place, issue one of the *clear* commands described here. This command:

```
clear ip bgp [* | ip-address | peer-group]
```

will tear down BGP sessions with the specified neighbors. Once the sessions are reestablished, the routing tables will reflect the current filter lists. However, the neighbors will lose routes learned from each other, disrupting traffic between the peers during session reestablishment. Cisco offers a new, softer approach that enables new policies to take effect without resetting the BGP TCP connection. This command:

```
clear ip bgp [* | ip-address | peer-group] [soft [in|out]]
```

is less harsh. The *in* option applies the current filter list on prefixes in the BGP table and the *out* option causes updates to be sent again.

Intermittent connectivity between end-stations is often the result of a flapping interface. Check the output of the *show ip bgp neighbor* command—an increasing version number indicates a problem in the infrastructure between the peers.

You may encounter a seemingly bizarre situation in which you are able to get to some parts of the Internet but not others. This may be because of the way ISPs advertise or block various prefixes depending on the length of the prefix. This can be a messy situation to troubleshoot, but there are several Internet sites that allow one to trace routes to any IP address. These sites are also called "looking-glass sites." *http://www.nanog.org* provides a wealth of data with pointers to other sites, including looking-glass sites. You can also check out *http://www.merit.edu*.

Also, some ISPs will tell you what routes they are seeing for your network numbers if you call and ask. AT&T even maintains a router on which you can check routes (*telnet route-server.cerf.net*), which will respond to *show ip route* commands (no password is required).

Summing Up

It's hard to remember that BGP is based on the simple DV algorithm. Instead of one metric (as in the case of RIP or IGRP), the protocol uses multiple attributes to choose the best path.

The environment on which I focused in this chapter—the use of BGP by ASs such as TraderMary to connect to one or more ISPs—is even simpler in that only a few attributes are necessary to implement most routing policies. The essentials in this environment are deciding on the optimum routing policy for inbound and outbound traffic given the client's topology and requirements, and using BGP to implement this policy well, so that failures and load-balancing issues are adequately addressed.

ISPs typically employ BGP in more complex ways, especially with route reflectors and confederations (to solve the problem of I-BGP meshes). This chapter did not focus on these issues.

CHAPTER 8
Administrative Controls

Chapter 1 classified the routing processes running on every router into three categories: (1) the processes responsible for running the routing protocols (EIGRP, OSPF, etc.); (2) the processes that take routing information from these routing protocols and build the routing table, exchange (redistribute) routing information between routing protocols, and filter routing information between peers; and (3) the processes involved with the forwarding of IP packets.

The bulk of this book is devoted to the description of routing protocols, which constitute the first set of processes. The third set of processes uses the rules of longest prefix match and classful versus classless route-lookup behavior, which I have already discussed at length.

The second set of processes is constituted of the controls that an administrator can exert over the routing process. This chapter describes these controls, which span all routing protocols. Instead of discussing these controls separately in the context of each routing protocol, I have reserved this discussion for this chapter, where I will talk about these controls just once.

The most common administrative control is the filtering of routing information between peers, over interfaces, or between routing protocols. Routing information may be filtered for any number of reasons: to stop sending routing updates to servers, to partition the network, to prevent routing loops, etc. These administrative controls are described in the section "Filter Routing Information."

If a router learns a route via multiple sources, it uses a default hierarchy of administrative distances to assign preference to one source over another (as discussed in

Chapter 1). This hierarchy can be adjusted as described later, in "Rate the Trustworthiness of a Routing Information Source." This control is used to create *floating static routes*.

For various reasons, networks often run multiple routing protocols. This requires the exchange of routing information between the routing protocols so as to present a cohesive, integrated network. The controls for this exchange of routing information are described in the section "Redistribute Routes."

When a router knows of multiple equal-cost paths to a given destination, it will install all the paths in its routing table, up to a default maximum. This default maximum number of paths to a single destination can be adjusted as described in "Maximum Number of Paths."

Filter Routing Information

The administrative control over updates entering and leaving a routing process has common elements across all routing protocols. As Figure 8-1 shows, both incoming and outgoing updates may be filtered.

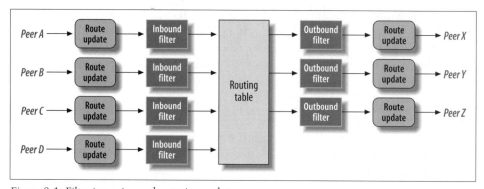

Figure 8-1. Filter incoming and outgoing updates

There are several approaches to filtering routing information. We will describe these approaches, along with a potential use of each, in the following sections.

Block All Updates on an Interface

The *passive-interface* command blocks all updates from being sent on the specified interface(s). The syntax of the command (in router configuration mode) is:

```
passive-interface type number
```

Consider the example of router *R*:

```
hostname R
...
interface Ethernet0
```

```
description * EIGRP Network *
...
interface Ethernet1
description * RIP Network *
...
router rip
passive-interface ethernet0
...
router eigrp 109
passive-interface ethernet1
```

This command allows router *R* to participate in a RIP process with routers connected on *Ethernet1* and an EIGRP process with routers on *Ethernet0*.

This command cannot be used with BGP.

Filter the Routes Sent out in Updates

The *distribute-list out* command may be used to filter the routes announced in updates to peers. The syntax of the command (in router configuration mode) is:

```
distribute-list access-list-number out [interface-name | routing-process]
```

There are two options: updates can be filtered when sent out of an interface or when redistributed between routing processes. An access list (as specified by *access-list-number*) is used in either case to specify the routes to be permitted or denied.

The following is an example of the first option. Router *R* is applying access list 1 to filter the RIP updates being sent out on *Ethernet1*:

```
hostname R
...
interface Ethernet1
description * RIP Network *
...
router rip
distribute-list 1 out interface Ethernet1
```

Our second example shows how routes can be filtered when conveyed to another routing protocol. Router *R* is running EIGRP and RIP. The routes learned from RIP are being redistributed into EIGRP. Access list 2 specifies that networks 146.100.0.0 and 11.0.0.0 are permitted to cross over from RIP into EIGRP; all other network numbers are blocked.

```
hostname R
...
interface Ethernet0
description * EIGRP Network *
...
interface Ethernet1
description * RIP Network *
...
router rip
passive-interface ethernet0
```

```
...
router eigrp 109
redistribute rip
distribute-list 2 out rip
...
access-list 2 permit 146.100.0.0
access-list 2 permit 11.0.0.0
```

Filter the Routes Received in Updates

It is not possible to control the routes being advertised by a peer, but it is possible to restrict the routes that are installed in the routing table. You can do so by applying the *distribute-list in* command to a routing process, using an access list to specify the routes to be permitted or denied:

```
distribute-list access-list-number in [interface-name]
```

In the following example, router *R* will not install 146.100.0.0 when it is received in an EIGRP update on *Ethernet0*:

```
hostname R
...
interface Ethernet0
description * EIGRP Network *
...
interface Ethernet1
description * RIP Network *
...
router rip
passive-interface ethernet0
...
router eigrp 109
 distribute-list 3 in Ethernet0
...
access-list 3 deny 146.100.0.0
access-list 3 permit 0.0.0.0 255.255.255.255
```

Apply an Offset to a Routing Metric

When there are several paths to a destination and one path is less desirable, an offset may be applied to (increase) the metric on the less favorable path. This subcommand applies to RIP and IGRP updates only:

```
offset-list [access-list-number] {in | out} offset [interface-type number]
```

The command must specify whether the offset applies to incoming or outgoing updates (using the *in* or the *out* keywords).

You can associate an access list with the command to specify the routes to which the offset applies. Optionally, you can also specify an interface type and number to indicate that the offset applies only to updates sent/received from a specific interface.

Rate the Trustworthiness of a Routing Information Source

As I discussed in detail in Chapter 1, administrative weight is the trustworthiness of a routing information source. When a route is known via more than one source, the source with the lower administrative distance is installed in the routing table. The following subcommand:

```
distance weight [[ip-source-address ip-address-mask] [access-list-number]]
```

is used to specify administrative weight. Without the options, the command applies to all routes known via the routing protocol. Thus, in the following example, a distance of 10 is attached to all RIP-derived routes and a distance of 20 is attached to all EIGRP-derived routes:

```
hostname R
...
router rip
distance 10
...
router eigrp 109
distance 20
```

You can use the optional filters to attach an administrative weight to only the routes derived from routing sources that pass the filters. Thus, the *distance* command in the following code:

```
router rip
network 11.0.0.0
distance 160 11.1.1.0 0.0.0.255
```

attaches a distance of 160 to RIP routes derived from sources in the IP address range 11.1.1.0 through 11.1.1.255. The use of the optional filters in the *distance* command is discouraged; unless it is carefully planned, it can cause problems with routing loops.

Redistribute Routes

Ideally, you should run only a single IGP in any given network. However, as networks evolve they often end up running multiple routing protocols. How does this happen? After all, shouldn't the routing engineer select one routing protocol and stick with it as the network grows?

Consider a network running RIP. The network is to be extended to support a new business area, and the routing engineers decide not to use RIP for the extension because of its long convergence times. Instead, they deploy EIGRP on the extension, while continuing to use RIP on the *legacy* network.

In another scenario, consider two corporations that merge and ask their network engineers to join their networks. One network may have been running OSPF and the other IGRP. The two routing domains in this scenario are described in Figure 8-2.

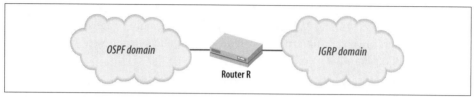

Figure 8-2. A network with two routing domains

For the network in Figure 8-2 to remain cohesive—i.e., for end-stations in one domain to reach end-stations in the other domain—router *R* must perform some kind of "translation," taking the routes from the OSPF domain and conveying them into IGRP, and vice versa.

This "translation" of routing information from one domain (or routing protocol) to another is known as *route redistribution*. Note that route redistribution is a one-way translation of routing information from one routing protocol to another. The two-way translation of routing information from one routing protocol to another and vice versa is referred to as *mutual redistribution*.

The translation of routing information during route redistribution is akin to the translation of texts between languages, such as French and English. A French-to-English translator must know both languages; a router doing route redistribution must run both routing protocols. Thus, router *R* in Figure 8-2 must run IGRP and OSPF if it is to redistribute between IGRP and OSPF.

Every translation between languages leads to a loss in nuance, feeling, and depth: how can you ever translate "Shalom"? Route redistribution usually results in some loss of routing information: how can an OSPF IA route with a metric of 1,575 be represented in IGRP? This can lead to problems. In fact, the careless use of route redistribution commands is a sure recipe for disaster. In the following section, I'll describe the commands used in route redistribution and some common pitfalls.

How to Redistribute

This section describes the Cisco IOS commands used in route redistribution. Route redistribution commands allow the network engineer to (a) specify which routing protocol to redistribute into which other protocol, (b) specify which routes to translate between the routing protocols, and (c) specify the attributes of the routes in the new routing protocol. So, for instance, if the routes are being imported into OSPF, it should be possible to specify that the redistributed routes should be AS-external type 2 with a metric of 100.

The *redistribute* command appears as follows in router configuration mode:

```
redistribute protocol [process-id] {level-1 | level-1-2 | level-2}
[metric metric-value] [metric-type type-value]
[match internal | external type-value] [route-map map-tag]
[weight weight] [subnets]
```

The *protocol* keyword specifies the source protocol from which routes are being redistributed. The source protocol may be bgp, igrp, ospf, static, connected, rip, isis, etc.

The *process-id* specifies the autonomous system number of the routing process. Note that no *process-id* value is needed for RIP.

The *{level-1 | level-1-2 | level-2}* keyword is used only for isis routes.

The *metric-value* specifies the metric to attach to the redistributed routes. Remember that route metrics do not translate between routing protocols. It is usual to assign a fixed metric to all routes when redistributing them into another routing protocol. In the upcoming example, a metric of 100 is attached to the routes redistributed from RIP. If a metric-value is not specified in the command, a default value of 0 is assumed.

The *type-value* applies to OSPF, which defines two types of external routes: type 1 and type 2.

The *match* keywords apply only when OSPF routes are being redistributed into another protocol. The keywords specify which types of OSPF routes to redistribute: *internal*, *external*, etc.

You can use a *route map* to control details of the redistribution or to specify the attributes of routes when translating between protocols. In the following example, RIP is being redistributed into OSPF. The route map *only-2-hop-routes* is used to enforce the policy that only two-hop routes be redistributed into OSPF. These routes are accepted into OSPF with a metric of 100 and as type 1 external routes.

```
router ospf 2
redistribute rip route-map only-2-hop-routes
!
route-map only-2-hop-routes permit
match metric 2
set metric-type 1
set metric 100
```

The *weight* keyword is used only when redistributing into BGP, to specify the Weight attribute of the redistributed route.

The *subnets* keyword is used when redistributing into OSPF to specify which routes to import from the specified protocol.

If you are experienced with RIP, you may have noticed an exception. RIP automatically redistributes all static routes with a metric of 1. In other words, static routes appear to RIP to be directly connected.

Since IGRP's metric is a vector, the specification of the metric of the redistributed routes takes on a variation:

```
default-metric bandwidth delay reliability loading mtu
```

Many Pitfalls...

Route redistribution exposes the network to the risks of routing anomalies. Consider the network in Figure 8-3. Routers *R1* and *R2* perform mutual redistribution, exchanging routes between the two domains. Let's say that domain 1 is using EIGRP, and domain 2 is using OSPF. *R1* and *R2* are redistributing EIGRP routes into OSPF and OSPF routes into EIGRP. The network engineer has selected two routers for this redistribution for redundancy.

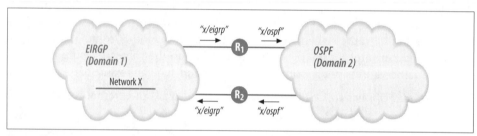

Figure 8-3. A routing anomaly as a result of route redistribution

Now, consider network X in domain 1. *R1* advertises X into domain 2. *R2* learns X (via OSPF) and redistributes this information into domain 1. It may appear to routers in domain 1 that X is reachable via *R2*! Such routing anomalies sometimes take the shape of routing loops.

Other routing anomalies include nonoptimal routing, "black holes," and missing routes. These problems are often a result of carelessly redistributing routes without paying attention to the details of the differences between routing protocols. For example, RIP Version 1 is a classful protocol and cannot carry subnet mask information. If an OSPF domain is using VLSM, how will the OSPF routes look to RIP? Or, if you are redistributing IGRP into OSPF, how should the IGRP metric be translated into the OSPF metric?

... and a Couple of Strategies

Do not run multiple routing protocols!

If you have to run multiple routing protocols (and use route redistribution), there are a few guidelines to follow:

1. Do not run multiple routing protocols on overlapping topologies.
2. Redistribute in one direction only.

3. Use distribute lists to control which routes to accept—there are examples of this in the earlier section "Filter Routing Information."

4. Avoid mutual redistribution (a common cause of routing loops). When mutual redistribution seems necessary, see if you can redistribute in one direction and use a default route in the opposite direction. Thus, in the example in Figure 8-3, redistribute EIGRP into OSPF and (in place of redistributing OSPF into EIGRP) define a default route in EIGRP pointing to the OSPF domain.

5. Avoid mutual redistribution at multiple routers like the plague.

6. Whatever redistribution strategy you decide to undertake, try to test it in a lab environment before inflicting it on a production network.

Maximum Number of Paths

If the path to a destination is known via more than one equal-cost path, the routing table will install multiple paths in the routing table and balance traffic over those paths. To override the default maximum number of paths (which is 6 for the current IOS releases) that can be installed in the routing table, use the following command in router configuration mode:

```
maximum-paths maximum
```

Note that this command does not apply to BGP, which installs only one route to a destination.

Summing Up

The administrative controls described in this chapter are useful tools for the network engineer to have in her back pocket. To ensure that the network engineer is not being constantly called on to use these tools to "patch" the network, it is important that the overall routing architecture be simple and elegant. Toward this end, it may be prudent for the network engineer to pay attention to the following:

• Hierarchy of design, reflecting a hierarchy of IP addresses

• Route summarization, reducing the size of the routing table

• Using only a small number of routing protocols in the network, as it is difficult to be familiar with the vagaries of several different routing protocols or to handle multiple route redistributions

Further, since all IOS versions exhibit bugs, limit the number of IOS versions used in the network.

Index

We'd like to hear your suggestions for improving our indexes. Send email to *index@oreilly.com*.

BGP-4 (*continued*)
  load balancing, 191
  LOCAL-PREF attribute, 186
  MED attribute, 184
  message types, 172–173
  metrics, 167
  neighbor relationships, 168
  network statement, 174
  NEXT-HOP attribute, 182
  ORIGIN attribute, 180
  peer specification, 163
  redistribute static statement, 174
  route filtering, 192–194
    AS-PATH, filtering by, 194
    prefix (address/mask), filtering
      by, 192
  route maps, 178–180
  routing policies, 158
  routing tables, 167
    transferring routes into, 173
  synchronization with I-BGP, 176
  troubleshooting, 200–202
  updates, attributes of, 178
  Weight attribute, 185
Border Gateway Protocol 4 (see BGP-4)

C

checksum, 79, 124
CIDR (Classless Inter-Domain
      Routing), 102, 158, 160–162
  ip classless command, 162
  route aggregation, 162
Cisco
  documentation, xii
  IOS commands, route redistribution, 208
  MD5 support, 99
  proprietary routing protocols, xii
  routers, serial interface configuration, 47
classful route lookups, 60
  vs. classless route lookups, 103
classful routing protocols, 42
  vs. classless routing protocols, 101–103
Classless Inter-Domain Routing (see CIDR)
composite metrics, 39
  IGRP, 44
confederations, 176
contiguous networks, 116

convergence, 19
  DUAL, 69, 75–78
    diffusing computation, 77
    local computation, 75
  speeding up, 22
    IGRP, 55
core routers, 6

D

database description (DD) packet, 129
DCs (demand circuits), 143
DD (database description) packet, 129
dead-interval, 125
debug commands, 93
debug ip ospf adjacency command, 154, 155
debug ip ospf events command, 155
default bandwidth and delay values, 40
default routes, 28, 57, 140
  creation, 58
  multiple routes, 59
default-information-originate keyword, 147
delay, 39
  default values, 40
  path, 43
  unit of measure, 41
delay command, 40
demand circuits (DCs), 143
designated router (see DR)
Diffusing Update Algorithm (see DUAL)
Dijkstra's algorithm, 114
  SPF (Shortest Path First) algorithm, 5,
      108
directly connected networks, 2
discretionary attributes, 178
distance command, 207
Distance Vector algorithms (see DV
      algorithms)
Distance Vector protocols (see DV protocols)
distribute-list in command, 206
distribute-list out command, 205
distribution routers, 6
DR (designated router), 125, 126
  election, 126
DUAL (Diffusing Update Algorithm), 69,
      71–78
  convergence, 75–78
    diffusing computation, 77
    local computation, 75

N

NAPs (network access points), 159
NBMA networks, 148–150
neighbor command, BGP, 168
neighbor relationships, 69, 128, 168
    BGP, verification under, 165
    BGP-4, 168
    EIGRP, verification under, 90
neighbor router ID list, 126
network access points (NAPs), 159
network administration
    IOS commands, route redistribution, 208
    multiple routing protocols,
        managing, 207
    routing controls, 203–211
    routing information, translation between
        domains, 208
    steady state, 53
network logs, 92
network LSAs (type 2), 119, 134
network mask, 124
network statement, 174
networks
    C and R attributes, 13
    directly connected, 2
    IGRP, design, 57
    internal addressing, devices, 162
    monitoring state of, 53
    private addresses, 162
next hop IP addresses, 94, 99
NEXT-HOP attribute, 182
no auto-summary command, 174
nontransitive attributes, 178
no-redistribution keyword, 148
no-summary keyword, 148
notification message, 173
NSSA external LSAs (type 7), 120, 137
NSSAs (not so stubby areas), 119, 147

O

offset lists, 31
offset-list command, 206
opcode field, 79
open message, 172
Open Shortest Path First protocol (see OSPF)
optional attributes, 178
options field, 125
ORIGIN attribute, 180

OSPF (Open Shortest Path First) protocol, 6,
    107–156
    ABR (area border router), 118
    administrative requirements, 156
    ASBR (autonomous system boundary
        router), 118
    backbone area, 117
    backbone router, 117
    configuration, 109–113
    DCs (demand circuits), 143
    default routes, 140
    design, 150–153
    Dijkstra's algorithm, 114
    functioning, explanation of, 121
    hello packets, format of, 123–126
    hello protocol, 122
    high-speed networks, calculating
        costs, 114
    interface state, 128
    internal router, 118
    metrics, 113
    NBMA networks, 148–150
    neighbor relationships, 128
    network command, 111
    packets, 121
    regular area, 117
    route summarization, 137–140
        ABR (inter-area summarization), 138
        ASBR (external route
            summarization), 139
    route types, 120
    show ip ospf interface command, 112,
        113
    stub areas, 145
    topological database, 119
    troubleshooting, 153–155
        area IDs, 153
        debug commands, 155
        failure to start, 153
        logs, 155
        LS database, using, 155
        overloaded routers, 154
        route summarization, 154
        SPF overruns, 154
        verification of neighbor
            relationships, 153
    VLs (virtual links), 141–143
outgoing interfaces, 44

Routing Information Protocol Version 2
(see RIP-2)
routing protocols
algorithms, 5
classful, 42
vs. classless, 101–103
dynamic, 10
features of, 6
flat, 107
hierarchical, 107
routing tables, 7–8
administration, 203–211
BGP, size under, 167
BGP-4, transfer of routes, 173
body, 8
IGRP route labels, 36
longest prefix match, 8
timer values, 18, 54
RRs (route reflectors), 176
RTO (retransmission timeout), 71

S

sequence fields, 79
serial interface configuration, Cisco
routers, 47
serial links and subnet masking, 95
show interface command, 3, 39
show ip bgp neighbor command, 171
show ip eigrp topology command, 74
show ip ospf database command, 155
show ip ospf interface command, 112, 113,
153
show ip route command, 2, 4, 43
show ip route destination-network-number
command, 68
show log command, 155
SIA (stuck-in-active), 78, 91
singly-homed networks, 159
split horizon, 23
SRTT (smoothed round trip time), 71
static routing, 3
static routes, 3
floating, 204
stub areas, 118, 145
stub ASs, 158
stuck-in-active (SIA), 78, 91
subnet masks, 26
24- vs. 30-bit, 95
(see also VLSM)
subnets keyword, 209

subnets, zero subnets, 102
sub-subnetting, 96
successor, 72
summary LSAs (type 3), 120, 134
switching modes, 19
synchronization, 176
system routes, 41

T

timer values, 18
topological address allocation, 161
topological database, 116
topology tables, 66, 71, 73–75
TOS (types of service), 114
totally stubby areas, 119, 146
TraderMary network, 10
transit networks, 133
transitive attributes, 178
troubleshooting
BGP, 200–202
EIGRP, 90–93
OSPF, 153–155
type-value, 209

U

update message, 173
update packets, 41, 70
update timer, 20
updates, reliable transmission of, 69

V

Variable Length Subnet Masks (see VLSM)
variance command, 52
VLs (virtual links), 141–143
VLSM (Variable Length Subnet Masks), 26,
82, 102
EIGRP, support by, 82–84
OSPF, support by, 148, 150, 152
RIP-2, support by, 95, 102

W

Weight attribute, 185
weight keyword, 209
well-known attributes, 178
wildcard-mask, 111

Z

zero subnets, 102

About the Author

Ravi Malhotra (*iparch@yahoo.com*) began working for AT&T Bell Labs in 1986, doing R&D work. Since then he has taught data communications at universities, managed IP networks for several large financial houses, and written several magazine assignments. Mr. Malhotra possesses degrees in Electrical Engineering and Computer Science.

Colophon

Our look is the result of reader comments, our own experimentation, and feedback from distribution channels. Distinctive covers complement our distinctive approach to technical topics, breathing personality and life into potentially dry subjects.

The animal on the cover of *IP Routing* is a zebu. Zebus are a type of *Bos indicus* cattle, characterized by a large fatty hump over the top of the shoulder and neck, loose skin under the throat, and large, drooping ears. They are an intermediate size for beef cattle—bulls generally weigh from 1,600 to 2,200 pounds and cows from 1,000 to 1,400 pounds—but have comparatively long legs and are extremely hardy. Zebu cattle breeds include Gyr, Guzerat, Indu-Brazil, Nelore, Red Zebu, and Gray Zebu. They originated in India and are thought to be the world's oldest domesticated cattle. Zebus were introduced into the U.S. (where they are called Brahman cattle) in the mid-19th century as draft animals, but they later interbred with other cattle breeds and produced hybrids that were bigger, grew faster, and were better suited for milk and beef production. These hybrids exhibited greater resistance to heat, disease, and cattle ticks than ordinary domestic cattle and consequently tended to fare better than the cattle the colonists had brought from Europe.

Rachel Wheeler was the production editor and copyeditor for *IP Routing*. Tatiana Apandi Diaz was the proofreader. Matt Hutchinson provided quality control, and Camilla Ammirati provided production assistance. John Bickelhaupt wrote the index.

Ellie Volckhausen designed the cover of this book, based on a series design by Edie Freedman. The cover image is a 19th-century engraving from the Dover Pictorial Archive. Emma Colby and Melanie Wang produced the cover layout with Quark-XPress 4.1 using Adobe's ITC Garamond font.

Melanie Wang designed the interior layout, based on a series design by David Futato. Neil Walls converted the files from Microsoft Word to FrameMaker 5.5.6 using tools created by Mike Sierra. The text font is Linotype Birka; the heading font is Adobe Myriad Condensed; and the code font is LucasFont's TheSans Mono Condensed. The illustrations that appear in the book were produced by Robert Romano and Jessamyn Read using Macromedia FreeHand 9 and Adobe Photoshop 6. The tip and warning icons were drawn by Christopher Bing. This colophon was written by Rachel Wheeler.

Whenever possible, our books use a durable and flexible lay-flat binding.

How to stay in touch with O'Reilly

1. Visit Our Award-Winning Web Site

http://www.oreilly.com/

★ "Top 100 Sites on the Web" —PC Magazine
★ "Top 5% Web sites" —Point Communications
★ "3-Star site" —The McKinley Group

Our web site contains a library of comprehensive product information (including book excerpts and tables of contents), downloadable software, background articles, interviews with technology leaders, links to relevant sites, book cover art, and more. File us in your Bookmarks or Hotlist!

2. Join Our Email Mailing Lists

New Product Releases
To receive automatic email with brief descriptions of all new O'Reilly products as they are released, send email to:
ora-news-subscribe@lists.oreilly.com
Put the following information in the first line of your message (not in the Subject field):
subscribe ora-news

O'Reilly Events
If you'd also like us to send information about trade show events, special promotions, and other O'Reilly events, send email to:
ora-news-subscribe@lists.oreilly.com
Put the following information in the first line of your message (not in the Subject field):
subscribe ora-events

3. Get Examples from Our Books via FTP

There are two ways to access an archive of example files from our books:

Regular FTP
• ftp to:
  ftp.oreilly.com
  (login: anonymous
  password: your email address)
• Point your web browser to:
  ftp://ftp.oreilly.com/

FTPMAIL
• Send an email message to:
  ftpmail@online.oreilly.com
  (Write "help" in the message body)

4. Contact Us via Email

order@oreilly.com
To place a book or software order online. Good for North American and international customers.

subscriptions@oreilly.com
To place an order for any of our newsletters or periodicals.

books@oreilly.com
General questions about any of our books.

cs@oreilly.com
For answers to problems regarding your order or our products.

booktech@oreilly.com
For book content technical questions or corrections.

proposals@oreilly.com
To submit new book or software proposals to our editors and product managers.

international@oreilly.com
For information about our international distributors or translation queries. For a list of our distributors outside of North America check out:
http://www.oreilly.com/distributors.html

5. Work with Us

Check out our website for current employment opportunites:
http://jobs.oreilly.com/

O'Reilly & Associates, Inc.
1005 Gravenstein Hwy North
Sebastopol, CA 95472 USA
TEL   707-829-0515 or 800-998-9938
      (6am to 5pm PST)
FAX   707-829-0104

International Distributors

http://international.oreilly.com/distributors.html • international@oreilly.com

UK, EUROPE, MIDDLE EAST, AND AFRICA (EXCEPT FRANCE, GERMANY, AUSTRIA, SWITZERLAND, LUXEMBOURG, AND LIECHTENSTEIN)

INQUIRIES
O'Reilly UK Limited
4 Castle Street
Farnham
Surrey, GU9 7HS
United Kingdom
Telephone: 44-1252-711776
Fax: 44-1252-734211
Email: information@oreilly.co.uk

ORDERS
Wiley Distribution Services Ltd.
1 Oldlands Way
Bognor Regis
West Sussex PO22 9SA
United Kingdom
Telephone: 44-1243-843294
UK Freephone: 0800-243207
Fax: 44-1243-843302 (Europe/EU orders)
or 44-1243-843274 (Middle East/Africa)
Email: cs-books@wiley.co.uk

FRANCE

INQUIRIES & ORDERS
Éditions O'Reilly
18 rue Séguier
75006 Paris, France
Tel: 33-1-40-51-71-89
Fax: 33-1-40-51-72-26
Email: france@oreilly.fr

GERMANY, SWITZERLAND, AUSTRIA, LUXEMBOURG, AND LIECHTENSTEIN

INQUIRIES & ORDERS
O'Reilly Verlag
Balthasarstr. 81
D-50670 Köln, Germany
Telephone: 49-221-973160-91
Fax: 49-221-973160-8
Email: anfragen@oreilly.de (inquiries)
Email: order@oreilly.de (orders)

CANADA

(FRENCH LANGUAGE BOOKS)
Les Éditions Flammarion ltée
375, Avenue Laurier Ouest
Montréal (Québec) H2V 2K3
Tel: 1-514-277-8807
Fax: 1-514-278-2085
Email: info@flammarion.qc.ca

HONG KONG

City Discount Subscription Service, Ltd.
Unit A, 6th Floor, Yan's Tower
27 Wong Chuk Hang Road
Aberdeen, Hong Kong
Tel: 852-2580-3539
Fax: 852-2580-6463
Email: citydis@ppn.com.hk

KOREA

Hanbit Media, Inc.
Chungmu Bldg. 210
Yonnam-dong 568-33
Mapo-gu
Seoul, Korea
Tel: 822-325-0397
Fax: 822-325-9697
Email: hant93@chollian.dacom.co.kr

PHILIPPINES

Global Publishing
G/F Benavides Garden
1186 Benavides Street
Manila, Philippines
Tel: 632-254-8949/632-252-2582
Fax: 632-734-5060/632-252-2733
Email: globalp@pacific.net.ph

TAIWAN

O'Reilly Taiwan
1st Floor, No. 21, Lane 295
Section 1, Fu-Shing South Road
Taipei, 106 Taiwan
Tel: 886-2-27099669
Fax: 886-2-27038802
Email: mori@oreilly.com

INDIA

Shroff Publishers & Distributors Pvt. Ltd.
12, "Roseland", 2nd Floor
180, Waterfield Road, Bandra (West)
Mumbai 400 050
Tel: 91-22-641-1800/643-9910
Fax: 91-22-643-2422
Email: spd@vsnl.com

CHINA

O'Reilly Beijing
SIGMA Building, Suite B809
No. 49 Zhichun Road
Haidian District
Beijing, China PR 100080
Tel: 86-10-8809-7475
Fax: 86-10-8809-7463
Email: beijing@oreilly.com

JAPAN

O'Reilly Japan, Inc.
Yotsuya Y's Building
7 Banch 6, Honshio-cho
Shinjuku-ku
Tokyo 160-0003 Japan
Tel: 81-3-3356-5227
Fax: 81-3-3356-5261
Email: japan@oreilly.com

SINGAPORE, INDONESIA, MALAYSIA, AND THAILAND

TransQuest Publishers Pte Ltd
30 Old Toh Tuck Road #05-02
Sembawang Kimtrans Logistics Centre
Singapore 597654
Tel: 65-4623112
Fax: 65-4625761
Email: wendiw@transquest.com.sg

AUSTRALIA

Woodslane Pty., Ltd.
7/5 Vuko Place
Warriewood NSW 2102
Australia
Tel: 61-2-9970-5111
Fax: 61-2-9970-5002
Email: info@woodslane.com.au

NEW ZEALAND

Woodslane New Zealand, Ltd.
21 Cooks Street (P.O. Box 575)
Waganui, New Zealand
Tel: 64-6-347-6543
Fax: 64-6-345-4840
Email: info@woodslane.com.au

ARGENTINA

Distribuidora Cuspide
Suipacha 764
1008 Buenos Aires
Argentina
Phone: 54-11-4322-8868
Fax: 54-11-4322-3456
Email: libros@cuspide.com

ALL OTHER COUNTRIES

O'Reilly & Associates, Inc.
1005 Gravenstein Hwy North
Sebastopol, CA 95472 USA
Tel: 707-829-0515
Fax: 707-829-0104
Email: order@oreilly.com

O'REILLY®

TO ORDER: **800-998-9938** • *order@oreilly.com* • **www.oreilly.com**
ONLINE EDITIONS OF MOST O'REILLY TITLES ARE AVAILABLE BY SUBSCRIPTION AT **safari.oreilly.com**
ALSO AVAILABLE AT MOST RETAIL AND ONLINE BOOKSTORES